Pra

"Need-to-read inside infor
line—the best source in the
LLP

"The *Inside the Minds* series is a valuable probe into the thoughts, perspectives, and techniques of accomplished professionals..." – Chuck Birenbaum, Partner, Thelen Reid & Priest

"Aspatore has tapped into a goldmine of knowledge and expertise ignored by other publishing houses." – Jack Barsky, Managing Director, Information Technology and CIO, ConEdison Solutions

"Unlike any other publisher—actual authors that are on the front lines of what is happening in industry." – Paul A. Sellers, Executive Director, National Sales, Fleet and Remarketing, Hyundai Motor America

"A snapshot of everything you need..." – Charles Koob, Co-Head of Litigation Department, Simpson Thacher & Bartlet

"Everything good books should be—honest, informative, inspiring, and incredibly well written." – Patti D. Hill, President, BlabberMouth PR

"Great information for both novices and experts." – Patrick Ennis, Partner, ARCH Venture Partners

"A rare peek behind the curtains and into the minds of the industry's best." – Brandon Baum, Partner, Cooley Godward

"Intensely personal, practical advice from seasoned deal-makers." – Mary Ann Jorgenson, Coordinator of Business Practice Area, Squire, Sanders & Dempsey

"Great practical advice and thoughtful insights." – Mark Gruhin, Partner, Schmeltzer, Aptaker & Shepard PC

"Reading about real-world strategies from real working people beats the typical business book hands down." – Andrew Ceccon, CMO, OnlineBenefits Inc.

"Books of this publisher are syntheses of actual experiences of real-life, hands-on, front-line leaders—no academic or theoretical nonsense here. Comprehensive, tightly organized, yet nonetheless motivational!" – Lac V. Tran, Senior Vice President, CIO, and Associate Dean, Rush University Medical Center

"Aspatore is unlike other publishers...books feature cutting-edge information provided by top executives working on the front lines of an industry." – Debra Reisenthel, President and CEO, Novasys Medical Inc.

ASPATORE

www.Aspatore.com

Aspatore Books, a Thomson business, is the largest and most exclusive publisher of C-level executives (CEO, CFO, CTO, CMO, partner) from the world's most respected companies and law firms. Aspatore annually publishes a select group of C-level executives from the Global 1,000, top 250 law firms (partners and chairs), and other leading companies of all sizes. C-Level Business Intelligence™, as conceptualized and developed by Aspatore Books, provides professionals of all levels with proven business intelligence from industry insiders—direct and unfiltered insight from those who know it best— as opposed to third-party accounts offered by unknown authors and analysts. Aspatore Books is committed to publishing an innovative line of business and legal books, those which lay forth principles and offer insights that, when employed, can have a direct financial impact on the reader's business objectives, whatever they may be. In essence, Aspatore publishes critical tools—need-to-read as opposed to nice-to-read books—for all business professionals.

Inside the Minds

The critically acclaimed *Inside the Minds* series provides readers of all levels with proven business intelligence from C-level executives (CEO, CFO, CTO, CMO, partner) from the world's most respected companies. Each chapter is comparable to a white paper or essay and is a future-oriented look at where an industry/profession/topic is heading and the most important issues for future success. Each author has been carefully chosen through an exhaustive selection process by the *Inside the Minds* editorial board to write a chapter for this book. *Inside the Minds* was conceived in order to give readers actual insights into the leading minds of business executives worldwide. Because so few books or other publications are actually written by executives in industry, *Inside the Minds* presents an unprecedented look at various industries and professions never before available.

INSIDE THE MINDS

Understanding Your Client's IP Needs

Leading Lawyers on Mitigating Financial Risks, Defining IP Standards, and Avoiding Common Mistakes

ASPATORE

Mat #40756104

BOOK AND ARTICLE IDEA SUBMISSIONS

If you are a C-level executive, senior lawyer, or venture capitalist interested in submitting a book or article idea to the Aspatore editorial board for review, please e-mail TLR.AspatoreAuthors@thomson.com. Aspatore is especially looking for highly specific ideas that would have a direct financial impact on behalf of a reader. Completed publications can range from 2 to 2,000 pages. Include your book/article idea, biography, and any additional pertinent information.

©2008 Thomson Reuters/Aspatore

All rights reserved. Printed in the United States of America.

Inside the Minds Project Manager, Andrea Peterson; edited by Eddie Fournier; proofread by Melanie Zimmerman

Aspatore books may be purchased for educational, business, or sales promotional use. For information, please e-mail West.customer.service@thomson.com.

ISBN 978-0-314-19506-7

For corrections, updates, comments, or any other inquiries, please e-mail TLR.AspatoreEditorial@thomson.com.

First Printing, 2008
10 9 8 7 6 5 4 3 2 1

CONTENTS

Grady M. Garrison and John R. Branson   7
Of Counsel and Shareholder,
Baker Donelson, Bearman, Caldwell & Berkowitz PC
KEY ISSUES IN IP LAW: PROTECTING THE CLIENT

Michael Barclay   21
Partner, Wilson Sonsini Goodrich & Rosati
PROPER IP PROTECTION: KEY ISSUES AND CHECKLISTS

Phillip E. Adler   35
Partner, Loeb & Loeb LLP
ADVISING CLIENTS IN TRANSACTIONAL IP

Alejandro J. Fernandez   57
Of Counsel, Broad and Cassel
A SURVEY OF IP MANAGEMENT

John C. Alemanni   75
Partner, Kilpatrick Stockton LLP
*UNDERSTANDING YOUR CLIENT'S IP NEEDS
IN A CHANGING ENVIRONMENT*

David A. Allgeyer   87
Partner, Lindquist & Vennum PLLP
IP: COMPONENTS, CASES, AND QUESTIONS

Keith J. Grady   107
Chair, IP Litigation Group,
Polsinelli Shalton Flanigan Suelthaus PC
*WORKING WITH CLIENTS TO
PROTECT AND ENFORCE THEIR IP ASSETS*

Greg L. Berenstein   123
Partner, **Barnes & Thornberg LLP**
THE CRITICAL ROLE OF EDUCATION BETWEEN
LAWYER AND CLIENT IN THE IP SPACE:
LISTEN AND LEARN, THEN SPEAK

Anne Brown, Ph.D.   133
Partner, **Thompson Hine LLP**
ADVISING CLIENTS IN IP MATTERS FROM THE
PERSPECTIVE OF A LIFE SCIENCES PRACTITIONER

John Arado   151
Partner, **Wildman, Harrold, Allen & Dixon LLP**
UNDERSTANDING YOUR CLIENT'S
TRADEMARK AND OTHER IP NEEDS

Paul D. Ackerman   163
Partner, **Dorsey & Whitney LLP**
CREATING LONG-TERM VALUE

Appendices   177

Key Issues in IP Law:
Protecting the Client

John R. Branson
Shareholder

Grady M. Garrison
Of Counsel

Baker Donelson, Bearman, Caldwell & Berkowitz PC

ASPATORE

Overview of IP Enforcement

Government agencies are involved in two different phases of protecting intellectual property (IP) rights: securing ownership rights and enforcing ownership of those rights.

The U.S. Patent and Trademark Office reviews applications for patents and federal trademarks, and issues patents and federal trademark registrations. A patent grants its owner the right to exclude others from making, using, offering for sale, or selling an invention in the United States or importing the invention into the United States. 35 U.S.C. §271 (2003). On the other hand, trademark rights are created when a party first uses a mark in commerce to identify its goods or services. The federal registration provides its owner with certain benefits and exclusive rights in the United States. There are also procedures for registering trademarks in each state that offer more limited protections within the state.

Although the U.S. Copyright Office registers copyrights, copyright protection is created automatically when an original work of authorship is fixed in a tangible medium of expression. A copyright registration is a condition precedent for filing a copyright infringement suit.

U.S. IP law has limited application to prevent infringing activities in foreign countries. For example, a U.S. patent does not prevent another party from using the patented invention or making products by a patented process in a foreign country. For this reason, it will often be advantageous to file applications for protection in individual countries. Most foreign countries have designated agencies with which to file trademark and patent applications. However, in most foreign countries, there are no formal copyright registration procedures.

Parties seeking to enforce IP rights have recourse through the judicial system and certain non-judicial tribunals. Federal courts have exclusive jurisdiction over patent and copyright infringement litigation. Federal Lanham Act (15 U.S.C. §1051, et seq.) cases (trademark-related) are usually filed in federal court, although state courts have jurisdiction to decide them. State courts decide trade secret misappropriation cases, although federal courts have concurrent jurisdiction, if there is diversity of citizenship between the parties and the amount in controversy exceeds $75,000, exclusive of interest and costs. 28 U.S.C. §1332.

Remedies for patent, trademark, and copyright infringement include injunctive relief, and seizure and destruction of offending articles. Prevailing copyright plaintiffs may recover their actual damages, or alternatively, the defendant's net profits, and, in some instances, statutory damages that range from $750 to $30,000 per work infringed, as the court deems appropriate. If the infringement was innocent, the statutory damages may be reduced to $200 per work infringed. If the infringement was willful, the statutory damages may be increased to $150,000 per work infringed. A prevailing patent infringement plaintiff is entitled to damages not less than a reasonable royalty. 35 U.S.C. §284 (2000). Remedies for trademark infringement include, subject to the principles of equity, the defendant's profits and damages sustained by the plaintiff. The court may increase the profits and damages or reduce the profits under appropriate circumstances. 15 U.S.C. §1117 (2004).

Parties may oppose trademark applications and seek to cancel trademark registrations in proceedings initiated before the Trademark Trial and Appeal Board.

In most countries, the first to file a patent application has priority. By contrast, the United States has a first-to-invent system that allows under certain circumstances the first to invent to challenge the application of another party that was the first to file. The Board of Patent Appeals and Interferences of the Patent and Trademark Office may determine which of multiple applicants claiming the same invention in separate applications is entitled to the patent.

The International Trade Commission is empowered to exclude items from being imported into the United States if they are "made, produced, processed, or mined under, or by means of, a process covered by the claims of a valid and enforceable United States patent" (17 U.S.C. §1337(1)(B)(ii)). –Not valid cite.

Compulsory Licensing Under the Copyright Act

The U.S. Copyright Act, 17 U.S.C. §101, et seq., provides for compulsory licensing and mandatory royalty rates in certain instances:

- *Compulsory License for Making and Distributing Phonorecords, 17 U.S.C. §115*: Once a recording of a non-dramatic musical composition has been distributed to the public in the United States under certain circumstances, the Copyright Act makes a compulsory license available to parties wishing to distribute their own recordings of the composition, including by digital means, to the public for private use in exchange for a statutory royalty fee. The compulsory license covers the musical composition, the music, and accompanying lyrics, but not the sound recording. A copyright license must be obtained separately to reproduce a sound recording.

- *Non-Commercial Broadcast Transmissions, 17 U.S.C. §118:* A non-commercial broadcasting entity may obtain a compulsory license, in exchange for a statutory fee, to transmit any published non-dramatic musical works and published pictorial, graphic, and sculptural work. The procedures for obtaining the compulsory license and the license's terms and rates are determined by the Copyright Royalty Board.

- *Secondary Broadcast Transmissions, 17 U.S.C. §111:* Certain secondary broadcasts transmissions are subject to a compulsory licensing and statutory fee scheme according to the Copyright Act. Both the Copyright Office and the Federal Communications Commission regulate these secondary broadcast transmissions.

- *Digital Audio Transmission, 17 U.S.C. §114:* Certain subscription and non-subscription digital audio transmissions can receive a statutory license to perform a sound recording publicly if the transmission meets certain restrictions.

- *Satellite Transmissions, 17 U.S.C. §119:* Certain satellite carriers, including super-stations and network stations, are eligible for a statutory license and fee scheme for some secondary transmissions of copyrighted works. Eligibility for these statutory licenses is determined by both copyright law and Federal Communications Commission regulations.

Standards for Obtaining Protection

To obtain a patent, an applicant must meet higher legal standards than applicants seeking copyright or trademark registrations. An invention must be novel, useful, and non-obvious according to statutory standards. 35 U.S.C. §101. An invention cannot be patented if (a) "the invention was known or used by others in this country, or patented or described in a printed publication in this or a foreign country, before the invention thereof by the applicant for patent" or (b) "the invention was patented or described in a printed publication in this or a foreign country or in public use or on sale in this country more than one year prior to the application for patent in the United States". 35 U.S.C. §102.

To determine if a claimed invention was obvious, the Court of Appeals for the Federal Circuit had developed a "teaching, suggestion, or motivation" test under which a patent claim was determined to be obvious only if the prior art, the problem's nature, or the knowledge of a person having ordinary skill in the art revealed some motivation or suggestion to combine the prior art teachings. However, the Supreme Court recently held that it was legal error to transform the general "teaching, suggestion, or motivation" inquiry into a formalistic conception of obviousness (*KSR Intern. Co v. Teleflex Inc.*, 127 S.Ct. 1727, 1741 (2007)). Instead, the court held that the "objective reach of the claim," not the applicant's motivation or avowed purpose, controls whether the claim is obvious. Id..

Although the full impact of the *KSR* decision will not be determined until the lower courts have applied the test for obviousness to the facts of particular cases, it is likely that the validity of existing patents, if asserted against third parties, will be more rigorously tested, and inventions will prove more difficult to patent.

The Copyright Office does not conduct a substantive examination of submissions to determine if they infringe on any other registered material. Rather, the registration procedure is more of a legal formality with minimal requirements. In most cases, a registration can be obtained by submitting a completed application form (which is standardized), paying a fee, and providing a copy of the work.

The Patent and Trademark Office trademark examining attorneys do a substantive review of each trademark application. An examining attorney may reject an application on several bases, including that the applicant's mark, as used on or in connection with the specified goods or services, so resembles a registered mark as to be likely to cause confusion. 15 U.S.C. §1052 (2006). The examining attorney must conduct a search of registered marks and pending applications with earlier effective filing dates to isolate potentially confusing marks. The examining attorney may also refuse registration on several other substantive bases, including that the mark is immoral, deceptive, or scandalous; suggests a false connection with persons, institutions, beliefs, or national symbols; is merely descriptive or deceptively mis-descriptive; is primarily geographically descriptive; is primarily geographically deceptively mis-descriptive (e.g., the mark "California Mix" for a mix of fruits and nuts not originating in California); is primarily merely a surname; or comprises any matter that, as a whole, is functional. Id.

A patent examiner will conduct a thorough examination of an application, including conducting an independent search of prior art that could indicate that the invention is obvious or not novel. The examiner must consider searching domestic patents, foreign patent documents, and non-patent literature, which includes the Internet. Manual of Patent Examining Procedures §904.02. None of these sources can be eliminated from the search unless the examiner can justify to a reasonable certainty that no references are likely to be found in the sources eliminated. Id. The searches should include both the claimed subject matter of the invention and the disclosed features that might reasonably be expected to be claimed.

Protecting a Company's IP

Companies concerned with maximizing the value of IP must be systematic in their approach. The first measure that should be taken is to identify the particular assets that are owned by the company. Some of these may be obvious, while others may not be. The value of the brand name for a product will be apparent, but the patentability of a product or process in research, or the trade secret nature of a singular source of supply of a critical compound or ingredient, may not be. An IP protocol should be adopted to identify the assets and delineate measures required to protect them. Enforcement of the protocol should be entrusted to a key management officer or committee.

The protocol should include affirmative procedures for protection of existing rights through appropriate registration, maintenance of those registrations, use of confidentiality agreements and self-help procedures, and policing of rights through the use of internal resources and external policing services.

Defensive measures should be taken to avoid infringing others' IP rights. These can include conducting freedom-to-operate searches to determine if patents have been issued that would prevent a company from using inventions or technology in certain ways, and conducting trademark searches to see if a confusingly similar mark is already being used in commerce. A company can then evaluate whether it should go forward as planned, adjust its plans, or possibly work to negotiate a license agreement with the owner of any conflicting patent or trademark rights.

There are several specific recommendations we routinely make to clients: conduct a cost/benefit analysis, pick your battles, monitor the marketplace, docket properties and be aware of deadlines, do not let details slip through the cracks as to transactions, mergers, and new attorneys, be aware that IP is expensive to maintain in terms of patent maintenance payments and trademark affidavits and renewals, and be sure you understand the proper usage of "TM," "©," "®," and patent markings and notices. Parties may give notice to the public that an invention is patented by marking the item with the word "patent" or the abbreviation "pat." together with the number of the patent. If the patent application is pending, a party may mark the item "patent pending" but is not required to do so. It is important for the attorney to ask clients how they want to manage their continuing IP protections. These things must be done by someone who knows what to do and how to do it—a paralegal at the very least, who can be in-house or at an outside firm.

The Most Common Legal Defense Needs of IP Clients

The most common legal defense needs of a client in this practice area include favorable evidence on the issues of likelihood of confusion (trademarks); avoidance of substantial similarity/no access (copyright); inequitable conduct, design-around versus infringement, and obviousness (patents); public domain and non-infringement (trade secrets); and the client needs to understand that all of this can be very expensive and should budget accordingly. For example, according to a survey conducted in 2007 by the American Intellectual Property Law Association, the median estimated cost of litigating IP cases (whether involving patents, copyrights, trade secrets, or trademarks) in which $25 million or more is at stake ranges from $1 million for copyright infringement to $5 million for patent infringement, per side.

A legal review with respect to a company's IP identifies possible problems and solutions, and suggests procedures to prevent those problems in the future. Unlike the case with real property, a client may not always recognize all of the IP it owns. A review by counsel can assist the client to identify unknown problems and update or improve procedures for ongoing maintenance tasks.

Examples of potentially problematic situations include clients who think copyrights protect ideas, or who do not realize a work must be registered for there to be a suit for copyright infringement; clients who do not know about maintenance of patents or trademarks; or clients who do not understand how to keep a trade secret a secret.

The review process can best be managed through interaction with a "gatekeeper" at the client company, who can pull together all of the files, and is generally familiar with all of the IP the client thinks it has. In most cases, we will briefly research patents and trademarks for the client before the review. We do not use pre-prepared checklists, because each situation is different.

In addition to the gatekeeper referred to above, the legal review process entails working with in-house counsel, marketing people, and, if applicable, inventors or creators. The primary goal in meeting with these individuals is to find out what rights are involved and what their relative worth is to the client and what, if anything, the client is doing already to protect them.

Key Questions

The key to representing clients in protecting their IP rights is to determine what they are really trying to protect. As noted above, clients do not always know exactly what types of IP they have. They might think they need a patent to protect an architectural plan, or a trademark to protect a book they have written.

Figuring out how much the client is willing to spend (or should be willing to spend) to protect IP rights is also important. For example, it might not be worth the cost of obtaining a patent if a client does not want to take the effort and face the costs of enforcing the patent rights. Many clients do not understand how expensive patent litigation can be. Some think their obtaining a patent means no one will infringe, or if there is an infringement, that it is a simple and inexpensive matter to get it stopped. Many are not aware that the standard for obtaining preliminary injunctions to prevent infringement recently has heightened considerably. *See Erico Int'l Corp. v. Vutec Corp., et al*, 516 F.3d 1350 (Fed. Cir. 2008). Clients may not know that the standard for enhanced damages for infringement was also raised in the case of *In re Seagate Technology*, 497 F. 3d 1360 (Fed. Cir. 2007). There is also the possibility of a serious counterclaim for infringement by the plaintiff, or even an antitrust or *Walker Process* claim, all of which should also be pointed out to the client.

Important questions to ask the client include: When did they begin using an invention? Who invented it? How long has the client (or someone else) been using the invention? When was the first commercial sale of an invention or product? How much is it worth? Will they sue (once they know what kind of expenses to expect)? What documentation is available to back up claims? Is the client aware of other uses or similar uses? Who created copyrighted material? Was there an employment or a work-for-hire situation? (Absent an assignment, an individual author owns the copyright in a work unless that individual executed a binding work-for-hire agreement or was an employee who created the work during the course and scope of employment, in which event, the employer owns the copyright.) How quickly can the invention become obsolete? What prior art was disclosed to the examiner? What is the market for the product? What is really novel from prior art? Is it really novel and "non-obvious" and therefore patentable, within the meaning of *KSR International Co. v. Teleflex, Inc.*? In *KSR*, the Supreme Court revised the test for meeting the applicable statute's test for innovation, which had been known as the "teaching, suggestion, or instruction test." In *KSR*, the court ruled that courts should be guided by "common sense," including consideration of the practical realities of what is going on in the marketplace, rather than rigid adherence to any particular formula. The court propounded this common sense test, which seems to increase the subjectivity of the analysis, but then stated that the issue of obviousness is a legal issue, which a trial judge can decide on a motion for summary judgment. While the decision is too recent for its effect to be predicted with any certainty, it seems likely that defendants will have an easier argument of obviousness. Many clients do not yet understand the extent to which *KSR* tightened up the obviousness analysis.

Investigating Industry Factors and Monitoring Trends

There are several important industry-related factors that must be identified and investigated in the course of an IP analysis (i.e., whether it is common to have patents in the client's industry, how common it is to license technology in the industry, the client's relative market share, the market share associated with the invention/mark, whether there are other uses of a similar mark, and whether something a client considers to be a trade secret really qualifies as a trade secret).

To identify these industry factors, we will talk to the client, review new IP publications, and review general publications. The rate at which key industry factors change is different for each industry, but all of them seem to be speeding up due to the recent communications revolution and the globalization of business. Now that virtually instantaneous communication has become so affordable and intelligent, educated people living almost anywhere can bring their mental faculties to bear on a problem. Shipping is so much faster and cheaper than it ever has been, and the pace of innovations in business and technology seems to have picked up considerably.

The best sources for monitoring overall IP trends in order of priority include legal publications, business publications, industry conferences and symposia, and appropriate Web sites. It is always better to spot a trend before the client knows about it, and then alert them to it.

The area of IP law that is changing most rapidly is patent law, as is evidenced by the *KSR*, *Erico*, and *Seagate* cases. These cases represent major shifts in patent law. There has not been anything like that type of activity recently in the other areas of IP law. IP litigation also seems to be on the rise in China—greater numbers of patents are being granted, which generates more lawsuits. We inform clients of changes in this area through newsletters, copies of articles, seminars, and personal visits.

Financial and Legal Risks for IP

IP can be a critical piece of the client's whole business model. However, it is important to warn a client in advance of the costs and risks of IP litigation.

The degree of financial and legal risk in this area is measured by the value of the IP in the market, the legal risk that the law will change since the patent was obtained or even since an IP litigation case started, as well as the staggering expense to litigate. It is also important to consider whether the client wants to put its IP at risk by suing. After all, a patentee who sues runs the risk that the patent will be invalidated or that the court will find there is no infringement. A trade secret may be found to be in the public domain or may have to be disclosed to the defendant (or at least a third-party intermediary) to evaluate whether the defendant has misappropriated—some clients might prefer to negotiate a license rather than run the risk of disclosing a critical secret. At the very least, with costs for these cases running into hundreds of thousands and even multiple millions of dollars, the client must understand that the costs might outweigh the value of the IP or even overwhelm the entire business. Analyzing these risks entails preparation (i.e., a review of the facts and law, especially the facts) and experience.

Handling an IP Litigation Matter

To understand the legal needs of IP clients, it is important for the attorney to listen and observe—an IP client may have no clue about what type of IP is involved in a matter, or how best to go about protecting it. To properly advise the client, one must understand the market in which the product/service is offered, and understand the relative value of the particular IP to the client. The lawyer cannot always eliminate the possibility of bad results, but he or she can eliminate bad surprises.

Perhaps the most complicated IP client situation we ever handled involved the representation of a plaintiff in federal district court in a trade secret misappropriation case involving cutting-edge technology. While the private suit was being litigated, patent applications related to the technology were pending in the Patent and Trademark Office and various international patent offices. There was tension between preservation of certain trade secrets associated with the technology and the publication of the patent applications, which described embodiments of the technology. The parties to the litigation negotiated what proved to be a very onerous protective order preventing the plaintiff's key in-house technical personnel from reviewing the defendant's accused technology and assisting counsel in misappropriation analysis. Sophisticated economic expertise was required to determine what "reasonable royalty" would have been negotiated by the parties in a hypothetical licensing situation in accordance with the Georgia Pacific factors (various industry and economic factors are reviewed for a determination of what license terms would have been negotiated by the parties immediately before the infringement began).

It is always important first for the IP attorney to understand the client's IP so he or she can form a legal strategy that best meets the client's goals and expectations. When a client's IP assets include, for example, a machine that performs a patented process, we might visit the factory and observe the machine to get a better understanding of how the process works.

Using Outside Experts

We work with attorneys outside our firm when a client needs to secure foreign trademark registrations or patents. For our clients, we coordinate applications and maintain records of all the docketing information and deadlines for their U.S. and foreign IP assets in our centralized system.

Other outside experts we consult on these matters can vary widely, depending on the type of IP and the legal situation at issue. In the past, we have consulted with economists and damages experts who can help determine the value of an asset; scientists and engineers who can help us understand and explain certain inventions; and economists and marketing professors on market surveys in such trademark cases. The costs associated with experts are typically based on hourly rates—and they are not inexpensive. They can easily get into six figures.

Key Technologies

There are several key technologies we use to assist us in IP matters. For our trademark and patent clients, we use services to conduct trademark availability and patent prior art searches. These services review a variety of sources and can help alert us to conflicting or other uses that would prevent a client from being able to receive a trademark registration or patent.

Performing these searches at an early stage can alert clients to avoid infringing others' IP rights, and save the client time and money it might spend marketing or developing a product for which it cannot obtain a patent or desired trademark. We also use a trademark monitoring service that alerts us to any uses that might infringe a client's trademark rights.

John R. Branson is a shareholder in Baker Donelson, Bearman, Caldwell & Berkowitz's Memphis office. He concentrates his practice in all types of litigation, and he is a member of the firm's intellectual property and commercial litigation groups. He has extensive experience in a variety of areas. He also has participated in a number of arbitrations and numerous judicial and non-judicial mediations.

Mr. Branson holds an AV rating from Martindale-Hubbell. He has presented numerous seminars on topics such as Chancery Court practice, trial strategy, business litigation, proof of damages, debt collection, collection of judgments, use of private investigators, surreptitious recording of evidence, and others. He earned his B.B.A. in marketing from the University of Mississippi and his J.D. from the University of Mississippi Law School.

Grady M. Garrison, *of counsel in Baker Donelson, Bearman, Caldwell & Berkowitz's Memphis office, concentrates his practice in the areas of intellectual property law and franchise law. He has experience in trademark, copyright, franchising, antitrust, and trade regulation matters, and licensing, litigation, and transactional issues related thereto.*

Mr. Garrison is a member of the International Bar Association, the American Bar Association, the Tennessee Bar Association, the Tennessee Intellectual Property Law Association, the Memphis Bar Association, and the Memphis Area Franchise Association. He has an AV peer review rating from Martindale-Hubbell and is listed in The Best Lawyers in America *for franchise law and intellectual property law. He earned his B.A. from Vanderbilt University, his J.D. from Memphis State University, and his L.L.M. from New York University. He is an adjunct professor of franchise law at the University of Memphis School of Law and of copyright and licensing at the University of Memphis School of Music.*

Acknowledgment: *The authors express their gratitude for the invaluable assistance of Wendy Robertson Esq. and Laura P. Merritt Esq., of Baker Donelson, Bearman, Caldwell & Berkowitz.*

Proper IP Protection: Key Issues and Checklists

Michael Barclay

Partner

Wilson Sonsini Goodrich & Rosati

ASPATORE

Introduction

This chapter discusses a number of intellectual property (IP) issues from the standpoint of an IP attorney in private practice. I handle litigation, strategic counseling, and licensing, primarily in the areas of patent, trade secret, and copyright law. I also have a master's degree in electrical engineering, and I worked as an engineer before going to law school. Therefore, when working on cases that deal with the intersection of law and technology, I can offer my clients expertise in both the legal and technological issues that are involved in a case.

This chapter first gives an overview of the IP legal needs of companies, by type of IP, by type of company, and by the company's approach toward IP protection. Next, I discuss some mistakes to avoid and best practices for a start-up company or other company that is still developing its IP strategy. The chapter then discusses various offensive and defensive IP strategies, and it gives some examples of complicated IP disputes. Some recent trends in IP law are then presented. Finally, the chapter includes a brief discussion of the agencies that regulate IP protection, as well as some sources for IP information. (In addition, four checklists for IP planning in the four areas of IP protection are included as Appendices B, C, D, and E.)

Legal Needs of Companies in the IP Realm

There are a number of different categories of legal needs for companies that are concerned with IP. The major categories include:

- *Patents:* procurement (patent prosecution), offensive patent litigation, defensive patent litigation, patent clearance (where possible in the particular industry), inbound and outbound licensing
- *Copyrights:* registration program (for companies that rely heavily on copyright protection), employee assignment programs, offensive and defensive litigation
- *Trademarks:* registration program, enforcement program (as needed for key trademarks), offensive and defensive litigation
- *Trade secrets:* secrecy program, new employee intake procedures, offensive and defensive litigation

- *Internet companies:* If the company is involved with Web hosting or similar activities, it needs to have good Web procedures, and be in compliance with the Digital Millennium Copyright Act, 17 U.S.C. §§512, 1201–1205, 1301–1332; 28 U.S.C. §4001.

- *Biotech/pharmaceutical companies:* Companies that are involved with Food and Drug Administration-approved drugs or devices need to have familiarity with abbreviated new drug application procedures. (Very briefly, under the Hatch-Waxman Act, 21 U.S.C. §355, a company wishing to market a generic drug can file abbreviated new drug applications to get Food and Drug Administration approval of their version of the generic drug. The owner of a patent that covers the generic can then file an infringement suit under 35 U.S.C. §271(e) to try to block approval of the application.)

This list can be prioritized in several ways:

By type of company:

- Companies with a heavy technology focus will be most concerned with patents and trade secrets.
- Companies with a heavy marketing focus will be more concerned with trademarks.
- Companies with a media/content focus will be most concerned with copyrights and trademarks, and perhaps Web issues.
- Web companies will be concerned about Web issues, copyrights, and trademarks.
- Biotech/pharmaceutical companies will be concerned about abbreviated new drug application issues, patents, and trade secrets.

By IP philosophy:

- An offensively minded company that wants to enforce its IP aggressively will be more interested in patent procurement and offensive litigation capabilities.
- A defensively oriented company will be more interested in patent clearance and other IP avoidance procedures, and in defensive litigation.

Broadly, a company might be offensively minded if it has a large patent portfolio and wishes to try to use the portfolio to generate licensing revenue. IBM, Texas Instruments, and Lucent are examples of companies of this type. Other offensively minded companies could include companies that once had a significant manufacturing business and no longer do, but have developed a patent portfolio that can be exploited. Defensively minded companies are ones that do not fit into either of the above categories, and prefer to focus on their technology instead of patent enforcement.

Mistakes to Avoid

A start-up company is typically founded by people who once worked somewhere else. Therefore, they have to be careful that their previous company or some other party does not have a claim with respect to ownership of any of their IP.

Companies often fail to get assignments of copyrights from outside vendors. They may assume that if they hire an outside vendor to write a computer program or do an ad campaign, they will automatically own the copyright. However, that might not be the case unless they get a copyright assignment. This again is a mistake some start-up companies make before they have implemented control procedures over such IP matters.

Another mistake that is commonly made in this area occurs when people spend money applying for patents that are not going to be economically efficient in the long term. You need to patent what your competitors are likely to be doing in the future to protect your own technology. However, it does not make sense to patent something if you are the only one who is involved in producing it. For example, a company may have produced a very odd technology or a solution to a very unique problem nobody else is likely to get involved in, and it could be a waste of money to patent such a technology. When considering patent issues, it is always important to look at the big picture.

IP Best Practices

Indeed, the decision of whether to patent something is generally less dependent on the idea itself than on what the competition is doing. Surprisingly, many software companies will patent a software process although they are unable to get access to the internal workings of their competitor's source code. If examination of the code is needed to prove infringement, it could be very difficult in such a case to determine if your competitor is infringing on your technology. You also need to determine if there is going to be an easy way to design around your patent. If a competitor can design around your patent very easily and at minimal cost, your patent is not worth very much.

For clients in the electronics industry, it is a good idea to make sure there are copyright notices on your manuals, data sheets, and source code if you think they are likely to be copied. If you decide trademark protection is worthwhile (e.g., if your product is being sold directly to consumers and brand differentiation is important), you need to do a search and apply for federal registration of your important marks. Finally, it is important for every technology company to have a trade secret protection program in place.

Therefore, when trying to understand your IP needs, there are several key questions a company's management team must consider:

- What will be the key technologies that will govern our business in the future? Can we obtain patent protection to control these technologies against our competitors? Do we have those technologies in-house, or do we need to acquire them?
- Do we have features that differentiate our products from our competitors' products? If so, can we patent those features? Can our competitors design around the patent easily, making patent protection not worthwhile? Can the infringement be detected by inspecting the competitor's product, or is it something purely internal to the product that would require access to the competitor's confidential information (such as source code) to detect infringements?

Offensive and Defensive IP Strategies

When meeting with a new client about an IP issue, I always want to learn everything I can about their technology and what their company does. This includes an examination of what the competitive landscape is like. Who are their competitors, and what are they currently doing and developing? I tend to work for electronics or computer industry clients, and clients in these industries have unique needs and areas of concern. For example, certain fields in the computer and electronics industries have a lot of patent activity, while others have less, and some fields have more aggressive competitors than others. If a client is considering the possibility of entering into a field where there is already an existing competitor who is inclined to sue every other competitor that comes along, it might be best to avoid that field. By contrast, getting into a field where companies are frequently cross-licensing technologies is much easier to deal with from an IP protection perspective. Understanding both the client's technology and the competitive landscape helps the IP attorney determine what that particular client should be doing in terms of protecting their own IP, and what they should be doing in terms of avoiding IP claims by other people.

The second step in the process of working with a new client on an IP matter is to evaluate the most effective offensive and defensive strategies. First, you need to consider what sort of IP budget the client can afford, and then consider what types of IP protections are cheap and easy to obtain. You need to determine what forms of IP protection they should definitely invest in, and what forms of protection they should not or cannot spend as much money on. In terms of offensive strategies, most companies usually want to obtain some type of patent protection for their key technologies, if for no other reason than because it makes their investors happy and gives them a form of protection they can use if they need to.

Companies should also definitely have a trade secret program in place, and make sure everyone has signed the proper non-disclosure and confidentiality agreements. Trade secret protection can cover not just technical products and processes, but also many things that are not patentable, such as business plans, marketing research, and customer lists.

Clients might also need copyright protection if their products include works of authorship, such as written materials where the expressive nature of the text is important, or music, video, or artwork. Other companies who sell directly to consumers and need to establish a brand to differentiate themselves from their competitors may find they are in a field where trademarks (for products) or service marks (for services) are going to be an important offensive investment.

For example, companies that are heavily involved in marketing will primarily be concerned with trademark rights. Issues for such clients include: Does the company have trademarks or service marks worth protecting? Does the company select distinctive terms for those marks? Does the company have a trademark registration program? Does the company perform clearance searches before investing heavily in a new mark? Has the company invested so much money in its present corporate name and product name that having to change it would be an expensive problem?

In terms of defensive strategies, it is always important to consider the client's technology and the competitive landscape. For example, in the semiconductor industry, there are typically tens of thousands of patents. Therefore, there is little you can do that will enable you to successfully design around everyone else's patents. On the other hand, some industries will have a limited number of competitors with a limited number of patents. Therefore, it may be possible to study those competitive products and design your product around them so it does not infringe.

In the realm of trade secrets, you want to be sure you are not doing anything to acquire trade secrets of a previous employer—either a previous employer of the founders, or of any other individuals the company hires. Every company should have a very strong policy with respect to new employees not bringing trade secrets into the company. In the area of copyrights, it is important for the client to figure out if they are likely to be infringing on someone else's copyrighted material, such as a computer code. Companies should also conduct a trademark search before they adopt a company name. I tell early-stage companies that if they do not care what their company name is and they do not mind changing it in the future, they should not spend a lot of money on a trademark search. But if they plan to immediately start developing a brand name, they had better make sure the name is available everywhere they want to use it, which could even be worldwide.

The process of obtaining IP protection is typically easier to budget, because you can decide what you want to do and how much to spend. Conversely, the costs of taking prophylactic defensive measures are always variable and hard to predict, because you do not really know what is going to happen down the road (i.e., whether you will get sued).

Legal Defenses and Risks for IP

The main risk situation in the IP realm is getting into a field that has very aggressive competitors from a legal standpoint. For example, during the 1990s, many of the companies in the field programmable gate array industry would repeatedly sue each other, resulting in multiple patent suits. (Eventually these suits were settled, but only after years of expensive litigation.) Conversely, many software companies have never had patent suits with respect to their core technology, because all of the competitors in that industry have many patents. Even though they could probably sue each other on a frequent basis, it would be a war nobody would win. Competing software companies will generally build up their IP portfolios on the understanding that they will not sue each other, even if infringement is suspected, because at the end of litigation both parties would simply get a cross-license, and neither side would recover its legal fees.

Another risk in the IP area is not having a good defense in a patent suit. Some of my clients that have been in a particular industry for a long time have faced a situation where a new company comes along and sues the client for infringement with respect to some aspect of the new company's patented technology. My client may claim they were doing whatever is protected by the new company's patent long before that new company ever got started, but when I ask them to show me samples of their old product, they may find they no longer have them. It is a good idea for clients to keep a museum of what they have done in the past, because it might prove to be useful later on.

Resolving a Complicated IP Dispute

One of the most complicated IP litigation matters I have ever handled was a case in the early 1990s involving Conner Peripherals, a disk drive company that was eventually acquired by Seagate. Conner and IBM got into a patent suit involving about twenty patents related to both companies' disk drives. This massive suit went on for several years—there were literally hundreds of depositions in the case. At one status hearing, the judge said he was "convinced" that "this was the largest patent infringement suit in the history of the United States." The case eventually settled only when Conner obtained a new patent that threatened not only IBM's disk drive business but also its laptop business, and this change in the dynamics of the case forced a settlement.

Another complicated IP case that did not settle was the computer copyright case of *Lotus vs. Borland. Lotus Development Corp. v. Borland International*, 49 F.3d 807 (1st. Cir. 1995), aff'd by an equally divided court, 516 U.S. 233 (1996). Lotus Development Corp. had a spreadsheet program called Lotus 1-2-3 that included a set of menus or commands for operating the spreadsheet on a computer. Menu options such as "Worksheet," "Copy," "Move," "File," "Print," and so forth would appear at the top of the DOS computer screen. Our client, Borland International, came out with competing computer spreadsheets called Quattro and Quattro Pro, which had their own set of menus that Borland felt were superior to Lotus's.

The problem was that Lotus had a big, established base of users who were used to the Lotus menus and had even written macros, or automated step-saving programs, that were dependent on the Lotus menus. Therefore, Borland included a feature in its program so you could change the user interface of the Borland program so it used the same menus Lotus did. We never found out if Lotus had ever applied for a patent on its menu structure or hierarchy, but Lotus tried to enforce its rights to its menu structure through copyright law. What made this case complicated was that copyright law is intended in the computer context to cover expressive elements of computer code, and Borland did not copy any of Lotus's code. Borland wrote its own code. The issue in this case centered on the menus each company was using, and menus are merely methods to operate a computer. They are not like a traditional copyrighted work of authorship, such as a book or play.

Nevertheless, Lotus sued Borland for copyright infringement. The issues in this case were enormously complicated in terms of what the law in this area was, and what it should be. The case involved questions such as "What types of IP should be patentable instead of copyrightable?" as well as antitrust implications with respect to Lotus having a big base of customers who were essentially "locked in" to using Lotus's menus, if it was found that Lotus could dictate who could use Lotus's menu hierarchy.

The law in this area was rapidly developing at the time this trial occurred. Borland lost at the trial court level and won on appeal, then the Supreme Court agreed to hear the case, and Borland won there as well.

Recent Trends and Changes in IP

Two years ago, the most important IP issues involved patents. The Supreme Court was taking up many cases and overruling the Federal Circuit with respect to many of its decisions. This situation came about because the Federal Circuit Court of Appeals, which hears all the patent appeals in this country, was seen to have overextended patent law in the direction of providing too much protection for patent holders, and many people were concerned that patent laws were getting out of hand. In one well-known patent case, the popular BlackBerry device was about to be shut down because the people who made it had lost a patent lawsuit. *NTP, Inc. v. Research in Motion Ltd.*, 392 F.3d 1336 (Fed. Cir. 2004). A shutdown was avoided only when Research in Motion paid NTP more than $600 million to settle the dispute.

Apparently, in reaction to the Federal Circuit case law, the Supreme Court started cutting back on certain aspects of patent protection. Notable cases included:

- *eBay Inc. v. MercExchange L.L.C.*, 547 U.S. 388 (2006). In this case, the Supreme Court unanimously overruled the Federal Circuit's rule that a winning patent owner would almost always get an automatic injunction once it won at trial. (The threat of such an injunction forced the large settlement in the BlackBerry case.) Because of this ruling, many companies that do not practice their own patents have been denied injunctions after winning the trial, and instead merely awarded royalties.

- *MedImmune Inc. v. Genentech Inc.*, 127 S. Ct. 764 (2007). In this case, the Supreme Court made it easier for an accused infringer to challenge a patent by filing what is known as a "declaratory judgment" action against the patent owner, for a declaration that the patent is invalid and/or not infringed.

- *KSR Int'l Co. v. Teleflex Inc.*, 127 S. Ct. 1727 (2007). This case made it easier to challenge a patent as being obvious, and overruled decades of Federal Circuit precedent.

- *Microsoft Corp. v. AT&T Corp.*, 127 S. Ct. 1746 (2007). This case limited the ability of a patent owner to recover damages for infringing products that were manufactured and sold outside the United States.

Apparently, in response to the willingness of the Supreme Court to review and reverse Federal Circuit doctrines that the Supreme Court believed went too far, the Federal Circuit has recently started to retreat from merely issuing pro-patent positions. For example, in a 2007 case decided after the above Supreme Court cases, the Federal Circuit made it more difficult to prove willful infringement. *In re Seagate Technology LLC*, 497 F.3d 1360 (Fed. Cir. 2007).

At the present time, there is a great deal of litigation over copyright protection for Web-based technology. Much of this litigation centers on the Digital Millennium Copyright Act. Various Web-based companies are engaged in battles with content providers such as entertainment and record companies over what those Web-based companies can do on the Internet in terms of searches and providing links to content. Many content providers want to limit the ability of people to get content over the Internet unless the content providers provide the access to the content themselves, or at least are guaranteed a royalty for every Internet use. The law is still very much unsettled in this area.

Domestic and International Regulatory Agencies in the IP Realm

With respect to patents and trademarks, the most important regulatory agency in the United States is the U.S. Patent and Trademark Office, which regulates patents and federal trademark registrations. Most states also have trademark offices that will issue a state trademark, although those types of marks are not worth as much as a federal trademark that covers the whole country. The U.S. Copyright Office is a division of the Library of Congress that regulates copyrights. There is no federal organization or state agencies for the regulation of trade secret protection. Therefore, this area is typically protected by common law or state statutes.

There are also some worldwide organizations that deal with patents, trademarks, and copyrights. In Europe, there is the European Patent Office, which provides patent protection in Europe. There is a Patent Cooperation Treaty that enables you to file for what can amount to a worldwide patent application, but this process entails applying for patents under the national patent offices of the individual countries you are interested in. Copyright and trademark protection is issued on a country-by-country basis.

The "How To" page on the U.S. Patent and Trademark Office's Web site (uspto.gov/main/howdoi.htm) has a number of useful links with respect to patent and trademark regulations. For copyrights, see these links:

- copyright.gov
- copyright.gov/circs/circ1.html (copyright basics)
- copyright.gov/help/faq/ (frequently asked questions)

Sources for Monitoring IP Trends and Other Helpful Resources

There are a number of useful sources for monitoring IP trends, depending on the industry the client is in. For example, the *BNA Patent, Trademark, and Copyright Journal* is the most useful single journal for monitoring legal trends, because it has both a daily and weekly service that does a very good job of reporting on a number of different IP areas across the country. It reports on current legislation and court decisions, and what is happening at seminars. For more details, see the *BNA Patent, Trademark, and Copyright Journal* at bna.com/products/ip/ptcj.htm and *Patent, Trademark & Copyright Daily* at bna.com/products/ip/ptdm.htm.

The *IP Law 360*, a somewhat newer resource, is also very useful. It sends daily e-mail updates, and you can check out updated content on their Web site. This resource tends to focus on court decisions, but it also has useful information on legislation, and it usually features guest articles on a daily basis. For more information, visit ip.law360.com/default.aspx.

The blogs and Web sites in this area are of varying types and quality, depending on what you are interested in. Some of these resources include:

- Patently-O (patentlaw.typepad.com/patent)
- The Federal Circuit home page (cafc.uscourts.gov)
- A blog devoted to litigation in the Eastern District of Texas, where many patent suits are filed (mcsmith.blogs.com)
- The Trademark Blog (schwimmerlegal.com)
- Eric Goldman's technology and marketing law blog (blog.ericgoldman.org)
- PATNEWS from bustpatents.com
- Peter Zura's patent blog (271patent.blogspot.com)
- The U.S. Patent and Trademark Office Website (uspto.gov)

Several sources that are not focused solely on IP law, but are of general interest to legal practitioners and report on IP issues on occasion, are:

- The Volokh Conspiracy (volokh.com) is more of a general legal blog, but it mentions IP decisions from time to time.
- SCOTUSblog (scotusblog.com/wp) is a place to look for Supreme Court decisions.

Finally, many if not all IP cases require expert witnesses on a variety of topics. Some expert witness consultants include:

- Silicon Valley Expert Witness Group: svewg.com
- National Expert Witness Network: newnexperts.com
- IMS Expert Services: ims-expertservices.com
- NERA Economic Consulting: nera.com
- Cornerstone Research: cornerstone.com

Final Thoughts: Understanding Competitive IP Situations

Be prepared. That is the best way to deal with your competitors in terms of IP. If you have a really new and novel technology that competitors are going to steal, you need to anticipate that situation and make sure you have the proper IP protection in place to stop that from happening. Similarly, if your competitors are aggressive, you need to make sure you are going to be in a position to deal with IP litigation on an economical basis when it happens.

To protect clients in this area, you have to understand the particular client, their industry, and their technology in order to understand what IP will be able to do for them relative to their competitors, and what their competitors might be able to do against them in terms of IP.

Michael Barclay is a member of Wilson Sonsini Goodrich & Rosati. He practices in the fields of patent and intellectual property litigation, particularly in electronics-related areas. He has litigated patent, trade secret, copyright, and trademark cases in a wide variety of fields, including semiconductors, computer graphics, computer disk drives, cable television descramblers, and computer software.

Mr. Barclay received a B.A. in physics and an M.S. in electrical engineering from the University of California at Berkeley, and his J.D. from UCLA Law School in 1979, where he was an associate editor of the UCLA Law Review. Prior to entering the legal field, he was employed at Intel Corporation and at Hughes Aircraft Company, where he designed CMOS, EPROM, and CCD integrated circuits, processes, and solid state devices.

Mr. Barclay is a member of the State Bar of California and the Institute of Electrical and Electronics Engineers. He is admitted to practice before the U.S. Patent and Trademark Office, the U.S. District Courts for the Northern, Central, Southern, and Eastern Districts of California, the U.S. Courts of Appeals for the First, Ninth, and Federal Circuits, and the U.S. Supreme Court.

Dedication: *This chapter is dedicated to the memory of Daniel Barclay.*

Advising Clients in Transactional IP

Phillip E. Adler

Partner

Loeb & Loeb LLP

ASPATORE

Many otherwise knowledgeable colleagues and clients both inside and outside of the legal profession have a tendency to classify intellectual property (IP) lawyers as a group of professionals who speak with a single voice. However, patent lawyers are not merger and acquisition lawyers, merger and acquisition lawyers are not necessarily skilled in matters involving the development and commercialization of software, and practitioners who are heavily involved in licensing are not necessarily trademark or copyright experts. My voice, my specialty in a specialized field, has been the acquisition and implementation of major information technology (IT) systems, also commonly referred to as enterprise software systems.

I am fortunate to have had a diverse background. I have close to forty years of concurrent experience in the areas of mergers and acquisitions and IP, and I have represented both those who acquire IT systems and individual software properties, and those who develop and distribute such systems and properties. Related areas in which I practice include outsourcing of IT departments and, more recently, a strong overlay of work involving the design and development of Web sites, privacy issues that arise with increasing frequency with respect to the operation of Web sites, and the creation and use of digital rights management and protections for the delivery of content over the Internet.

Representing the Client in IP Acquisitions

When representing a client that is acquiring a new IT platform to run its business, I will be called upon to understand the nature of the legacy systems and what it is that has been promised to the client, both from the business and legal standpoints and from the technology perspective as well. For example, many hospitals are currently involved in the process of acquiring very large, expensive, and complex IT systems governing the entire spectrum of their operations. Such acquisitions often may consist of a two-part process: coupled with negotiating the terms of the licenses and the support agreements for the IT system to be acquired, I am also called upon to negotiate the consulting or implementation agreement with either the software vendor or a consulting firm. Therefore, legal counsel is essentially representing the client in connection with two very different kinds of agreements, all the while seeking to establish a certain degree of accountability on the part of those who would profit greatly by the licensing and implementation relationships. This is where the marriage of IP and merger and acquisition skills is critical, because at that point counsel is dealing with both commercial and technology issues.

The tension between the two kinds of relationships becomes all too quickly obvious: the software vendor will insist that its system works each and every time and that problems, if any, arise only in the customization and implementation, as to which, claims the software vendor, only the customer should be at risk. The implementation/customization teams will respond, on the other hand, that they are merely consultants, and that any problems must lie with the software vendor or the customer. In the absence of experienced legal advisers, the allocation of risk will fall squarely and exclusively on the customer. A bad place to be if you are the customer. So my thesis can be briefly summarized: there are methods through which the allocation of risk can be shared, at least to some extent, if you care to spend the time and effort.

I am also engaged by those who did not go through the rigors of carefully negotiating these kinds of agreements. After a few years into the project, such a client may come to the realization that it has a financial and technological disaster on its hands. A chief executive officer or general counsel of a business will ordinarily engage legal counsel in a $5 to $30 million project outside of the technology area. But all too often, if a decision is reached that an enterprise must acquire a new IT platform, executive management may simply assume—often based on input from the head of technology—that the terms of such acquisitions are non-negotiable, or that negotiation of such terms is unnecessary. Such an assumption, however, is likely to be incorrect and may prove to be a costly error.

In our firm, we put together multi-disciplinary teams to handle troubled acquisitions of IT platforms. Typically, a litigation partner (having both technology and licensing experience) and I will work in tandem to seek remedies for the client. And while it may be demanding work for the lawyers, it is a far more difficult process for the client, because the implementation of what the client had set out to achieve will, at a minimum, be delayed for many years, and no one likes to return to senior management or the board and tell them there is a serious problem. The message here should be clear: engage qualified legal counsel in the formative stages rather than the disaster recovery stages.

Representing the IP Owner

Conversely, I may be engaged by an emerging software company that is undertaking the design, development, and distribution of its own products. In that case, I will work with the client to establish its initial business model and legal structures, and its policies and procedures for IP protection. The client and I will typically review in considerable detail the variety of possibilities that are available. It is important to consider a number of key questions, some examples of which include:

- What are the preferred distribution channels for the type of IP product involved?
- Is the license term perpetual or renewable?
- What are the usage implications (run time or authorized users)?
- Is there an application service provider component?

In many cases, the industry itself and/or a dominant competing product may have already set the standard for how the client's product will be distributed, and clients often tend to select those elements that have been previously established in the market, rather than trying to experiment with a different business model.

Frequently, our conversations will center on the degree of tolerance within the emerging client's marketplace for various types of contractual IP protections. In other words, what is the perceived level of tolerance or lack of tolerance that prospective customers will exhibit in relation to the degree of IP protections for the client's products? A number of topics are common. For example, will customers accept the requirement for the installation of new release versions in order to continue to be eligible for product support? Will customers require source code escrows? Will customers accept strong limitations of liability? Fortunately, the IP marketplace tends to allow for a greater degree of protection for those who design, develop, and distribute software than is often available for more tangible products in other industries, perhaps because more clients in the software industry have consulted with lawyers upon the inception of their businesses due to the intangible nature of the underlying IP, and due to the nature of the license relationship, as contrasted with a product sale.

I believe the most difficult lesson to impart here is the absolute need for the emerging enterprise to separate marketing and sales materials from its contractual obligations, and to censor the client's natural enthusiasm for a new product so it does not become "over-promised." Accordingly, I recommend that legal counsel review from time to time the text of marketing materials, and that such materials be expressly excluded from the contractual documents. Interestingly, this problem is not limited to the emerging enterprise, and actually can be a plague for the mature business as well. It is one I have been able to exploit routinely when representing the customer for such software, as will be discussed below.

Major Challenges in IP Negotiations

One of the principal challenges an IP attorney faces when representing a client who intends to acquire a major IT system is that of the client expectations, sometimes expecting too much from the product, but more often demanding too little from the software vendor or project implementation team. While you may not be able to induce Microsoft to accept changes in the terms of its licensing agreements, if the project is big enough (i.e., many hundreds of thousands, if not millions, of dollars), almost all of the mega-licensors of this world will very grudgingly agree to negotiate some of the terms in their standard documentation, even though they will initially tell you they will not do so. The client needs to appreciate that this is not just a "make work" project for zealous legal counsel, but that it genuinely represents a value-added effort to establish accountability and risk sharing in connection with the project. Client education of what is possible in relation to these issues is extremely important, following which the client may then intelligently decide whether it wants to spend the time and money to negotiate these terms. Of course, some will elect not to do so, and some of those will wish they had.

The percentage of major IT initiatives that experience very significant cost overruns and material schedule delays is astonishingly high. And the percentage of major developmental projects (i.e., those having a relatively high degree of customization or custom development and build factors) that fail altogether or do not reach scalability or other key metrics is even higher. Needless to say, many clients do not want to hear this from their legal counsel, or entertain this advice at all. And it's certainly not the kind of information glowingly presented in your annual report. Understanding that there is a material element of risk in these projects is perhaps the single most important advice I can provide, as this information will drive other discussions and considerations that are discussed below.

Another challenge in the domain of IP negotiations results from the enormous rate of change in technology-driven industries. What you knew to be a problem a few years ago, at least from a practical standpoint, may no longer be an issue today. This rate of change cannot be overestimated. It was not that long ago, for example, that I was in the audience when a chief visionary officer (that wasn't his title, but it seemed to be his job description) spoke of governments and businesses, individuals and communities, electronically wired together in every form of business and personal expression, as a challenge to our collective future landscape. All this from the spokesperson of one of Silicon Valley's most forward-looking enterprises. Yet those words had hardly escaped his mouth when they had become obsolete. The lesson may be that legal counsel and business leaders alike need to understand better the relationship between our customary legal issues and the nature of our clients' particular technologies. It also is important for practitioners and business leaders alike to understand where the risks may become manifest in any given transaction and in any new technology, and the protections that can be employed to mitigate such risks. This process requires a degree of candor among the members of the technology, business, and legal teams that, quite often, is simply lacking. But therein lies the goal.

As globalization and the concentration of vendors in the various IP-centric industries increases, processes that influence almost every facet of our lives and commercial practices, the acquisition and implementation of major IT systems is and will continue to be affected. From the client standpoint, the license and implementation agreements for the acquisition of IT systems will become increasingly difficult to negotiate based on the disparity in bargaining power and the lack of viable alternative choices. This is not a populist diatribe, but simply a fact of current economic life that must be recognized and overcome to the extent possible by a variety of techniques.

Prominent among those is the use of request for proposal/request for quotation procedures. When using this process, counsel also may consider offering up an acquiring party form of license that must be used by the successful bidder. Keep the competition in play as long as possible. These techniques can help level the playing field in the context of projects having significant scope and dollar value.

The globalization and concentration of vendors not only affects those who are acquiring IP, but it also presents an increasingly formidable entry barrier for emerging enterprises. Many entrepreneurs who have succeeded in developing and placing a viable product into commercial production will have a choice of whether to try to continue to go at it alone, or sell or license product rights to one of the major software players, knowing that if they do not, the potential acquiring party will threaten to obtain rights to someone else's product or develop a similar product internally. Indeed, in negotiating an "inbound license" to a major software company, creating what is essentially a private label relationship, the leverage is entirely in the hands of the acquiring party. Therefore, legal counsel's role is often reduced to protecting the young entrepreneur from himself or herself, while at the same time knowing when and where some flexibility can be achieved. A guiding presence, reminding the entrepreneur that there is a reason his or her product has been chosen, can mean more than any negotiation with the acquiring party.

However, these challenges, while difficult to overcome, are what make IP enterprises and IP legal practices alike exciting. Legal counsel must be capable of handling any issues on a technological level. When legal counsel reviews the request for proposal or request for quotation with the client's technical team, we must be able to recognize and discuss any technology problems that affect the legal relations. At the same time, counsel must have a sense of transactional realities—what will work and what will not. Therefore, we must be able to employ two very different skill sets in support of our clients.

Effectively Negotiating an IP Agreement

As suggested above, many problems in this practice area occur simply because the client did not bring legal counsel into the process before signing agreements for IT system acquisitions. Skilled counsel can assist clients in mitigating a variety of risks. For example, I was recently brought in to assist the in-house counsel of a publicly held company that was in the process of restructuring its IT platform. One of the projects involved a comparatively low-tech, high-volume software solution. When I reviewed the proposed license agreement, I discovered the license stipulated that the software would work in accordance with the product specifications. I then asked the client, "Have you reviewed the product specifications? If so, are they adequate? Do they contain performance metrics satisfactory for your purposes?"

A momentary digression. On the one hand, "product specifications" for software traditionally consist of "functional specifications" describing what tasks a product will perform. On the other hand, "performance specifications" or "performance metrics" are frequently absent from the product specifications. Performance metrics are especially important, as they delineate how much volume the product can be expected to produce, what the response times will be correlated to the volumes and the number of concurrent users, as well as the expected up-time of the platform. Indeed, the existence or lack of performance metrics can often represent the difference between accountability for the failure of an IT project on the one hand, or the result that there may be no recourse for such failure on the other hand. This is the other most important piece of advice I can provide to any client from the acquisition perspective.

Returning to my example, the client told me, "Well, we haven't seen the specifications, so we don't know what they consist of, and the vendor won't let us see them until we sign the license." We then scheduled a conference call with the vendor. I asked the vendor, "Where are the specifications?" The vendor said, "We don't give them out until you sign up." I said, "We don't sign up until we review the specifications." After some grumbling, the vendor finally agreed to provide the specifications. However, we soon received a call back from the vendor, who told us they did not have specifications of any kind for that particular product line. I then told the vendor, "Your license says the product will work in accordance with the specifications, and now you are telling me there are no specifications, and therefore there is no accountability on your part." At that point, I instructed the vendor that my client's technical team would work with the vendor's technical team to develop mutually agreeable performance specifications detailing the minimum standards under which the product would operate. Although there was again some considerable grumbling, the vendor ultimately agreed, and we signed the licenses following completion of the specifications. As it turned out, one of three major project elements failed to perform as per the agreed specifications, and we demanded that the vendor return the relevant part of the client's money. Had we not structured the licenses in the manner I have described, the client would have been left with no recourse for a product that simply did not perform appropriately in the real world. Instead, the client received a check for half a million dollars without the necessity and expense of litigation.

Interestingly, the project manager for this client was initially resistant to the entire line of inquiry because he was concerned it would unduly delay the project, but I made it clear that I was hired by the general counsel to protect the company, not one individual's project schedule.

Another element lies in project timing. For more than thirty years, IT vendors have played the "end of quarter" or "end of fiscal year" game, claiming that, "Once we're in a new quarter (or year), the favorable pricing we've quoted for you is off the table." Whether the client is willing to play software poker is always an interesting moment. But by just a little better timing in the project cycle, you can avoid this problem entirely. Needless to say, my answer to this dilemma is simply to reply, "Next-quarter business is better than no business at all." But you will need client buy-in that it will simply not stand for this kind of treatment.

Understanding Your Client's IP Needs

IP Categories, Prioritization

The major categories of legal needs for the preservation and protection of IP rights are determined from the nature of each client's particular business. Accordingly, clients are better served by encouraging IP counsel to explore directly and personally the nature of the client's businesses so we in turn can best protect that which is of the greatest importance to our clients.

For example, while a client may have obtained patent protection involving a critical element of its world beating widget, it nevertheless may need to develop an IP protection program covering any number of areas ancillary to its main IP asset. This IP infrastructure could quite easily include any of the following tasks:

- Obtain trademark rights to the name "world beating widget."
- Consider copyright protection of slogans for the "world beating widget."
- Determine if the client's IT department has used any open-source code in connection with the development or operation of the widget, and consider any implications if such was the case.
- Establish standardized work-for-hire and non-disclosure agreements for the use of independent contractors and third-party consultants.
- Develop institutional invention/patent policies for the client's employees.
- Review product licensing/sale policies and contracts for the widget, with a view to the preservation of IP rights.
- Review key employee contracts, with a view to protection of the IP owned by the enterprise.
- Review Web site terms and conditions for IP and privacy protections and related matters.

Obviously, each of these examples has a different weighting in terms of importance. And the client's needs will be better served if a number of these examples had been in place prior to the creation of the widget. The foregoing is presented only as a series of examples to be considered, reminders really, of the broad range of the kinds of IP protections that may be useful and available for the protection of IP beyond that required for the initial IP invention itself.

A related inquiry: is the IP an occasional byproduct or one small component of a larger business, or is the IP key to what generates a material part of the client's revenue stream? Prioritization needs to be driven by the client's business needs, and the applicable business model. The larger the client, the more likely that outside counsel will be restricted to services on a project-by-project basis. Yet legal counsel is most effective when we are provided with the opportunity to explore and respond to the larger picture.

Therefore, when IP counsel considers the legal needs of a new client, we should explore the characteristics of the industry involved, the client's business generally, and the specific role of the IP in the potential revenue stream for the enterprise, in order to determine the appropriate expense level for the protection of the IP. Consequently, to protect the client and its budget, we need to:

- Identify the categories of legal protection that may be required.
- Understand the role of the IP in the client's business, and then make appropriate recommendations concerning the client's budget for legal services.
- Isolate the relevant portions of the IP infrastructure for which protection should be obtained within the client's specified budget. Propose the most cost-effective means of protecting the IP infrastructure.
- The prioritization of IP protection should occur initially based on the client's business judgment as to the relative importance of the respective IP rights to the overall financial and operational success of the enterprise. Ideally, these kinds of decisions are made with the advice of IP counsel.

Harvesting Information

I do not believe the use of checklists is the best means of harvesting the information necessary to establish an IP protection program or to counsel IP clients effectively. I typically borrow from the merger and acquisition experience and recommend that in-person (if feasible) or telephonic due diligence meetings with various client business leaders will provide a more comprehensive picture of what the client may need, including the exposure of differing opinions within the client team concerning the relative values, future prospects, and expected life spans for key elements of the client's respective IP assets.

All too often, the task of responding to checklists is delegated by the client to those persons with the least seniority, or who are perceived to have the most time available for such purposes. This is not necessarily the person with the broadest vision in the enterprise. Moreover, such delegation is likely to reflect only the information available to that one person. Instead, I recommend obtaining the personal views of several business leaders, to include representatives from (i) in-house legal counsel, if any, (ii) IT, (iii) sales and marketing, and (iv) research and development. Consensus is not necessary, but reliable information is critical. The client will benefit indirectly as well. A more in-depth and analytical, if not personal, viewpoint will be expressed to legal counsel behind closed doors than will ever be provided to a subordinate for a checklist.

When I refer to "due diligence," I do not mean reviewing the IP equivalent of minute books, contracts, and licenses. I have in mind conversations, posing leading questions, conducting a friendly deposition, and encouraging personal views of the business model, the nature of the IP, and the direction of the client's business. It is important to learn the business from the eyes of those who lead it. Counsel will be able to fill in the legal blanks as things proceed.

Consideration of Industry Factors

I certainly recommend obtaining documents in current use by various competitors when considering the kinds of IP protections that may be warranted for a client's particular product or industry. Such reviews might include consideration of the kinds of customer sale contracts, licenses, warranty and support policies, and other critical contracts in general use within the industry for competing products. It is important for legal counsel to understand what the norm is in each particular industry to engage with the client in the "marketing" versus "legal protection" discussions, particularly as they relate to the permissible depth and nature of contracts to protect the client's IP.

The determination of the nature, degree, and type of IP protection can often involve a number of independent moving parts, such as (i) the type of protection that may be available for the particular IP, (ii) the client's budget for ongoing protection, (iii) the client's need for protection, (iv) the ease of entry/difficulty of entry into a given field or industry, (v) the velocity of change in the given field or industry, and (vi) the prevalence of work-arounds to avoid the kind of IP protection that might otherwise be selected for the particular IP involved. Of these six factors, the last three, in particular, involve familiarity with the client's industry, not just the client's business.

Again, I believe an in-depth due diligence review with key business leaders at the client level becomes the most effective means of determining the relevant industry factors. To be effective, counsel certainly needs to see the industry, overall, and the client's place in that industry, in particular, through the client's eyes.

Monitoring IP Trends

Attorneys by nature, practice, and training are experts on what has occurred in the past. However, we are challenged, perhaps as never before, by the rapidity of technological change. Monitoring the prevailing trends—legal, business, and technological—is a much more demanding inquiry today than in the past. Correspondingly, vast amounts of information can be accessed through the Internet today as never before. Therefore, the range and speed of change has created both unparalleled challenges and opportunities to the IP practitioner.

The social networking Web sites that have become so prominent during the past few years provide a contemporary example of unanticipated change, having interest to IP practitioners well beyond the highly publicized infringement cases. As a result, an increasing number of major multinational corporations is beginning to explore how they may harness or encourage customer interaction through company-sponsored sites. And all of these kinds of activities involve knowledgeable IP-, media-, and content-savvy corporate, entertainment, and legal executives and legal advisers with the foresight to lead rather than follow.

Learning how to cope with and recognize those particular trends that may affect any given client will often take the practicing lawyer out of his or her comfort zone. Here are a few useful tips to consider:

- Clients and IP counsel should consider the means by which third parties may be able to appropriate the client's IP and forge it, steal it, alter it, duplicate it, disclose it, physh it, spam it, regulate it for public use, create private and moral rights to it, and so on.
- Clients and IP counsel should anticipate the frailties and vulnerabilities facing the client's IP in order to fashion legal solutions accordingly.
- From counsel's perspective, talk to your clients. They already think you are pretty smart, or they wouldn't be your clients. Try to envision what their innovation promises to be, consider what their product vulnerabilities may be, and discuss what factors the client fears the most.
- All concerned need to be prepared for the expansion of conventional laws to new IP. Privacy-related issues (see the recent legislative activities regarding DNA test results, as just one example) represent an area ripe for future expansion.

Recommendations

While any generic recommendations gain relevance only through application to the specific problems and facts involving each individual client, the nature of the IP, and the position of the client and its technology within its particular industry, I have nevertheless set forth some recommendations and further reflections in the following sections in the hopes that they may be of some assistance to IP counsel and their clients.

The following are some general recommendations for best practices in the IP practice area:

- Once the client has been provided with forms of agreements dealing with work for hire, confidentiality, and similar topics to be signed by third-party contractors and consultants, counsel and the client should periodically discuss whether and to what extent these protections are being systematically placed into everyday use by the client.
- Counsel should be correspondingly encouraged to review the forms of such agreements in use from time to time against the "master form" that was originally supplied to the client. These types of

agreements frequently morph over time in the hands of those who are charged with implementing them. A change is made for one particular contractor, and that changed form then unknowingly and unintentionally becomes the client's new template.

- Once the client has been provided with an employee invention policy, related provisions for the client's employment manuals, and implementing forms covering employee inventions, counsel likewise should be periodically encouraged to audit the level of compliance by the client.

- In this regard, when representing emerging enterprises, look back as well as forward. Confirm that the founders and former key employees have assigned to the enterprise all rights and interests to key IP in accordance with prior understandings and agreements. It is surprising how often this will arise as an impediment to a future sale, merger, or initial public offering.

- As mentioned above, there is a broad range of medium- to higher-end software, the business and legal terms of which *are* negotiable. Indeed, as also previously noted, even if you will not be able to achieve any success with one or two major players, you will be able to level the playing field to some extent with a surprising number of other major vendors.

- The same is true for the engagement of professional services incidental to the acquisition of IT platforms. Such services are provided under outsourcing contracts, implementation contracts, development contracts, Web site contracts, and other consulting contracts, many of which are as important as the licenses for the underlying IP. And often the cost factor is equal to or greater than the license fees for the underlying IP. Failure at least to consider, if not pursue, some degree of risk sharing and accountability for the success of the project in connection with the engagement of such services may not be a prudent decision.

- Clients often consider the related statements of work and specifications accompanying the licenses or customization and implementation contracts for IT platforms, or for major Web site projects, as the exclusive province of the IT team. Nothing could be further from the truth. First, the legal terms of the design, development, implementation, and similar contracts cannot really be separated from the transactional detail of what will be performed or provided by the contractor. Second, it is all too common for such attachments to provide that the terms of the attachment supersede the terms of the principal agreement. And the terms of the attachment may well allocate all risks for performance and completion of the tasks under the attachment on the client, rather than shared as appropriate between the contracting party and the client. Last, such attachments may often directly or indirectly include other very material legal terms.

- Contract negotiations to include the presence of the legal team should be started earlier in the overall process than is often thought to be necessary. Otherwise, the pressure on the business team at the end of the selection/contracting process will leave the legal team arguing not only with the vendor, but also with the client's own business leaders whose project schedule is placed in jeopardy due to extended negotiations of the remaining business and legal terms.

- Legal counsel should be consulted on the importance and best practices to control the use of open-source software. The critical element here is not so much "how" to control this use, but rather to educate the client on the need for such controls, and the basis under which that need arises.

- Legal counsel should review and assist in the preparation of requests for proposals and requests for quotations. These practices will help protect the client's IP acquisition in a variety of ways, including: (i) identify and help preserve what the client may develop or own as contrasted with what may be licensed from others, (ii) if the client intends to require the vendor to use a form of agreement created for or by the client, as licensee or buyer, this is the appropriate time to make such a requirement known, (iii) this is where the inclusion of relevant performance metrics and the creation of risk-sharing and accountability begins, and (iv) to the extent that the client has specific legal terms and conditions peculiar to its business or industry, special terms adopted by its general counsel, or unique legal issues, these should be specified and vendor education and buy-in should take place at this time, as a condition to the vendor response to the request for proposal or request for quotation.

Risks of IP Management

The legal and financial risks in IP management may increase dramatically in the circumstance when the risks themselves are vaguely perceived, if at all. The failure to perceive the risks involved occurs more often for IP created or acquired for internal operations, rather than with respect to IP portfolios developed as part of the ongoing business of the enterprise. I think of the former as "internal" or "enterprise" IP, and the latter as "product" IP. Clients whose business models are directly involved in the design and development of product IP or the creation of IP-dependent products are more likely to understand and pursue appropriate levels of IP protection.

However, clients who acquire enterprise IP as an incidental result of conducting business largely unrelated to the creation of IP products are often at risk of failing to recognize the need for IP-related protections. Additionally, businesses that principally *develop* enterprise IP for internal use only may stand the greatest chance of failing to recognize the need for IP protection programs.

Another common risk occurs when acquiring enterprise licenses for IP used in the process of creating the enterprise's products. Frequently such licenses contain restrictions on the field of use that are considered reasonable at the time. Clients are often willing to accept such restrictions because they believe they will never enter into other product lines that would make such restrictions untenable. However, if their business goals change or the product lines change, they may realize the mistake they have made, but at that point, it may be too late or too expensive to correct the mistake, or the rights they need might not be available.

Specific Recommendations for Business Leadership

- A word about custom IT projects: don't. Or think twice about recommendations to develop independently, either internally or by contract, a new-generation IT system, or to substantially customize an existing IT system. And then, "just say no." The road to IT ruin is paved with such projects.
- If the project warrants a consultant, clients often choose one who has advised others with respect to acquisitions involving the same

IP. This selection criteria should apply equally to your selection of legal counsel. More and more general counsel will tell you that today they engage lawyers, not law firms.

- Consider early on with your legal and consulting teams the general parameters of what level of risk you are willing to underwrite, and what level of protection is likely to be achievable, in relation to the type of project and the track record for the vendor of the IP. Bear in mind the general recommendations discussed above concerning major IP undertakings.

- Consider the extent to which some degree of accountability for the proper operation of the IT platform can be allocated to the vendor of the IT platform and to the provider of implementation or consulting services.

- As also anecdotally noted above, the determination of mutually agreed performance metrics is the keystone for the successful IT project. Yes, the software itself usually will be accompanied by some form of product specifications. Such specifications serve only as the starting point for your protection. Such matters as scalability (both concurrent user access and volumes) and speed of processing, benchmarked for volumes as well as system performance (and single versus multiple instances), should be considered for your platform and embodied in performance metrics for which there is some degree of accountability and remedy.

- Last, don't lose sight of the responses received during the request for proposal/request for quotation process, as well as other "sales cycle" information that is commonly provided by the vendor. Do you really want to hear, "Well, yes, that's what we said, but…"? I routinely require the vendor to incorporate by reference their responses to the request for proposal/request for quotation and even sales literature providing product descriptions and product functionality as part of the IT platform specifications. You can easily imagine what those discussions sound like, particularly concerning inclusion of the sales cycle marketing material, and it is not pretty. In the final analysis, either such information is accurate and worthy of inclusion as part of the product specifications, or it is inaccurate. In either circumstance, the client benefits from this exercise. What you might not imagine is the degree to which this process causes the vendor to "correct" information previously delivered, and to resize the recommended hardware and related products. Certainly, if that resizing is necessary to protect the vendor, the additional capacity will likely protect the client as well.

After-Care

Finally, a few words of advice concerning support (maintenance) relationships. So-called service level agreements are common in outsourcing relationships, and on occasion they are offered in acquisition or support agreements for IT platforms as well. Basically, these tend to be liquidated damage provisions, providing very modest credits to the customer upon the failure of the IT system to achieve various benchmarks, such as system up-time. My approach is to require that service level agreements are not exclusive remedies if the triggers occur more than a stated minimum number of times within any rolling six- or twelve-month period. This response is strongly resisted, as the service level agreement is offered to limit the vendor's liability, not as a means of making the customer whole.

Probably the most common ongoing issue in support relationships today involves the conflict that develops between the vendor's requirement that the customer install new versions and releases within a given period of time or within a specified number of versions in arrears. While this requirement may appear to be fair, it nevertheless may result in the concomitant requirement for the customer to install and run new versions or releases of third-party products the customer does not want to deploy at all or within the time required. There is often no "right" or "wrong" here, but to understand the problem is the first step in negotiating at least more favorable terms than those offered in the conventional support agreement.

Another example of issues to consider with respect to support agreements involves the potential legal effects of change orders or amendments that may create unintended changes to existing agreements. Even those clients who are scrupulous in their use of legal counsel in the negotiation and documentation of the principal license agreements neglect to involve legal counsel in connection with ongoing project change orders and amendments to support agreements. Yet those same change orders or amendments may contain assumptions, terms, or conditions that will significantly alter the legal relationship between the contracting parties.

A few years ago, through a series of "amendments" ostensibly related to the support agreements with its customers, an international software vendor of major repute effectively altered (to its customers' significant financial detriment) the entire fabric of the pricing structure under its license agreements with respect to the usage charges payable for its software. The tech personnel, being unaware of the subtle nature of these changes, blithely signed amendment after amendment, until the crisis became apparent. This points to the need for improved processes between IT leadership and staff on the one hand, and legal counsel on the other hand.

Another example can be found with a service level agreement under an outsourcing contract that included both the personnel and IT equipment and software licenses of a client. I had occasion to revisit the contract a number of years into what was a long-term relationship. Upon inquiry as to what the client's experience had been under the service level provisions, I was told by the client, "Whoops, we forgot about that." Common attrition in the workplace environment can leave the IT department without the personnel who negotiated and understood the nature of key contracts. The absence of legal summaries or other processes for maintaining control over the rights and remedies available at a day-to-day level under such contracts should be examined.

It is not at all uncommon for the long-term expenses under the support relationship to exceed the original license fees for the IT platform. And once acceptance has occurred for the customer's IT system, the client is left only with the support relationship. It seems self-evident that as much attention should be paid to the support relationship as with any other aspect of the license agreement. Yet this is seldom the case. This should be seriously reconsidered by IT departments, both large and small.

Phillip E. Adler is a partner with Loeb & Loeb. His practice concentrates on the acquisition of enterprise-wide information technology platforms and systems (ranging from $1 to $50 million), the licensing of client software to major entertainment and software companies for internal and private label use, major information technology outsourcing relationships, digital rights protection for licensors or users of media downloads, and dispute resolution and project analysis. He also deals with Web site development contracts, privacy and security policies, matters regarding loss or theft of customer data, patent licensing and commercialization, and more.

A Survey of
IP Management

Alejandro J. Fernandez

Of Counsel

Broad and Cassel

ASPATORE

Intellectual property (IP) constitutes a major asset of many companies. Yet IP frequently is ignored entirely until a company believes its IP is infringed by a competitor, or when it runs afoul of another's IP rights. This chapter provides an overview of basic IP-related issues, techniques for identifying and managing IP, and advice for avoiding infringing the IP rights of others.

A Quick Look at Basic IP Principles

IP is generally categorized into patents, trademarks, copyrights, and trade secrets. Each of these categories has unique issues associated with it. Nevertheless, there are legal issues common to most of these categories. These common legal issues include protecting IP from infringement by others, avoiding the infringement of others' IP, and acquiring and maximizing the value of IP.

Categorizing a Client's IP Assets

The first step in assisting a client on an IP-related matter is determining which category of IP is relevant—patents, trademarks, copyrights, trade secrets, or something else. Many times clients seek legal counsel in the field of IP because they have created something they believe is new and innovative. Asking a few preliminary questions quickly clarifies the area of IP most relevant to that new and innovative creation. What is the client's creation? Is it a product or process? Or is it a name used to identify a product or service? Determining which type of IP applies is often an interesting inquiry, as clients frequently confuse copyright and trademark protection, or trademark and patent protection. Once the relevant category of IP is established, a more detailed fact-gathering takes place.

When advising a client seeking patent protection for an innovative product or process, there are several baseline questions that merit consideration:

1. What problem did the client face that led to the creation of the invention?
2. Has the invention been disclosed?
3. Is the invention currently in use?
4. Who was involved in the development of the invention?

Answers to these questions inevitably lead to more questions. For example, in a case where a client has disclosed an invention, it is critical to know when the disclosure took place, whether a non-disclosure agreement was in place, or whether it was a public disclosure. These facts drastically affect patentability.

When advising a client seeking trademark protection, initially ask these questions:

1. Is the mark in use, or does the client intend to use it in the future?
2. What goods or services are going to be offered in connection with the mark?
3. Is the mark used in commerce in more than one state or internationally?
4. Has the client performed an appropriate trademark search?

When advising a client seeking copyright protection, the main questions to ask include:

1. Who is the author of the work in question?
2. Was the work created under a work-for-hire agreement, or was it performed by an employee within the scope of their employment?
3. Has the work been registered with the U.S. Library of Congress?
4. Are there multiple parts to the work?
5. If the work is a software program, are there multiple versions of it?

Answers to these questions often bring to light other issues. For example, if there are multiple parts to a work, who created each part?

When advising clients regarding trade secret matters, there are several questions to consider:

1. Is the trade secret really a secret?
2. Does the so-called secret constitute valuable information that derives its value from the fact that it is a secret?
3. Can the secret be discovered by reverse engineering of an end product, by independent investigation or research, or through publicly available data?

4. What steps have been taken to keep the information a secret? This question is particularly important, because the failure to take reasonable steps to protect the information effectively results in abandonment of the secret.

5. Are there appropriate employment agreements in place with respect to all employees who have access to the secret?

Ownership and Infringement: Two Common Legal Landmines

The most common issues that arise in the IP realm are ownership and infringement. However, those issues do not equally apply to all forms of IP. Each category of IP has its own unique legal landmines. A dispute over ownership can have drastic effects on copyright or patent assets, but typically not trademarks. Further, infringement is front and center in trademark and patent law, but does not apply to trade secrets.

Several factors drive the common legal issue of ownership in IP cases. In some cases, the inventor/author of IP is not necessarily the owner of the IP. Similarly, the company whose employee invents or authors the IP does not necessarily own it. As a result, there can be some confusion with respect to ownership. To be more specific, when dealing with copyrights, a key legal issue is authorship—who authored something and whether they own it. The concept of independent creation is specific to copyrights—multiple people may create the same thing, and each will have independent rights to that creation as long as they created it. For example, if someone writes a poem and another person happens to come up with the same exact poem, we are each entitled to our own copyright protection as long as there is proof that there was no copying involved.

A key factor that drives many cases is the value of the IP. Many times IP represents the crown jewels of a company. Indeed, in some cases it's worth billions of dollars. In those cases, inventors and companies may fight to the very end to determine and/or gain ownership of such an invention. To avoid these disputes, it is important to implement appropriate policies for protecting IP. Specifically, clients should be advised to have very clear employment and assignment agreements in place so the most common ownership issues do not plague them.

Infringement is another common problem when asserting IP rights. In simple terms, a party claims infringement when another is violating its IP rights by unlawfully replicating or using the protected matter (usually a copyrighted work, patented product or process, or trademark). Freedom-to-operate searches and infringement analysis both assess the IP rights of others as compared to a client's IP assets. The major difference is that freedom-to-operate opinions are completed early in the development of a product or trademark in hopes of avoiding a costly infringement suit later.

Generating a freedom-to-operate opinion usually requires conducting a very costly search. For example, depending on a client's industry, a freedom-to-operate search of preexisting patent rights usually costs between $30,000 and $50,000. Clients are often reluctant to pay for such a costly process, but they should be advised that conducting a freedom-to-operate search in the early stages could save them a substantial amount of money in the long run. Indeed, all too often clients plow forward in the development process without performing a search to avoid expense, only to be confronted with a cease-and-desist letter down the road. At that point, they may be forced to pay royalties to another party or undergo substantial redesign efforts that could have been easily avoided at an earlier state, had they known about an existing patent. In many cases, infringement can be avoided by making small tweaks in technology, but those adjustments are not possible at the end of the research and development cycle. Once the product has gone to market, it can be very expensive to go back and retool or redesign it. Therefore, an attorney's priority with respect to freedom-to-operate searches is to get an opinion sooner rather than later, which may be difficult if the client is adamant about keeping costs low. This is more often the case for small to mid-sized businesses and individual inventors, because in many cases they barely have the resources to file a patent application, let alone perform a freedom-to-operate search.

If a client foregoes a freedom-to-operate opinion, they may ultimately be forced to pay for an infringement analysis later on. Infringement analysis is similar to a freedom-to-operate opinion and is commonly done when a client receives a cease-and-desist letter claiming patent infringement. When conducting infringement analysis, the product accused of infringing the patent is compared to the claims of the patent itself. Then a legal determination is made as to whether the product infringes, and the client is advised accordingly.

The Risks: What Can Happen Without a Sound IP Strategy

When clients fail to understand and protect their IP assets, they risk a variety of business and legal repercussions, including the loss of rights and the financial repercussions, the costs of defending an infringement claim, and paying damages.

<u>Loss of Rights and Financial Repercussions</u>

A serious risk for clients in the IP area is the loss of rights. When a company inadvertently abandons IP by not filing patent applications in a timely manner, or not taking the proper steps to keep information confidential, its rights to that IP can be forfeited. The loss of rights can impact clients financially, especially when ownership issues arise. For example, employees can easily walk away with millions of dollars in IP rights if appropriate contractual relationships are not put into place in advance.

<u>The Various Consequences of Defending an Infringement Suit</u>

Arguably, the most serious risk for clients with respect to IP involves the infringement of the IP rights of others. Patent infringement suits are incredibly expensive to defend, at a cost of at least $1.5 million. In addition, infringing another party's IP in the context of copyright and trademark cases can result in increased damages and attorneys' fees in cases of willful infringement. Moreover, criminal charges can be brought for copyright infringement and theft of trade secrets. Injunctive relief is another possible penalty: a client can be stopped by the courts from manufacturing products that may be core to its company, or from identifying those products with certain trademarks, although this once powerful tool has been limited to some extent by recent case law.

Paying Damages

The degree of financial risk is greatly determined by the availability of statutory damages, the extent of the infringement, and the type of IP that is infringed. For example, a patent may be infringed on only one occasion, yet the infringement results in enormous damages. In other cases, a patent may be infringed millions of times, yet a much smaller amount of damages is awarded. In the area of copyrights, statutory damages can be awarded for each instance of infringement, and those damages can be very costly. The intent of the infringer must also be taken into account. If clients infringe something willfully, they will face greater damages than if they inadvertently blunder into an infringement. The amount of damage the infringement has caused to a competitor is also going to determine the degree of financial risk a client faces in IP litigation.

The IP Audit: Five Steps toward Developing an IP Strategy

One approach to maximize a client's IP assets and minimize their exposure to the risks outlined above is to conduct an IP audit. The audit process can be broken down into five important steps.

Step One: Getting a Lay of the Land—Fact Gathering

The first step in performing an audit of a client's IP portfolio is fact gathering. The goal is to become familiar with the client's business and how its IP assets play a role in giving the client a competitive advantage. Understanding the client's industry, identifying and interviewing the right people, and collecting the right documents are critical to the audit process.

An important thing to consider is that the information-gathering process sometimes presents a political and emotional challenge for employees. Indeed, whenever a legal review is conducted, employees are likely to feel threatened. That may be because they do not know what an audit entails, or they may be afraid that they have done something wrong. They may also feel that the search process is an invasion of what they consider their space, especially as it may involve looking at projects they worked on extensively, or reading their e-mails. Visiting a client and effected employees during the fact-gathering process does wonders toward overcoming these challenges.

Meeting with a person on a face-to-face basis often makes them feel much more at ease. Remember that the goal is to help them understand that the audit process will facilitate organizing a system—not point out things they have done wrong.

In addition, conducting fact gathering in person allows the opportunity for quick answers to any follow-up questions. Conversely, this process breaks down fairly quickly if information is gathered by e-mail, because if the client responds to a document request by sending the wrong document, additional follow-up is needed. As such, e-mail tends to be an inefficient means to conduct fact gathering as opposed to a face-to-face process where you can simply reach into the client's file cabinets and grab the information you need. If the files are very disorderly, simply tell the client you wish to take the boxes of documents back to your office, where you can organize them yourself. That saves the client the inconvenience of having to leaf through each document to answer your questions.

<u>Understanding the Industry</u>

Certain industry factors play an important part in analyzing a client's IP needs. For example, one key consideration is whether the client is in a litigious industry. There is a large amount of high-profile litigation in the medical device and pharmaceutical fields. As such, it is critical to ensure a client has freedom-to-operate searches and opinions performed before investing heavily into these fields. It is also important to consider who the main players are in the client's industry. For example, is it a highly fractured industry with many small players, or are there a few large and very aggressive players? Who are the client's main competitors?

Another important consideration is how quickly the industry changes. For example, is the client in the manufacturing industry where a particular process has been used the same way for a hundred years? Or is the client in the electronics and software fields, where the industry changes radically every eighteen months? Answers to these questions affect the type of protection that is appropriate for the client.

Another factor is whether the client's industry is regulated, since regulation can have a major impact on the client's IP rights. The Food and Drug Administration, the Federal Aviation Administration, or any number of regulatory agencies may have an impact on the client's marketplace. For example, the Food and Drug Administration regulatory approval process can affect the duration of a patent.

It is also important to understand any markets and jurisdictions the client is targeting for expansion. For example, if a client is trying to sell goods in China, they need to have a clear understanding of how the Chinese government enforces (or does not enforce) its IP laws. Similarly, if the client is marketing medical devices in Europe, it is important to know they cannot claim patent rights over a surgical procedure—they may be able to get protection for an instrument used in the procedure, but not the procedure itself. Accordingly, it can be just as important to know a client's history as it is to know the client.

Interviewing the Right People

When undertaking a legal review of a client's IP protection strategy, it is important to first identify and interview the people tasked with managing the company's IP. In a large company, those individuals may include executive or senior vice presidents. In a small company, the president is often the appropriate person, and in a start-up, the contact person may be a single inventor. The goals at this point are to develop a relationship with that contact person and determine the company's IP goals, as well as where the company presently stands in terms of reaching those goals. Quite often, the vice president or executive acting as the company's IP manager does not understand the benefits of IP protection. Additionally, the IP manager may be overworked and does not want the added responsibility of managing a very important part of the company's property. In those situations, educating the client is essential, as is helping them organize their IP-related tasks. That may require taking much of the work off their hands by taking the lead role on pending projects. Instructing the client on what needs to be accomplished is important, especially when things are in disarray and the IP manager is unsure of the status of the client's IP.

Collecting the Right Documents

The third component in gathering the information necessary for an audit consists of collecting all relevant documents—the client's contracts, disclosure records, and filings with government offices, such as the U.S. Patent and Trademark Office. Here the goal is to become familiar with the universe of the client's past and present IP holdings. Rather than worry about future events, the focus is on the IP actually in existence at the time of the audit.

The largest challenge in this area is when many small to mid-sized companies have not addressed their IP at all prior to the audit. Usually, their records are in complete disarray and/or documents are missing. When documents are requested, they may be overlooked by the client or are returned in draft or partial draft form. In some cases, the client may have prepared applications and planned to file them, but it is unclear whether the applications actually were filed.

Step Two: Putting It Together—Portfolio Organization and Assessment

The second step in the audit process is organizing and analyzing the client's information—portfolio assessment. The overall goal of this step, which is probably the most work-intensive step, is to quickly audit the client's IP protection and identify any time-sensitive matters. For example, failure to file for the appropriate registrations can lead to the loss of IP rights in certain circumstances. While this process applies to trademarks and copyrights, portfolio assessment is primarily focused toward the patent side of the client's portfolio, which is often more fact-intensive and requires more analysis.

Organizing IP Information

One of the outcomes of fact gathering is that you are able to categorize the client's IP and make a master list of all their current U.S. and foreign IP holdings, as well as their pending U.S. and foreign IP applications. After that, gather details with respect to the specific aspects of each of the client's standing patents or patent applications.

The core information that needs to be organized includes inventor names, the synopsis of the invention, the year in which it was developed or the dates on which the invention was developed, patent application serial numbers for patents that were actually filed, filing dates, due dates for maintenance fees, and expirations for patents. Any inventions for which patent applications have not been filed should also be reviewed closely, as well as any items in the research and development pipeline that may not have matured sufficiently to file a patent application, or those that are mature, but the leg work has not yet been done.

During this step in the IP audit process, it is especially important to get a sense for whether an invention has been used or publicly disclosed. Any time there is a use or public disclosure, certain statutory requirements are triggered, and filing deadlines are created. For example, in the United States, if you publicly disclose an invention, you have one year to file an application for that invention or it is abandoned to the public. Therefore, if some information about an invention was disclosed six months prior to the audit, a patent application must be filed within the next six months to avoid a loss of rights to the invention. Also, a disclosure at this stage may, and often does, impact foreign rights.

Next, all patent-related agreements collected during the first step should be analyzed to determine the impact of each agreement on either the patent portfolio or the client's ownership of its IP. This process will include a review of assignment agreements, third-party license agreements, and any government funding or grant documents. In many cases, those types of agreements have a disclosure requirement or specific provisions that affect how ownership is determined.

It is also necessary to determine whether there is any infringement of a third-party patent, copyright, or trademark rights. If a cease-and-desist letter is uncovered during fact gathering, it is important to know when it was sent, what actions have been taken to address it, and the general status of the situation. Were any freedom-to-operate opinions procured because of that letter? Were any design changes implemented?

The long-term goal of this step is to establish an appropriate client-specific policy for handling all IP-related matters going forward. The main challenges to achieving this goal once again include missing documents, unclear disclosure dates, poor record keeping, and general disorder. These difficulties can be overcome primarily through education, including implementing new and appropriate policies that will show the client the value of patents, trademarks, and copyrights, and the impact that ignoring IP protections can have (i.e., loss of rights or getting involved in an infringement suit scenario).

A high level of organization and attention to detail are critical to accomplishing these goals. Detailed charts of identified IP can be used to categorize IP assets into patents, trademarks, copyrights, and trade secrets. Also include on the charts any critical dates and important identifying information, such as serial numbers and project names. Assigning responsibility for certain tasks and putting them into a docket system is very important. Once docketed, important IP tasks will be properly handled and are less likely to be overlooked.

Prioritizing a Company's IP Legal Needs

In general, the most important driving factor in prioritizing a company's IP legal needs is the client's business goals, which should be identified as part of the IP audit analysis. Next, identify the client's core technologies, and determine whether they are protected appropriately. Simply put, the client's core technologies should receive IP protection resources before any non-core technologies.

However, at the outset of representation, deadlines for filing applications for IP protections will automatically prioritize your actions. When faced with limited resources and a looming deadline to file protection for an important form of IP, obviously the need to dedicate the resources in that area outweighs the areas that do not have deadlines. For example, if an invention has already been disclosed, obtaining protection for that invention should be given higher priority than an invention that has not been disclosed.

Finally, consider the client's budget. While they may have a lot of IP to protect, if they cannot pay for all forms of protection, choices must be made as to which protections should be pursued for which assets. In such cases, it is especially important to consider the client's business goals and core technologies.

Step Three: Preparing the Report—What to Recommend to the Client

The third step is to prepare an audit report for the client that will include an in-depth analysis of the client's IP portfolio. It will also include recommended IP policies, tailored form agreements, and a list of the steps the client must take to achieve critical IP goals. The report should set forth a "you are here" marker, and secondly provide a roadmap for how to go forward. This is an iterative process wherein the client and its attorney work together to develop an IP strategy. The report ultimately summarizes the findings of the audit, including the strategy envisioned by the client.

There are several key recommendations that commonly arise with respect to IP portfolio protection:

1. *Implement appropriate employment agreements that address IP ownership.* Many clients do not have those agreements in place, and only after an invention is fully conceived and put into practice will the client decide they need to determine who owns the patent rights. By that time, it is often too late to assign the IP to the client. Similarly, if the appropriate employment or "work made for hire" agreements are not in place with respect to copyrights, the ownership of the IP belongs to the author. All too often, clients do not understand that hiring someone to work on a project does not necessarily mean you are going to own the IP that is created by that employee in the course of their employment. Therefore, it is important to keep in mind that the company may lose its rights to own its IP under some circumstances, if appropriate steps with respect to creating employment agreements are not taken.

   In addition to protecting the client from inadvertently losing their IP rights, employment agreements also help clarify the relationship between the employer and the employee, or the company and the creator of the intellectual assets, to avoid future problems. If there is a clear agreement in place that says the employee has to sign over all rights to their inventions to the employer, employees are much more likely to honor that agreement. Merely having a policy or an unspoken rule to the effect that the employer owns all inventions is legally ineffective.

2. *Do not disclose inventions prior to filing a patent application, or without a non-disclosure agreement in place.*

3. *Register all copyrightable matter.* There are huge benefits to registering copyrightable matter with the Library of Congress, the primary benefit being that if a copyright application is filed before an infringement takes place, attorneys' fees and statutory damages are available. In addition, a copyright must be filed before an infringement suit. It is relatively inexpensive to file a copyright application—a fee ranging from $45 to a few hundred dollars buys quite a bit of protection for a copyrightable work.

4. *Use a multi-layered approach to IP protection.* A layered approach to IP protection is most effective, as it takes advantage of the different protections offered by patents, copyrights, and trade secrets. For example, patents can be used to effectively protect the functional aspects of software, but under patent laws, attorneys' fees are rarely awarded, whereas if someone infringes your copyright, there are statutory provisions for attorneys' fees and statutory damages if those copyrights are registered in a timely fashion. Consequently, having both types of protection in place protects the underlying idea under patent law, and gives the client leverage in a litigation scenario by having attorneys' fees and statutory damages available under copyright: statutory damages for copyright infringement can often be much higher on a per-infringement basis than a court-imposed damages award for patents.

Step Four: Moving Forward—Implementing Recommendations

The fourth step is to move forward with the client on this IP report roadmap. This process will involve filing any necessary patent, trademark, and copyright applications or registrations, and assuming responsibility for existing or pending filings. It is important to transition out any previous attorneys' records and documents with the appropriate offices, while getting all IP-related tasks into the docket system.

To ensure implementation and adherence to appropriate IP-related policies, a manual should be prepared that contains policies tailored to the specific client. Once the manual is prepared, ensure the client and their employees sign it. Over the following months, engage in frequent communication with the client and the IP manager to make sure the policies are actually being followed. In many cases, if you simply give the client an employee manual, they will thank you for it, shelve it, and never follow its instructions. Thus, it will not have the preventative effect it was intended to have.

Another way to make sure all recommended practices are implemented and managed is to engage in ongoing client education. This process can involve quarterly or annual presentations to client personnel who work in different areas. It is important that all employees understand the purposes of the policies so they can be as vigilant as the client's management team in enforcing them.

Good management and organizational skills are also important to the implementation process. The client's managers must be able to manage their employees with respect to ensuring the appropriate disclosures are provided at the appropriate times, rather than making inadvertent public disclosures. They must also have good organizational tools in place to avoid missing deadlines and any loss of IP rights as a result.

Step Five: Portfolio Maintenance—Monitoring IP Trends in a Changing Landscape

Finally, to effectively manage a client's IP portfolio, it is important to monitor IP trends. There are several helpful sources to consult on a daily, weekly, or monthly basis. The most important sources for IP-related information are the U.S. Supreme Court, the Court of Appeals for the Federal Circuit, which has exclusive jurisdiction over all patent-related matters, and the various state and circuit courts for decisions regarding copyrights, trade secrets, and common law trademark issues. The U.S.

Patent and Trademark Office Web site has vast sums of information regarding up-to-date regulations, policies, and fees.

Secondary sources include the American Intellectual Property Law Association's journal and initial public offering reports. In addition, several attorneys with a high level of expertise in different specific areas of IP have law blogs relating to upcoming patent reform issues and analysis of new cases. Other blogs relate to industry-specific groups that feature information on changes in the law in those areas, or positions particular clients have taken in briefs.

Patent law is a constitutional area, but all the Constitution says about patents is that they exist to promote the progress of the arts and sciences. Therefore, it is the courts that have the primary authority to interpret the laws and regulations under the Constitution, which means they must be the first source in a legal analysis. The U.S. Patent and Trademark Office is the federal agency that administers applications for patents and trademarks, and therefore, it has a high level of importance. Relevant journals provide legal analysis in terms of regulations and case law, and they help in identifying new legal trends. However, the downside to these journals is that they lag behind the state of the law in areas that are changing rapidly. Fortunately, blogs are very timely. In fact, if a new case is issued, often a number of law blogs will report on it within twelve hours. Blogs often provide very accurate information with respect to daily developments in the IP realm. However, in some instances, the rush to get online results in inaccurate information, or incomplete or fragmented analysis.

Creating a monitoring routine is essential to staying current and providing a client with sound advice despite the changing landscape of IP law.

An Illustration: The Changing Landscape of Patent Law

In recent years, ground-shaking changes have reshaped the patent landscape. These changes have mainly stemmed from Supreme Court decisions. Up until a few years ago, the Supreme Court had taken a laissez fair attitude to the decisions of the Court of Appeals for the Federal Circuit, which has exclusive jurisdiction over all patent appeals. However, the Supreme Court recently ruled in three cases that have greatly impacted the scope and patentability of inventions in the United States: (1) *eBay Inc. v. MercExchange, LLC*, 547 U.S. 388 (2006), (2) *KSR Int'l Co. v. Teleflex Inc.*, 127 S. Ct. 1727 (2007.), and (3) *MedImmune Inc. v. Genentech Inc.*,127 S. Ct. 764 (2007).

Arguably, the most important of these three cases was *KSR Int'l Co,* 127 S. Ct. 1727 (2007)., which modified the standard used to determine whether an invention is obvious. In effect, this decision cast doubt and uncertainty as to the validity of millions of patents issued under the previous standard. It also made it more likely that patent applications will be rejected by the U.S. Patent and Trademark Office for reasons relating to obviousness.

In *eBay Inc.*, 547 U.S. 388 (2006)., the Supreme Court unanimously decided a finding of patent infringement should not automatically result in an injunction. That is, infringers are no longer automatically enjoined from practicing a patented invention solely because they are found to infringe that patent. Finally, in *MedImmune,* 127 S. Ct. 764 (2007)., the Supreme Court considered the question of whether a patent licensee must breach the license agreement to have standing to challenge the patent's validity, among other things. The Supreme Court held that the plaintiff did have standing to sue, even though the license was not breached.

In sum, these cases changed the standard with respect to determining whether a technology is patentable, altered the leverage patentees have in forcing others to stop manufacturing a product or using a process, and affected whether a licensee can seek a declaratory judgment relating to the licensed patent. These Supreme Court decisions have thus affected millions of patents, infringers, and parties to license agreements.

In recent times, there has also been a proliferation of patent trolls—companies that do not actually manufacture products themselves, but rather are designed only to acquire and hold patents, and assert them against other companies in a particular sector. These patent trolls frequently send letters to big players in the software or electronics industry, accusing them of infringement and demanding royalties. With that said, it appears that the proliferation of patent trolls may be short-lived. It has generally been limited by the decision of the Supreme Court as discussed above.

Much of IP management involves the flywheel principle. That is, at the outset, a substantial effort is necessary to initiate movement of the flywheel. However, once set in motion, it takes much less effort to keep it in motion. Likewise, when first tackling IP issues for a company, a substantial effort is necessary to identify and organize IP. Thereafter, maintenance is generally straightforward. There are substantial benefits to managing a client's IP rather than ignoring it. The greatest benefits include the ability to exclude competitors from using protected IP, and avoiding inadvertently infringing the IP of competitors. These benefits directly translate into increased revenue and decreased costs.

Alejandro J. Fernandez is of counsel for the firm of Broad and Cassel. He is a registered patent attorney and is board-certified in intellectual property. He provides understandable, practical advice to clients facing complex intellectual property challenges. He frequently advises clients in the alternative energy, defense, automotive, medical device, and Internet sectors. He has managed intellectual property portfolios, prosecuted patents, provided freedom-to-operate opinions, and negotiated multimillion-dollar licensing agreements. In addition, he regularly advises clients in matters regarding domain name disputes, trademarks, copyrights, and trade secrets.

Dedication: *I would like to dedicate this chapter to Kelly Fernandez, a fine, outstanding editor.*

Understanding Your Client's IP Needs in a Changing Environment

John C. Alemanni

Partner

Kilpatrick Stockton LLP

ASPATORE

IP Concerns

The major categories of legal needs for companies concerned with intellectual property (IP) are general IP counseling, transactional services, and litigation. General counseling includes determining what a company has by, for instance, performing an IP audit, and helping a company determine and implement a strategy for protecting its IP.

Transactional work includes drafting of agreements and prosecution of trademark and patent applications before the U.S. Patent and Trademark Office. Agreements that typically require sections devoted to protecting, securing, or transferring IP include employment agreements, non-disclosure agreements, merger and purchase agreements, licenses, both inbound and outbound, and development agreements.

Litigation includes enforcement of a company's patents, defending against infringement actions, and filing declaratory judgment actions asking a court to find that a patent is invalid and/or not infringed.

Absent a pending lawsuit, counseling is probably the most important category of a company's legal needs. To successfully obtain and leverage IP, a company must understand what rights and opportunities it has, and have a strategy for obtaining and enforcing its IP going forward.

Litigation is important for a number of reasons. First, when a company is accused of infringing a patent, it can be enjoined from making, using, selling, or offering to sell the accused product or service. In some circumstances, if the injunction is put in place, the company will no longer be able to function in the market. Further, the threat of legal action with respect to a patent can raise concern for existing and potential customers, as well as financial markets. This concern can cause sales to decrease and available financing to dry up.

Transactional aspects of obtaining and protecting IP remain important. However, these categories of legal needs tend to be more routine in nature.

The one constant for all three of these categories of IP legal needs is the continual changes to the law. Other factors that have affected these categories include the globalization of all aspects of the economy and the relatively recent economic downturn and not-so-recent devaluation of the dollar.

Changes to the law have been most evident in patent law. The Supreme Court and the U.S. Court of Appeals for the Federal Circuit have clarified or modified some of the very basic tenets of patent law. For example, the Supreme Court has changed the standard for filing declaratory judgment suits in relation to patents. *Medimmune Inc. v. Genentech Inc.*, 127 S. Ct. 764 (2007). The prior test for obtaining standing to file a declaratory judgment suit in a patent context was that the defendant must have a "reasonable apprehension of suit." This standard might have been satisfied, for example, when a patent owner sent a letter to a company that included an allegation that a particular product infringed a specific claim in a patent. This test was eliminated by the Supreme Court. *See Medimmune*, footnote 11. This has obvious ramifications in relation to a company's litigation needs. It is easier to file a declaratory judgment action or to find oneself being sued in one. Clients are now often counseled to file a lawsuit prior to sending a letter to a potential infringer.

Another case that changed both counseling and litigation was the Federal Circuit decision in *In re Seagate Technology LLC*, 497 F.3d 1360 (Fed. Cir. 2007). Prior to the *Seagate* decision, IP attorneys would often counsel clients to take great care in reviewing competitors' patents to avoid risking a finding of willful infringement, which could lead to a trebling of damages and the imposition of the other party's attorneys' fees. Id. 1382. However, in *Seagate*, the court held that proof of willful infringement requires at least a showing of "objective recklessness." The court explained that, "a patentee must show by clear and convincing evidence that the infringer acted despite an objectively high likelihood that its actions constituted infringement of a valid patent Id. 1380.. The Federal Circuit further held that "the patentee must also demonstrate that the objectively defined risk was either known or so obvious that it should have been known to the accused infringer. Id. 1382.

From a transactional perspective, additional onus was placed on the attorney prosecuting a patent to make the examiner aware of potentially relevant material. In one case, the prosecuting attorney was held to have committed inequitable conduct, thus resulting in an unenforceable patent. *See McKesson Information Solutions Inc. v. Bridge Medical Inc.*, 487 F.3d 897 (Fed. Cir. 2007). What the attorney failed to do was to point the examiner specifically to material that was in the possession of the U.S. Patent and Trademark Office and to which the attorney had arguably provided adequate, if indirect, reference.

The Supreme Court has also lowered the bar to invalidate patents based on obviousness. *See KSR Intern. Co. v. Teleflex Inc.*, 127 S. Ct. 1727 (2007). The Supreme Court held that the former Federal Circuit Rule, referred to as the "teaching, suggestion, motivation test," was not mandatory. Prior to *KSR*, in order to provide a patent claim obvious by combining prior art teachings, some motivation or suggestion to combine the prior art teachings must have been present in the prior art, the nature of the problem, or the knowledge of a person having ordinary skill in the art. *See Graham v. John Deere Co.*, 383 U.S. 1 (1966).

Since the *EchoStar* decision in 1996, there has been uncertainty with regard to waiver of attorney/client privilege when relying on an opinion of counsel to rebut an allegation of willful infringement. *In re EchoStar Communications Corp.*, 448 F.3d 1294 (Fed. Cir. 2006). When a company relies on advice of counsel to rebut an allegation of willful infringement, the company waives attorney/client privilege as to that advice. But other documents sent to the company by outside counsel may be discoverable as well, including documents about the patent's validity, enforceability, or infringement. After *EchoStar*, it was unclear whether the waiver of the attorney/client privilege also extends to trial counsel. In *Seagate*, the Federal Circuit found that "the significantly different functions of trial counsel and opinion counsel advise against extending waiver to trial counsel." The court determined that the long-recognized and compelling need to protect trial counsel's thoughts, and the realization that in ordinary circumstances willfulness will only depend on an infringer's pre-litigation conduct, both weighed against extending waiver to trial counsel. As to work product, the court found that "the same rationale generally limiting the waiver of the attorney/client privilege with trial counsel applies with even greater force to so limiting work product waiver because of the nature of the work product doctrine."

Another issue that affects both counseling and transactional work is the tremendous backlog of applications before the U.S. Patent and Trademark Office. The office's management has unsuccessfully attempted to limit the number and scope of applications presented. *See Tafas v. Dudas*, 07–cv-0846 (E.D.Va 2007). However, these attempts have failed to decrease the backlog or increase the speed with which the U.S. Patent and Trademark Office responds to these applications.

Appendix F is an outline for performing an IP audit. The IP audit should include a review of all patents, trademarks, copyrights, and trade secrets. These include existing and potential rights. For instance, do any proprietary or novel systems or methods provide the company with a competitive advantage in the market? In addition, agreements such as licenses, non-disclosure agreements, and employee agreements should be analyzed.

Further, the IP audit should analyze management processes and IP policies. For instance, are inventors required to keep notebooks? Are inventors encouraged to provide disclosures, and are employees remunerated for helping the company identify and protect intellectual assets? Finally, leaving no stone unturned, the company should look at other assets, such as the company's Web sites and databases, to attempt to identify potentially valuable IP.

To be effective, the IP audit checklist should be developed earlier, when it is easier to set up policies and procedures, and capture all the information necessary. The IP audit should be performed by a combination of people. Management must be involved in the process for it to be successful. Management is responsible for initializing and controlling the IP audit. Management is also responsible for determining the short- and long-term goals to be achieved by the audit. Management determines the high-level market definition, which guides the breadth and scope of the IP a company pursues. Finally, management is responsible for setting a reasonable budget for the process.

Marketing should also be involved in the process. Marketing can provide marketing plans to help define the types of branding strategies that may affect the IP sought or maintained by the company. Marketing can also play a key role in determining the true value of an intellectual asset in the marketplace. Finally, marketing is probably in the best position to identify competitors and specific competitive products in the market. For all types of IP, it is critical to understand the marketplace to properly sculpt the IP rights a company pursues.

From a patent perspective, it is important to involve a research and development technical leader in the process. The research and development technical leader is able to explain the technology at the heart of the company's current products and provide insight into the company's product development plans. They may also be able to compare and contrast the company's products with those of competitors in the marketplace.

An IP expert, generally an IP attorney, is also important to the process. The IP expert can help educate the participants and organize the output into a coherent picture of the company's intellectual assets. The IP expert can help define specific goals based on the goals set out by management, define threats based on the competitive companies and products identified by marketing and research and development, and develop a strategy for attaining the goals set out by management.

The IP expert can also perform the steps involved in the actual IP audit, including developing an IP repository, completing the IP checklist, and defining metrics for valuation (e.g., return on investment, commercial potential of IP, and competitive advantage derived from IP). The patent expert can also help in the process of developing policies and an IP acquisition plan based on the results.

When the IP audit is complete, the IP expert should provide a copy of the completed checklist, a framework for an IP policy, and recommendations for change. Management should take these results and use them to educate the company's personnel and actively manage the IP portfolio moving forward.

The goal of an IP program is to provide the level of protection to intellectual assets that are equal to their commercial importance. Spending more is a waste of time and resources, but spending less can result in a failure to adequately protect the assets. An IP audit can help define the scope of an IP portfolio, including its strength, the cost to build and maintain the portfolio, and the value of the resulting IP assets.

One goal of the IP audit is to educate management regarding the types of IP protection that may be available to the company, the intellectual assets the company currently has, how those assets are protected, and how the company's position with regard to these assets may be strengthened. Further, company personnel spend substantial time and money developing intellectual assets, and it is important to protect those assets. Knowledge of those assets shows value to outsiders, such as potential investors. Once assets are identified, they may also be used to generate income.

Officers and members of the board of directors have a fiduciary duty to protect the assets of the company, including the intellectual assets, which are often, particularly in the case of a start-up, the company's most valuable assets. For an established company, an IP audit can provide valuable information for reorganizations of the company or for re-engineering specific processes within the company.

IP protection can be used for both offensive and defensive purposes. For instance, a company may use a patent on a basic technology as a barrier to entry. Or a company may use the threat of asserting its own portfolio of IP to avoid charges that the company infringes, which may lead to expensive litigation.

A company may face a variety of challenges. Often these challenges result from a failure to research, educate, or act. A company may be in a position in which they are unfamiliar with what competitors are doing. Failing to research when a competitor has filed a trademark or patent application can result in a tremendous waste of time, effort, and resources. For example, when a company begins the process of developing a new product, they often perform market research to determine whether the product has a realistic chance of succeeding in the marketplace. As part of this market research, the company often identifies competitors in the marketplace. These competitors may have obtained patents covering aspects of the products in the marketplace.

The company preparing to introduce a new product in this marketplace may want to obtain a clearance opinion to help ensure that entry into the marketplace will not result in a letter to cease and desist from making, using, selling, or offering to sell the new product. When a company requests a clearance opinion, a search of issued patents and pending patent applications is performed. The claims of these issued patents and pending applications are then analyzed to determine whether they cover the new product. The results of this analysis may be provided to a company in a form called a clearance opinion. While these opinions can cost tens, or even hundreds, of thousands of dollars, the cost may be worthwhile to avoid wasting millions of dollars in development and marketing costs.

Failing to educate personnel within a company can also result in the loss of rights. For instance, the marketing department may plan for release of a product or disclose it publicly if they are unaware that doing so can result in the inability to obtain protection for the underlying IP. It is similarly important to educate engineering personnel so they know what is patentable, when to disclose their inventions to the company, and why it is important to do so. Providing education to engineers can be particularly important in relation to the first of these.

Engineers often believe no invention is patentable. Once an engineer has accomplished a goal, they often believe the solution they have conceived is not patentable because the solution was obvious. However, the legal standard for obviousness is often substantially different from how an engineer views that term. Under 35 U.S.C. §103, a patent may not be obtained though the invention is not identically disclosed or described as set forth in Section 102 of this title, if the differences between the subject matter sought to be patented and the prior art are such that the subject matter as a whole would have been obvious at the time the invention was made to a person having ordinary skill in the art to which said subject matter pertains.

Finally, a failure to act can result in a missed opportunity. For example, the failure to file a patent application before the public disclosure of a product or process may preclude protection of the IP. Similarly, establishing a brand, but failing to register a trademark, can result in the loss of the brand identity a company works so hard to develop.

Trends and Changes

I remain current in patent law by attending seminars and continuing legal education classes, and by participating in organizations such as the Intellectual Property Owner's Association. I remain current in key technologies by subscribing to technical journals such as the Association of Computing Machinery's *Communications of the ACM*.

Several sources exist for monitoring IP trends. One of the best sources is the professional organizations, such as the Intellectual Property Owner's Association, whose daily e-mail update provides, among other information, a brief synopsis of decisions from the Federal Circuit. By constantly monitoring the relevant decisions from this court, the strategy in pending litigation matters and for preparing patent applications and responses to the Patent Office can be modified on an ongoing basis to provide the client with the most efficient and effective ways to protect their IP assets.

The laws concerning patentability of inventions and the enforceability of patents are changing the most rapidly. The Supreme Court has taken an active role in the last couple of years in shaping this area of law. *See, e.g.*, *KSR Intern. Co. v. Teleflex Inc.*, 127 S. Ct. 1727 (2007); *Medimmune Inc. v. Genentech Inc.*, 127 S. Ct. 764 (2007).

As discussed above, in *KSR*, the Supreme Court held that a patent claim can be proven obvious without some motivation or suggestion to combine the prior art teachings that may be found in the prior art, the nature of the problem to be solved, or the knowledge of one of skill in the art. The Federal Circuit had required such proof as part of the "teaching, suggestion, motivation" test. The Supreme Court held that while the test may provide helpful insight, it should not be applied as a "rigid and mandatory formula" because "the obviousness analysis cannot be confined by a formalistic conception of the words teaching, suggestion, and motivation, or by overemphasis on the importance of published articles and the explicit content of issued patents." The result of this holding is that it is now more difficult and expensive to prosecute and obtain patents, and easier to invalidate them.

Before *Medimmune*, in order to file and maintain a declaratory judgment suit against a patent holder seeking a declaration of non-infringement or invalidity, a company was required to have a reasonable apprehension of imminent suit. In *Medimmune*, the Supreme Court eliminated the "reasonable apprehension of suit" test. Prior to the *Medimmune* decision, a licensee was required to either terminate or breach a patent license agreement before seeking a declaratory judgment that the underlying patent is not infringed or is invalid. The Supreme Court also eliminated this requirement. *Medimmune Inc. v. Genentech Inc.*, 127 S. Ct. 764 (2007).

Because of the change to the standard for willful infringement, the need to obtain opinions of counsel has been reduced dramatically. Litigation, particularly from patent holding companies, seems to be on the rise. These companies occupy an asymmetric position in litigation since they have no ongoing business and thus no exposure to loss of revenue based on the company's IP. Two examples are the Blackberry (*Research in Motion Ltd. v. NTP Ltd.*, 418 F.3d 1282 (Fed. Cir. 2005)) and eBay cases (*MercExchange v. eBay*, 547 U.S. 388 (2006)) (holding that an injunction should not automatically issue based on a finding of patent infringement; a federal court must still weigh the four factors traditionally used to determine whether injunctive relief is appropriate in a particular case).

NTP is a patent holding company in Arlington, Virginia, that was incorporated to hold patents for a wireless communication system. NTP sued Research in Motion for infringement of these patents. In 2002, a jury in the U.S. District Court for the Eastern District of Virginia found that Research in Motion willingly infringed the NTP patents. Research in Motion and NTP subsequently settled the suit for $450 million. In a traditional patent litigation matter, Research in Motion might have sued NTP for infringement of patents that Research in Motion held. However, since NTP has no business other than asserting the patents at issue, the threat of a lawsuit provided no leverage for Research in Motion in its negotiations with NTP.

We inform clients of developments in the law and potential exposure in a variety of ways. The most effective way is with personal phone calls, e-mails, and in-person meetings. These can take the form of forwarding an interesting case or a complaint in a recent filing. We also provide case law updates as one-hour lunch presentations to clients and prospective clients. We also produce short summaries of recent developments and send those to distribution lists that include clients who have expressed an interest in the topic, or who may be affected by the development.

Understanding Clients' Needs

The unique aspect of understanding the legal needs of IP clients is the intersection of technology and the law. To understand the needs of IP clients, it is critical to understand the technology that is at the heart of the company. The particular technical background of the attorney may then be particularly suited to working with particular companies. The same may be true to some degree for other types of IP, particularly for software-related copyrights and agreements, but this is especially true for patent-related IP work. Not only does a strong background in the technology help the attorney understand the business of the company, but it also helps the attorney communicate with the personnel in the company. In my experience, it is much easier to address IP issues if the attorney speaks the language.

For example, to obtain patent protection, the attorney must understand the contours of the prior art, the invention, and the differences between the two. The attorney acts as part lawyer and part technical writer. It also helps if the attorney remains organized in the approach to communicating with the company's personnel. For instance, in taking an invention disclosure from an inventor, it is often useful to develop a history of the area of innovation before attempting to understand what the inventor has invented and why it is useful, novel, and non-obvious. Appendix G is an outline for an invention disclosure conference. The outline helps provide structure for the disclosure.

Technology certainly may be an issue for a corporate attorney helping a company navigate incentives or particular regulations within a jurisdiction. But for many practice areas, the technology at the heart of a company makes little, if any, difference to the way a matter is handled.

John C. Alemanni concentrates his practice in intellectual property law, with a primary focus on patent litigation, intellectual property strategy and licensing, and patent portfolio management and prosecution. He works with both established and emerging companies. He is a registered patent attorney and practices in a wide range of technologies, including software, computer peripheral devices and control methods, haptics, network security, bioinformatics, e-commerce, telecommunications, and electronics. He assists companies with a variety of intellectual property matters, including establishing patent programs and committees, analyzing patents held by competitors, conducting freedom-to-practice analysis, providing written opinions, negotiating and drafting license agreements, drafting patent applications and prosecution, and patent portfolio management.

Before joining Kilpatrick Stockton, Mr. Alemanni owned and managed a computer consulting firm, as well as a Web hosting firm. Besides managing the company, he performed various consulting roles, including client-server and Web-enabled application development and system integration, including custom browser-based user interfaces for PeopleSoft and SAP.

Mr. Alemanni is a member of the American Intellectual Property Law Association and its software and business methods committee. He is also a member of the North Carolina Bar Association, for which he is chair of the software and electrical engineering committee and past chair of the continuing legal education committee of the intellectual property section.

IP: Components, Cases, and Questions

David A. Allgeyer

Partner

Lindquist & Vennum PLLP

ASPATORE

A thorough understanding of intellectual property (IP) is an invaluable asset for any business operating in a competitive environment. While the major categories include patents, trademarks, copyrights, licenses, and trade secrets the company may own, IP contains a host of other related issues. Of these, the question of what properties warrant such attention, as well as the nature of competition's motives, are of the greatest importance. One consideration generally relates to understanding the competitors' IP, since this can interfere with the company's plans. Another concern is to develop a sound understanding of your own company's IP. Indeed, the list of issues may seem endless.

As the number of patents and other means of protecting IP grows, it has become increasingly important to review the IP held by others so the company knows the areas in which it is likely to face challenges or suits by others. While there has been some cutting back on the breadth of patent protection in the wake of a slightly narrowed approach to claims construction in the *Phillips* case, a revitalization of possible attacks on validity of asserted patents in the *KSR* case, and a decreased chance of liability for punitive damages after the *Seagate* case, patent litigation remains expensive and distracting.

KSR International Co. v. Teleflex, 127 S.Ct. 1727 (2007), represents the most significant change in patent law in decades. Before the Supreme Court's decision in *KSR*, court had required that a defendant prove there was a teaching, suggestion, or motivation to combine prior art references before they could be used to invalidate a patent for obviousness. *KSR* rejected this rigid approach in favor of an "expansive and flexible approach" using "common sense" when assessing whether an invention would be obvious to a person of ordinary skill in the art, and therefore invalid. *KSR*, 127 S.Ct. at 1729, 1742–43. This has significantly enhanced the opportunities for prevailing on an obviousness defense, reducing the protection of many patents.

Earlier, the Federal Circuit, which hears virtually all appeals in patent cases, diminished the breadth of the claims of many patents in *Phillips v. AWH Corp.*, 415 F.3d 1303, 1313 (Fed. Cir. 2005) (en banc). Claims are the portion at the end of the patent that defines the legal limits of the invention claimed in the patent. Before *Phillips*, some courts had given claim terms in the patent expansive readings, often based on dictionary definitions. In *Phillips*, the Federal Circuit noted that essential to any analysis is to determine what the inventor had actually invented, often using the patent specification as a guide. The patent specification is the portion of the patent that sets out an explanation and examples of the invention in detail. While the patent is not limited to only what the specification says, the specification is to be consulted as a key guide to understanding what was actually invented. This approach has diminished the reach of protection of some patents.

Finally, in *In re Seagate Technology, LLC*, 497 F.3d 1360 (Fed. Cir. 2007), the Federal Circuit made it much more difficult for a patent-owning plaintiff to prove the defendant infringed the patent willfully. A finding of willful infringement could lead to a court awarding treble damages. In earlier decisions, the Federal Circuit had imposed a duty of a party learning of a patent to seek an opinion of qualified patent counsel whether or not it would infringe before beginning infringing activity. In *Seagate*, the court required that a party alleging willful infringement "show by clear and convincing evidence that the infringer acted despite an objectively high likelihood that its actions constituted infringement of a valid patent." This significantly reduces the threat of a court trebling a losing party's damages in a patent infringement suit.

Nonetheless, care must be taken in patent-related matters. While their reach may have diminished somewhat, patent cases still can lead to extremely large verdicts. We have seen verdicts and settlements in patent cases in the hundreds of millions of dollars in recent years. And the cost of defending patent litigation itself is not insignificant, averaging more than $2 million for cases involving damages claims between $1 and $25 million. *AIPLA Report of the Economic Survey 2007* at I-90 (July 2007). The risk that a company found to be an infringer will be enjoined from further infringing and thus selling key products or services is also significant. While injunctions were at one time virtually automatic against an infringer at the end of a case, the standard for achieving an injunction was recently made more difficult by the Supreme Court in *eBay v. MercExchange*, 126 S. Ct. 1837 (2006), by requiring *inter alia* a showing of irreparable harm absent the injunction. Nonetheless, the risk of an injunction remains real in many cases.

Of course, if patents represent risks to an accused infringer, they represent great opportunities for patent holders who may enjoy a large verdict and elimination of infringing competition from the market. Owning patents also represents an opportunity for protection against an infringement charge. With a significant patent portfolio, a company accused of infringement may find that the accuser is infringing the company's patents, leading to leverage that can be used to settle the matter.

Trademarks, while often not as threatening as patents, can also provide a significant threat to a company. I recently represented a nationwide chain whose competitor challenged its use of its very name. The implications of losing the ability to continue using a nationwide trademark are, of course, staggering. Fortunately, the challenge was successfully averted, but the threat was significant. Damages can be significant in trademark cases as well, particularly where the plaintiff can show that the infringer's use of the infringing mark diverted business away from it. The cost of defending trademark infringement actions is also significant, reported as averaging $750,000 in larger cases. *AIPLA Report of the Economic Survey 2007* at I-995 (July 2007). Of course, it is critical for a company to protect its trademarks to keep others from profiting by misappropriating its good name and goodwill by using infringing marks.

Indeed, all forms of IP provide both risks and rewards for companies. This necessitates careful attention to understanding, maintaining, and enhancing the company's IP while understanding, planning for, and avoiding competitors' IP.

The Key Questions to Ask IP Clients

There are a number of relevant questions every company involved with IP—which is virtually every company—must ask of themselves. They include:

- What patents do you currently own? How do these patents relate to your core business? How do they relate to your competitors' business? What patents do you currently license from others? How do these patents relate to your core business? How do they relate to your competitors' business?

- What patents do you currently license to others? How do these patents relate to your core business? How do they relate to your competitors' business?

- What trademarks do you currently have registered? Which do you use? How do they relate to your business and your competitors' business?

- Do you license trademarks to or from others?

- Does you company have valuable trade secrets? (Virtually every company does.) What have you done to categorize them and protect them? Do you use covenants not to compete and confidentiality agreements? Are they systematically required and maintained? What are their provisions?

- How does the company identify the confidentiality obligations or invention assignment obligations of employees it has hired? Has the company signed any non-disclosure agreements, joint development agreements, or other agreements requiring it to keep certain information confidential? How does it monitor those obligations?

- Have your employees, where appropriate, signed assignment of invention/IP agreements? If you use independent contractors or advertising agencies to write software, ads, product literature, or other important documents, have they assigned the copyright to your company?

- Are there areas in which you innovate in which you should be, but have not been, systematically seeking protection in the form of patents, trademarks, or trade secrets? How do you document your innovations and history of products or processes?

- Who are your key competitors? What patents and trademarks do they own that may interfere with your business?

What Is Protected? What Should Be?

Current patents must be analyzed to determine what technology or methods are protected, to ensure maintenance fees are paid, and to ensure continuations are filed in a timely manner to keep the patents in place or broaden them as appropriate. Royalties on licensed patents must be accounted for and paid, and payments due on patents the company licenses must be tracked. Similar tracking must be done for trademarks.

Information on trade secrets is necessary to determine whether the company has IP in that area to protect, and if so, to determine what steps need to be taken to protect it. Trade secrets are easily lost if the company does not take the proper steps to keep the information secret, including limiting access to the information, requiring employees, vendors, and others, as appropriate, to agree to maintain the secrecy of the information, and ensure the monitoring of such information is also kept secret.

It is important for companies that use independent contractors for advertising, writing, Web site creation, software writing, and the like to make sure the authors assign the rights to the copyrights to the company. Absent such an assignment, they (and not the company) may own the rights to the original work. You will also want to explore whether the company has works that should be protected by copyright. This is particularly important, as registration is normally a prerequisite to enforcing copyrights in court.

Protecting IP: Means and Methods

Non-competition agreements are a major tool used to protect trade secret information as well as valuable customer relationships established at the company's expense. They need to be reviewed to ensure they are used consistently, that their provisions are enforceable under current law in key jurisdictions, that consideration has been provided, and that other requisites are met for their enforcement. If they are not in place, a program may need to be implemented. If the company does not have assignment of invention/IP agreements from employees, it must put in a program to get those agreements created and signed.

The questions regarding areas of innovation are critical to building up necessary protection. I had a client, for example, who had a competitor with an aggressive program of filing for patents. My client kept noticing this competitor seemed to be filing for patents on processes my client had used for years. We then determined my client needed to keep track of its innovations and systematically file for protection in key areas for three reasons. The first was to build up a portfolio to protect their innovations. The second was to have a portfolio for use in counterclaims in the event that the aggressive competitor sued them (as seemed likely, given their aggressive patent activity). The third reason was to provide proof of the date and time of my client's invention of technology, on which their competitor was otherwise likely to seek patent.

Information about proving innovation is gathered to be used as defense against claims of patent infringement by proving prior invention. Many companies show greater concern with the present and future than the past, so they tend to not maintain adequate records of prior products and processes sufficient to prove prior invention and use of technology, patented or not. It is critical to put in place a process to maintain such information so it is available if needed to defend the company.

Information on key competitors is used to perform necessary patent and trademark searches to see what type of patents, applications, and trademarks competitors either own or are seeking. This will then allow a company to determine whether it is likely to infringe prior IP owned by competitors as well as IP sought by competitors. This, in turn, will allow the company to plan whether to challenge the applications, if they mature into patents, by way of reexamination or in litigation, design around them, seek licenses, or otherwise deal with them. It may also alert the company to areas where it has innovations that are important to protect. The searches must be done on a periodic basis to allow ongoing analysis of these issues.

The Client's Role in IP

Generally, the client gathers what it understands regarding the IP it owns, but in each case, we also verify that they actually own the IP and that it is properly assigned and registered. Once this is accomplished, we go about working with them to understand what patents, trademarks, trade secrets, or other IP covering their products or services are critical.

Typically, the client will have some idea of the competitors' patents, but we will search for patents and trademarks assigned to competitors, to see what possible issues our client is facing—issues of which they may not be aware. Patent licenses, for instance, may or may not be registered with the U.S.

Patent and Trademark Office, so we will search databases for licenses, although we must rely on the clients to be comprehensive in this regard. Then there must be extensive follow-up to analyze their business needs and goals, and to craft an IP program that meets those needs.

The key factors for companies are who the competitors are now, who they are likely to be, what IP they own or are seeking, and where the market is likely going. The clients are generally able to identify their competitors, but in addition to searching trademark and patent databases, we can also verify competitors' patent filings in given classes and areas, which are now fairly easily searchable. Ownership of IP is sometimes identified by the clients, but we also need to perform searches to see what they have and what applications have yet to be filed.

The client generally has some idea of trends, but again, patent filings by competitor and class are another good indication of the areas that are likely to become important. The emphasis may change on these factors in the coming years, but identifying all forms of IP continues to be among the most important aspects of IP. Given some of the new trends in limiting patent protection, I believe we will see a little more emphasis on trade secrets in the coming years.

The Five Steps of an IP Legal Review

We must first determine from our client who the key people are with knowledge of IP, in all forms, and obtain any available summaries of IP, including issued patents, pending applications, trademark registrations, and trademark applications from such sources. This is critical to making sure our first meeting with them to go over their IP situation is productive. The challenge, of course, is to make sure knowledgeable people are involved, as representatives must include product managers, technical people, and executives.

The next objective is to gather up all publicly available patents, patent applications, trademarks, and trademark applications owned by the company and, from there, gather up the same information about their competitors and search the publicly available information to see who has IP of the same type or class. This needs to then be summarized and categorized in a meaningful way for discussion with the client team.

The third step is to engage in a series of meetings with company representatives to determine how existing or pending IP fits in with their business needs and goals, and to identify areas that could be better protected. The goal for such meetings is to focus resources on the important matters and set priorities. Another goal is to determine the competitor's apparent IP plans that may raise obstacle for the company. The ultimate plan here is to determine whether to design around the competitor's IP, move in a different direction, challenge the competitor's IP, or license it. This requires an analysis of what is possible and the cost of each alternative.

The first meeting will likely focus on patents and trademarks, but one should not neglect all aspects of a client's trade secrets, trade secrets program, non-competition agreements, and aspects of that program. Often, each meeting will focus on one particular aspect, depending on the company's situation. At the conclusion of this step, you will have identified seven major pieces of information, including:

1. A catalog of existing IP and importance of each item to the company

2. A catalog of the company's obligations with regard to IP, including licenses, confidentiality requirements, and so on

3. A list of the areas in which the company should be seeking additional IP and the preferred form of IP (i.e. patent, trademark, trade secrets, etc.)

4. Identification of an IP committee that will include technical and business representatives responsible for setting direction and approving decisions to seek IP and enforce IP and provide strategies regarding competitive IP (This committee must also, working with counsel, put in place a mechanism for documenting inventions/IP and, ultimately, providing ideas for worthy inventions to the committee for consideration.)

5. Identification of competitors and potential competitors, and their IP to watch

6. Identification of programs the company has in place or needs to put in place regarding non-competition agreements, confidentiality agreements, assignment of invention/IP agreements, trade secrets processes, and related matter

The above should all make its way into a database to allow quick access to company-owned IP, competitors' IP of concern, the company's pending IP, competitors' pending IP to watch, and the company's desired IP. The database also allows keeping track of deadlines, maintenance fees, and so on.

The next step is to apply for additional desired IP protection, with follow-through on monitoring and continuing to reevaluate the client's position and the competitive landscape. This process can include straightening out assignments and registrations of the same, initiating and keeping track of pending applications, and putting in place trade secret programs and invention programs (including confidentiality, non-competition, and invention/IP assignment agreements). This will also include periodic meetings with the companies' IP committee to perform evaluations of IP opportunities, and identify new areas in which to protect.

By the final stages of the process, the IP committee will be functioning and ongoing decisions will be made about seeking IP, its maintenance, enforcement, licensing, and formulation of strategies for dealing with potential threats from competitors' IP. Additionally, the company will ideally be expanding protection for trade secrets and related matters.

One major client representative we like to meet with for the above procedures, to establish a company's commitment to dealing with these issues, is of course the chief executive officer. Managers and members of the sales department are included when determining the IP related to the company's key business and direction.

Managers help assure that procedures and contracts are in place and monitored on an ongoing basis, while engineers and researchers are met with to learn the type of innovation going on and how to document and protect those efforts.

Monitoring IP Trends

The decisions of all critical courts must be monitored regarding patent, trademark, and trade secret matters. As far as overall trends are concerned, there is no substitute for staying current with the decisions of the U.S. Supreme Court, the Court of Appeals for the Federal Circuit, and important patent decisions in the trial courts. Summaries of those decisions are available on a subscription basis and through Westlaw and various blogs. While some of the key decisions can be spotted from the national media, particularly high-profile patent cases from the Supreme Court or the Federal Circuit, one cannot rely on that media alone. The issues tend to be complex, and the actual decisions themselves must be considered against the facts involved in the cases and traditional IP law. My younger associates are enthusiastic readers of blogs such as Patently-O.com and trademark blogs such as SchwimmerLegal.com, which typically report on important developments in the law on an ongoing basis. This is a good starting point for keeping up. I also belong to and subscribe to the publications of the American Bar Association's intellectual property section and the Federal Circuit Bar Association, among others, all of which have very useful publications on recent decisions and trends.

Regarding the competitive landscape, we perform a search for clients who have active IP programs on a weekly basis with the names of competitors and key technical terms in patent and patent application databases. A number of clients routinely send along trade journals for their industry that are helpful to review. Our searches also provide us with information from such journals if they are online.

This research allows us to identify any patent or trademark applications of interest, and to identify competitor applications. Moreover, it assists us in identifying "hot" technological areas where protection should be sought for client innovations. We also utilize a trademark watch service for our clients that allows us to evaluate possible challenges to trademark applications of competitors and others.

The Essentials of IP: What Every Client Should Know

The most common piece of advice I offer is this: concentrate on IP that is close to the core of your business. Look for opportunities to expand your IP value by licensing, and make sure you have the proper documentation in place concerning employees. And don't forget about your competitors' IP, which can cause you some unpleasant surprises if you don't pay attention to it.

I recall very clearly visiting a new client that had about 100 patent plaques on their wall. I said they must have a lot of litigation and licensing. They said they did not. Most of the inventions never made it into products. They sure could have used the million dollars they had spent on getting those patents in a better way. In short, focus is the key.

As for competitors, over the years I noticed that at first clients would often come to our firm because they had received a threat of IP litigation or had been sued. Once we finish a case, they start to come earlier so we can help them identify threats before suits and plan our way around them. The advice here is simple: learn about competitive IP to avoid surprises.

Developing IP: Tools and Tactics

All types of IP require emphasis on documenting ownership, development, and following up on applications and programs. Patents, on the other hand, have special requirements in a complicated, rule-driven application process that can be performed only by licensed and experienced prosecution counsel. It is therefore critical to make sure applications are timely made, and that follow-up takes place. Also, you must make sure inventions are assigned to your company, as patents are issued only in the name of individuals, so to own them you need to have them assigned to you. Competitors' applications must be watched to give the company time to determine whether issues of infringement are presented by their competitors' patents, and if so, whether there is a basis to challenge them, design around them, or license them outright.

Trademarks also have technical and timing requirements to obtain and maintain registrations. Key among these is the filing after five years of use to make the mark "incontestable." Competitors' use and registration of marks must be monitored, and new marks must be cleared before use.

Trade secrets can be particularly tricky from both a defense and owner's point of view. From a defense point of view, one must make sure new employees who may possess trade secrets will not use trade secrets of their former employers. Your company may well be liable for its employees' misappropriation or misuse of their former employers' trade secrets. You also will need to know whether prospective employees are subject to non-competition or confidentiality agreements, determine if they can abide by them, or whether you have defenses to their enforcement.

From an owner's point of view, an ongoing program of enforcing confidentiality, proper use of agreements, and diligence in protection is necessary to protect trade secrets. Trade secrets are a unique type of IP the company can create without filing or the like. All that is necessary is that the company has a valuable secret and takes steps reasonable to keep it secret. This takes a fair amount of effort, but it is often well worth it to protect what is sometimes some of the most valuable information the company owns. Care must be taken to enforce secrecy and document the steps taken. If the proper steps are not taken, the information can no longer be protected as a trade secret and can be used by competitors. It is not uncommon for companies to decide valuable trade secret information has been stolen from them. But if steps have not been taken to reasonably protect the information in the eyes of a court, there is no right to protect it.

The key to most defenses tends to be access to information. For patents, it is not uncommon, at least in some industries, that the company that has actually invented and used the technology in question before the inventor now claiming a right to the invention that is the subject of a patent did. The prior invention by the company may render the patent invalid, a complete defense to a claim or infringement. Or, as in many cases, the technology may have been known throughout the industry before the patentee "invented" it, which again could render the patent invalid. In these situations, you need to prove your company actually invented the technology and when, or that the technology was used earlier in the industry and when. Companies therefore need to have a system for documenting and maintaining a record of their activities so this can be proven.

The same is true for trademark use and trade secrets. The date of first use is critical for protection of trademarks. In the United States, the first to use the trademark is typically the owner of it, despite the date of registration. Therefore, it is critical to be able to prove when the mark was first used in commerce. With respect to the trade secrets, proving development and use of the trade secret is a key first step to establishing a right to protection. Proving steps to keep the secrets secret is also critical. Finally, in defending against a claim of trade secrets, proof of independent development or preexisting use of the alleged trade secret is key.

The common issue in this regard is in assigning someone responsible for preserving historic information and categorizing it in some way. Counsel can best direct the company as to what kinds of proof are most useful and necessary in this regard.

The Cost of IP

The most serious risks associated with IP generally include being precluded from selling products, including key technology critical to the company's business, being required to pay large damages claims, and being unable to protect the competitive advantage created by innovation if proper protection is not obtained.

The risks also include the cost of legal fees, distraction to the company, and the possible economic effect of an injunction or damages. To minimize the risks, we try to learn of IP risks before they actually arise by monitoring competitors' IP activities and IP situation so we have time to consider what poses a risk, the degree of risk (both financially and on a "win or lose" basis), and possible alternatives. The latter may include designing around, licensing, creating a standoff using the company's own IP, or challenging the IP of others.

In recent years, the size of patent verdicts has grown significantly. Some are in the tens or even hundreds of millions of dollars when courts award to patentees lost profits on lost sale. Of course, it can be disastrous for a company to face an injunction in the middle of a product launch, which can require the company to immediately stop selling the product. It can be equally disastrous to have a key product taken off the market by an injunction, particularly for companies that offer only a few products. Normally, careful planning can head off these types of disasters, particularly given the great amount of information about pending patent applications that is now available.

Of course, the registration of IP has expense associated with it. A typical patent application averages about $6,500. *AIPLA Report of the Economic Survey 2007* at I-21 (July 2007). But this can be in the tens or even hundreds of thousands of dollars, depending on the complexity of the technology, the length and intensity of the examination process at the Patent Office, and possible challenges after issuance by competitors.

Government Regulation of IP

Patents are issued by the United States and other national governments. There is now cooperation through the Patent Cooperation Treaty between the United States and many nations. Regulation is through the courts, except in the case of U.S. International Trade Commission proceedings, where this is done federally on an administrative level. The International Trade Commission is an independent federal agency that, among other things, directs actions against unfair trade practices involving patent, trademark, and copyright matters.

There has been a fair amount of activity in the patent area as of late. New rules were issued by the U.S. Patent Office making the patent application process more complex and useful to patent examiners. These rules were, as of this writing, held to be outside the power of the U.S. Patent Office to put in place, and so they are not yet in effect. Significant changes to the application process are, however, expected. Similarly, patent reform legislation has been proposed, although not yet enacted as of this writing, that could roll back some of the reach of patents and impose some limitations on damages and the like.

Trademarks are issued by the United States and other national governments, as well as by state governments. Trademark rights can also proceed at common law without registration in the United States as a matter of state law. Some regulation, particularly of counterfeit goods, is enforced by the U.S. government through the International Trade Commission. There is also regulation of trademarks in an Internet context by the World Intellectual Property Organization, for example, as well as in the courts.

Trade secrets are created as a matter of state law, usually by statute. Many states—though certainly not all of them—have enacted the Uniform Trade Secrets Act, although there are variations even in that. There are federal criminal laws, for instance, making it illegal to steal trade secrets.

Copyrights are regulated exclusively on a national basis, through the U.S. Copyright Office. They are enforceable through the court system as well as by the International Trade Commission, again typically in counterfeit situations.

Trends in IP: Where to Find Them

My practice possesses a variety of patent and trademark searching capabilities, including databases with docketing and reminder services to keep an eye on processing of applications and related matters. As noted, these are used to understand competitive risks and opportunities.

It is critical to know the changes in the legal landscape. I subscribe to three or four magazines on the topic and monitor the cases and legal backdrop to keep current on IP trends and key technologies. As such, I can say with confidence that patents are rapidly changing. The U.S. Supreme Court has changed the ease of challenging patents for obviousness, as noted above. The Federal Circuit has narrowed the breadth of patent claims, and made treble damages for willful infringement much more difficult to achieve, meaning patents provide less protection to their owners and slightly less of a concern for the potential defendant.

Meanwhile, as noted above, the patent rules were changed by the patent office, but the D.C. Circuit rejected the new rules. As also noted, Congress is considering a Patent Reform Act. Make no mistake about it though, patents are still critically important to many businesses.

Trademark law is in some flux regarding dilution of famous marks that may be getting easier to protect. This is good news for holders of nationally recognized marks, but it is of virtually no benefit to those with marks that have less recognition and national reach.

Understanding the Client's Needs

One of the more complicated situations I have handled involved a client in the specialized construction equipment industry—an industry with very little history of IP issues. A newer competitor began to apply for patents, some of them on processes my client had used for years, and so it became clear that the client needed to institute a complete IP program, particularly in the patent area.

I was quite familiar with the client, and I reasoned that we needed to learn about their product lines in depth, the history of their product development and methodology, as well as other areas for growth and innovation, and to strengthen protection in those areas in which the competitor was positioning. We had a meeting at the client site location with the chief executive officer and key marketing and technical people, and as a result, we put in place a program similar to the one outlined above. This included identifying IP the client had, identifying IP protection the client might obtain, identifying competitive IP, and determining whether to invalidate (sometimes with the client's own previous activities), design around, or take some other approach to competitors' IP actions. We then built up the client's IP portfolio and performed weekly monitoring of competitors' patent applications. We also unearthed trademark violations using metatags including our client's registered marks, which we put a stop to.

IP issues entail advantages and disadvantages uncommon to other areas of law. The information on our clients' and competitors' IP is largely public and searchable, so we can rely on our background and expertise to help clients understand their situation. There are also significant opportunities for planning and improving their position. Thus, one can be proactive to develop their IP portfolio and to plan for competitors' activities simultaneously.

One disadvantage is that there are no set rules for how best to proceed in this area. There are, of course, rules preventing infringement and rules for obtaining protection, but designing a program to protect IP and to avoid the IP of others requires one to be experienced and creative. This also provides opportunities, of course, to those who approach the problem creatively and diligently. Again, the key way to manage costs is to focus on critical IP and not simply seek IP protection for its own sake. One must also monitor competitors' IP so one can plan for what to do if competitors receive patents or other protection that can block your client's plans. It is much less expensive to deal with such issues after having the chance to plan, rather than being tied up in expensive patent litigation.

The Value of Expertise in IP

Our firm is involved in our clients' business development and IP development, but we do not apply for patents, preferring instead to hire firms with the very best credentials in a given area to manage that affair. We feel this is the best approach, as it is not possible for a mid-sized firm to build all the technical expertise desired in all the technology areas in which our clients are involved. We partner with these firms to provide a seamless approach to coordinating the various activities.

Remember to focus only on critical IP, related to your client's business and the competitive landscape. Know what issues you will be facing from competitors so you can plan for them. This will lower your costs and increase your IP effectiveness.

David A. Allgeyer is a partner with Lindquist & Vennum. For more than twenty-five years he has been practicing in the areas of intellectual property litigation, arbitration, and commercial litigation. He has litigated cases in state and federal trial and appellate courts throughout the United States involving intellectual property in the form of patents, trademarks, trade dress, trade secrets, and copyrights, as well as related issues of unfair competition. Based on his litigation experience, he helps clients identify and address contractual and commercial issues and disputes, general intellectual property protection and strategy, and intellectual property licensing.

As a member of the American Arbitration Association's commercial panel, Mr. Allgeyer has been appointed as an arbitrator in more than twenty matters concerning commercial and intellectual property disputes. The former chair of Lindquist & Vennum's commercial litigation and intellectual property practice groups, he currently heads the firm's litigation department. He also serves on the firm's management committee.

Mr. Allgeyer has been included in Best Lawyers in America in 2007 and 2008, as well as Chambers USA Guide for intellectual property litigation. He has been named a "Minnesota Super Lawyer" by Minnesota Law and Politics from 2002 to 2007. He has also been named one of "Minnesota's Top Intellectual Property Super Lawyers" by Law and Politics.

Working with Clients to Protect and Enforce Their IP Assets

Keith J. Grady

Chair, IP Litigation Group

Polsinelli Shalton Flanigan Suelthaus PC

ASPATORE

I am the chair of the intellectual property (IP) litigation group at my law firm. We assist individuals and businesses in enforcing their IP rights, and defend individuals and businesses when they have been accused of violating another party's IP rights. Our work includes: filing and defending lawsuits in state and federal courts and administrative agencies such as the U.S. Patent and Trademark Office and the Trademark Trial and Appeal Boards; negotiating settlements; creating licensing agreements; attempting to resolve potential disputes without litigation through mutually beneficial business arrangements; and examining creative solutions to help the client avoid the substantial expenses that can be associated with IP litigation. We handle all forms of IP litigation, including patents, trademarks, copyrights, trade secrets, non-competition agreements, non-disclosure or confidentiality agreements, and employment agreements.

Our services are always most helpful when we get involved at the outset of an IP matter. For example, if a client is considering what sort of IP to obtain, it is helpful for us to work with them to analyze their industry, as well as what their competitors are doing. We will look at the IP that is already in that particular industry, and then assist the client in devising a strategy that will help them make the best use of their IP. Obtaining a patent, for instance, is a substantial investment of time and resources. The attorneys' fees and costs to prosecute a patent usually begin in the range of $5,000 to $10,000, depending on the complexity of the technology, and they could get much higher in situations involving extraordinarily complex areas such as biotechnology and/or pharmaceuticals. It is also necessary for the inventors to invest their time and efforts in assisting the patent attorney in the drafting of the patent application. This process can be very time-consuming. Therefore, the decision to obtain a patent should not be taken lightly—the client needs to know what added value the patent will bring, and how it can give them a competitive advantage. Obtaining a patent on a new invention can prevent competitors from practicing that invention and secure a particular market segment for the business. Then the patent holder can undertake the marketing and educational efforts necessary to develop the market for a product covered by the patent, secure in the knowledge that none of its competitors can take advantage of the time and expense associated with those efforts by marketing a copy of the patented invention.

Major Categories of Legal Needs in the IP Realm

Clients always want to know what types of IP they can and should acquire, and this up-front acquisition issue involves a number of considerations. Does the client have IP already? What kind of IP would provide the client with the greatest protection? Would it be better for the client to obtain a patent or a trademark—or would a copyright be most effective? Is it better for the client to maintain its formula as a trade secret, because that form of IP will never expire?

Once the client decides what type of IP to acquire, the next step is to determine the best method of acquisition. For example, is there some form of IP you are already aware of in your industry that you can buy, or do you want to develop your own IP portfolio in an effort to rope off a certain area of an industry? Patents are often effective in helping a client achieve dominance in a particular industry or segment of an industry. However, if the client is a sales or manufacturing organization, trademarks will be very important, because branding is often the primary driver in selling certain products. Therefore, we frequently assist clients in developing brands and obtaining trademarks. For publishing companies, musicians, and some other industries, copyrights are a very important form of IP, because a copyright will protect their original works of authorship.

Next it is important to protect and enforce the IP you decide to obtain. If you know there are competitors on the fringes of a certain area in which you are involved, or you know other parties will soon be competing with your company in a certain area, a decision must be made regarding how you will enforce your IP. Are you going to file lawsuits, or embark on a licensing program? In some cases, you can use a hybrid of these two vastly different approaches. For example, you may decide to file lawsuits to enforce some forms of IP, while giving licenses for others. This decision often depends upon the size of the competitor and the threat to your company's market share.

The client also often needs to consider what are known as freedom-to-operate issues. In many cases, a company will come up with an idea for a new product or an improvement on an existing product, and they will want to know whether they can develop their idea and sell their product without infringing on anyone else's IP. We will look at the entire market area and each component part of the proposed product to determine whether any single part or combination of parts, or the whole product, is going to result in infringing on anyone else's IP. We will give the client a view of the landscape (i.e., what is out there in the industry, what sorts of IP might have an impact on the product they are considering, and whether there are specific patents that might pose a threat to their freedom to bring their product to the market). We will then work with the client to develop a strategy to avoid any potential infringement issues, and help them get their product to market in an effective way that will not subject them to a lawsuit down the road.

The counsel we provide is always evaluated on a case-by-case basis, depending on the client's industry and what they want to know. It is important to know who the major players/competitors are in a particular industry or product category, and what the client wants to achieve by obtaining and enforcing IP in a certain area. Do they want to carve out market share, compete with another company head to head, or prevent another company from doing something?

Key Agencies in IP Acquisition and Enforcement

The U.S. Patent and Trademark Office is the primary agency for acquiring IP in the United States. The office employs patent examiners who are responsible for analyzing patent applications to ensure that a claimed invention meets the conditions for patentability set forth in the Patent Act. These examiners become proficient in certain technological areas and examine patent applications in those areas. As a result, the examiners become familiar with the entire field, and this helps ensure that only new discoveries or advances in technology are patented. Generally, "any new and useful process, machine, manufacture, or composition of matter, or any new or useful improvement thereof," is eligible for a patent. *See* 35 U.S.C. §101.

The U.S. Patent and Trademark Office also employs examining attorneys in the trademark area to review trademark applications to make sure a proposed trademark is not, among other things, confusingly similar to a previously issued mark. *See generally*, 15 U.S.C. §1051 (2002). The purpose for this type of examination is to allow marks to issue that identify the source of the goods or services, but to prevent applicants from obtaining marks that are simply generic in the sense that they only describe a category of goods or services.

A separate agency, the U.S. Copyright Office, issues copyrights. A copyright may be obtained for "original works of authorship fixed in any tangible medium of expression, now known or later developed, from which they can be perceived, reproduced, or otherwise communicated, either directly or with the aid of a machine or device." *See* 17 U.S.C. §102(a). The statute sets out the specific categories of works of authorship for which copyright protection may be obtained, including (1) literary works, (2) musical works, including any accompanying words, (3) dramatic works, including any accompanying music, (4) pantomimes and choreographic works, (5) pictorial, graphic, and sculptural works, (6) motion pictures and other audio-visual works, (7) sound recordings, and (8) architectural works. Id.

Disputes related to patents, trademarks, and copyrights are normally heard in the U.S. district courts throughout the country. Additionally, the International Trade Commission plays a major role in enforcing IP in the U.S. that is related to imports. There is currently a great deal of litigation going on at the International Trade Commission level because it is viewed as a quick way to stop cheap knock-off products and illegal imports from coming into the United States.

U.S. patents are only enforceable in the United States. Therefore, companies or individuals involved in the global marketplace need to seek IP protection in other countries. Almost every country has its own patent law. To obtain patent protection outside of the United States, one must apply for a patent in the countries in which you want protection. It is important to ensure that a client who is interested in protecting their IP outside of the United States does what they need to do to obtain patent protection outside of the United States. In most foreign countries, publication of an invention before applying for a patent will prevent an applicant from obtaining patent protection. Accordingly, it is important to file a U.S. application prior to publishing any invention for which the inventor may want international patent protection. The Patent Cooperation Treaty makes this process somewhat easier. It provides for centralized filing of international applications such that a single filing can constitute filing in all member countries. Thereafter, the applicant will have to decide in which member countries to prosecute the patent, which must be done on a country-by-country basis.

Recent IP Trends and Litigation

The past ten years have seen a vast expansion in IP litigation, particularly in the patent area, but also in the trademark and copyright areas. Over the past few years, however, the protection of IP in the United States has been somewhat diminished by court rulings, particularly in the patent area. For example, the U.S. Supreme Court in a recent case, *KSR Int'l Co., v. Teleflex International*, 127 S. Ct. 1727 (2007), has made it easier to invalidate patents on grounds that the claimed invention would be "obvious" to one of ordinary skill in the specific field of technology. This type of validity challenge relies upon a combination of references, which taken together, show all of the limitations of a claimed invention. In the past, obviousness challenges were very difficult to prevail upon in patent litigation. However, it is now widely accepted that the *KSR* case has lowered the burden on patent challenges on obviousness grounds. Patent holders may now be discouraged from asserting a patent for fear that it may be invalidated. Indeed, this case may embolden businesses that want to copy the patented products of others to do so in the hopes that, if they do, they will be able to invalidate the other party's patent based on the new lower obviousness standard. Generally, this decision has had the effect of making some patents less valuable. The case will also end up making patent litigation more costly, because more obviousness challenges will be advanced by alleged infringers, causing the courts and the parties to engage in the fact-intensive inquiries necessary to resolve these claims.

Another important case in this area, *eBay Inc. v. MercExchange LLC*, 547 U.S. 388 (2006), has been viewed as limiting the availability of permanent injunctions as a remedy for patent infringement. In the *eBay* case, the court held that a patent holder must do more than simply prove infringement in order to obtain an injunction, whereas in the past courts presumed that infringement caused irreparable harm to the patent holder, and would therefore issue a permanent injunction against the infringer as a matter of course. However, a patent holder now must satisfy a four-part test, traditionally used in other areas, to obtain a permanent injunction. The factors are (1) irreparable injury to the patent holder, (2) the inadequacy of legal remedies, such as monetary damages, to compensate for the injury, (3) the balance of hardships must favor the party seeking the injunction, and (4) proof that the public interest would not be disserved by issuing a permanent injunction.

A third important case, *In re Seagate Technology LLC*, 497 F.3d 1360 (Fed. Cir. 2007) (en banc), has had an impact on the availability of enhanced damages for willful infringement. Prior to *Seagate*, a party had an affirmative duty of due care to avoid infringement, and it was generally accepted that an alleged infringer accused of willful infringement could defeat such a claim by proving reasonable reliance on a competent opinion of counsel. However, *Seagate* changed the standard for willful infringement, requiring the patent holder to prove objectively reckless behavior by the alleged infringer. The case further holds that there is no affirmative obligation to obtain an opinion of counsel regarding non-infringement.

A number of laws and regulations relating to patents, trademarks, copyrights, and unfair competition continue to be important to clients in this practice area, including the Lanham Act, a federal law that provides remedies for trademark infringement, and the Copyright Act, a federal law that provides remedies for copying a protected work. It is also important to be aware of the Code of Federal Regulations relating to patent prosecution, as well as the *Manual of Patent Examining Procedure*, a key resource patent lawyers use in obtaining patent protection for their clients.

Helpful Resources

To monitor trends in these areas, the attorneys in our firm receive a number of industry and trade publications, and we attend seminars and trade shows. I am a member of the American Intellectual Property Law Association and the IP law section of the American Bar Association, both of which circulate publications that are very helpful in keeping abreast of trends in these areas. Many local bar associations also have IP sections— our St. Louis bar association is one of the oldest in the United States, and it is very good on the IP front. Talking with other lawyers in my firm who are very knowledgeable is also helpful. We have a large patent prosecution group that we interact with on a frequent basis, and we keep each other aware of developing trends in various areas.

Industry experts are also helpful resources for the IP attorney. Some of the products that are the subject of IP litigation, such as medical devices, can be very complex and small, and therefore we need to find ways to explain the technology and to project images of the external and internal workings of these extremely small devices so they are easy for judges and juries to understand and see. To do so, we often work with engineers and other experts who can assist us in making those images more accessible and understandable. We also work with financial experts who have a high level of expertise in ascertaining the impact of infringement on a particular business, and how a company's competitive advantage can be damaged by acts of infringement.

Consulting with Counsel: Understanding the Client's Technology

The most important thing a client can do to ensure complete protection of their IP is to consult legal counsel early in the product development process, because there are a number of problems that can arise if you do not protect your ideas properly from their inception. There are a number of statutory bars in the patent area. For example, if you sell or show a product embodying the patented technology for a certain period before you file for a patent application, you may be precluded from obtaining protection.

Getting assistance from legal counsel early in this process is also essential in order to make an informed decision regarding what sorts of IP to pursue. Clients are usually very knowledgeable about their own industry, including what is being enforced and what is not, but they often need an attorney to help them navigate through the various minefields in the IP area. Consulting with counsel prior to bringing a product to market is a good way to do business, because it helps the attorney understand exactly what the client's technology consists of, what the client wants to protect, and why it is important for their business. Working with the client at the early stages of the development process also helps us understand how their product gives them a competitive advantage in their industry. Accordingly, when we attempt to enforce that IP, we will have intimate knowledge of the client's technology, what has occurred in the development process, how broad or narrow the client's IP coverage for that technology is, and what sorts of defenses the alleged infringer will assert.

If the client is in a particularly complex industry, such as the medical device industry or the pharmaceutical industry, their technology can be difficult to understand, and it requires a real commitment on the part of both the attorney and the client to spend the time necessary to convey the appropriate information and explain the technology. In other industries, such as some of the mechanical arts, the client's technology will be fairly straightforward and easy to understand. However, the challenge in those situations lies in determining how crowded the field is and where the client sees their product falling in terms of their competitors' products. Generally speaking, if a certain technology is not that complicated, there will be a lot of IP in that area, which makes it harder to develop new products without having to take a license with your competitors—and that is something they may not be willing to grant because of their desire to protect their niche in the market.

Determining a Client's IP Needs

When first meeting with a client in relation to an IP matter, I try to find out what they believe their IP needs are and what their ideas encompass, and after that we will look at the various forms of IP that are available to them for their particular ideas. It is important to determine how viable the client's ideas are and how likely it is that we would be able to obtain IP to protect those ideas, or whether we would need to go to someone else who has similar IP and talk to them about a licensing arrangement.

Generally, I try to find out from the client how important the idea is to their business, and what form of protection they want to obtain. I have been in situations where a client's idea can be protected with both a patent and a trademark; and it is generally a lot less expensive for clients to obtain a trademark on a product than a patent. Therefore, if a company is a start-up, they might want to make the financial decision to go with trademark protection rather than patent protection. I normally give the client various choices and options, and they then make their decision based on their resources, needs, and capabilities.

There are two primary areas of legal needs in this practice area. Obviously, when a client gets sued they need a lawyer to defend them against a claim of patent, copyright, or trademark infringement. Sometimes a situation will arise where one business has threatened another with a patent infringement lawsuit, and the business that has been threatened will then file suit against the patent holder to prevent future threats due to the devastating impact these threats can have on sales of a product. Either party in such a situation needs a lawyer to protect their IP, or to assist them in the difficult process of defending against patent infringement.

Another defensive mechanism lawyers can assist clients with is the freedom to operate situation, which involves being proactive and making a determination early on as to how to develop your product in such a way as to avoid infringing on other IP in your industry. Partnering with the client at an early stage in order to help them develop their product properly, while at the same time avoiding other IP in the industry, can assist the client in avoiding a lawsuit down the road.

Avoiding Financial and Legal Risks

The financial and legal risks of IP infringement can be very serious. For example, if a business is found to infringe a patent, they can be required to pay damages including lost profits to the other company based on sales the infringing party made, and if they are found to have willfully infringed a patent, the damages could be trebled. In a case of willful infringement, there is also a possibility of having to pay the other party's attorneys' fees, which can be very high. Furthermore, a party found to have infringed a patent could also have a permanent injunction entered against them, which would prohibit them from continuing to produce the product. If that product is a major product in your client's business, or is the entire business, the client may be forced to shut down.

There is an enormous drain on any company that is involved in IP litigation. Businesses make money by manufacturing and/or selling products, and when litigation occurs, they need to divert their resources from these areas to work with their attorneys. Indeed, litigation drains a company of key resources in terms of time, money, and effort. There is also an emotional investment on the part of the inventor who developed the IP and is worried about his or her ideas being copied or stolen. Consequently, it is always best to protect your IP investment early on, and implement key compliance practices in this area.

The Importance of Documentation

To protect IP properly and avoid litigation, it is important to fully document the inventive process. For example, a client should keep notebooks that document when an idea first came into being, who came up with it, how the idea went through its development phases, and who worked on the project going forward. Once the idea is fully developed, having the proper documentation in place will enable you to determine all of the inventors you need to list on a patent application.

Documentation of the initial conception, and the steps you took to reduce the invention to practice, can also be important in determining priority of your invention over other inventions in the marketplace. The United States does not have a "first to file" system, as is the case in Europe. Therefore, if I came up with an idea on December 31, 2007, wrote it down, went on vacation, developed the idea later in 2008, and ended up filing a patent on April 18, 2008, I might still have priority over someone else who came up with a similar idea on January 2, 2008, and filed right away, simply because my initial conception pre-dated that of the other party. Simply put, since I was the first to conceive of the invention and was diligent in my efforts to reduce the invention to practice and to document how I went about that process, I should be able to pre-date an earlier patent filing. Consequently, it is very important to document your chain of development every step of the way, because it can have a serious impact on your rights going forward.

It is also important to keep confidentiality safeguards in effect when you are in a business that thrives on IP. One of the most important aspects of IP protection is secrecy—you cannot have a trade secret if you do not keep it secret. Therefore, it is important to prevent employees and other parties from having access to information or materials that are highly confidential unless they sign an agreement not to disclose what they see. It is also important not to display products that are still in development without such an agreement, because it can have an impact on your ability to obtain a patent later on down the road. Indeed, ensuring that you maintain the confidentiality and secrecy of your inventions is an important business practice and can assist in the process of acquiring a patent on new technology.

Performing a Legal Review of a Client's IP Portfolio

The primary goals of an IP portfolio review are to determine what IP the client presently has, what they want to obtain, and to assist them in determining whether their ideas/technology are protectable. The client must determine how they want to protect their IP, taking into consideration how valuable it is, and how they want to allocate their resources for obtaining that protection.

The first step in performing a legal review of a client's IP portfolio is to do an IP inventory. We look at all of the client's IP properties in the three major categories—the patent area, the trademark area, and the copyright area—as well as any trade secrets. Then we look at what products they are trying to protect with that IP portfolio, and we try to ascertain what the client believes to be long-term or short-term products. In the United States, some product cycles can be very long or short, as consumers may have a short attention span with respect to certain products. Fads often arise in different industries, and a particular product may only be very popular for a short time—hula-hoops and the pet rock are examples of products that were enormously popular for a short time. Therefore, how the client views the life cycle of the product they are interested in protecting is important, because that will have an impact on how much they want to spend on obtaining, enforcing, and protecting any IP related to that product.

Where your client fits in the marketplace is also very important. In other words, are they a major player or an up-and-comer others will be looking to knock off? What are the relationships within the client's industry? Sometimes industries and competitors are very cooperative, sometimes they are very ruthless and litigious, and you need to know who is more litigious and willing to go to the mat for different types of IP, and who is not. Some companies have reputations for being unwilling to resolve cases without litigation, and once they embark upon litigation, they are unreasonable in their approach. It is important to be aware of those factors when you are advising your clients and reviewing their IP portfolio and strategies.

It is also important for the client to understand the costs that may be related to the review process. Therefore, I believe in speaking frankly and being up-front with the client about what I anticipate the potential costs of the process will be so they can determine whether it is worth expending those resources to do the type of IP review they want me to undertake. During the review process, you may find that analyzing complicated pieces of IP or technology can take you in different directions you could not foresee at the outset of a project, and when that happens, it is important to inform the client in a timely manner. Although you may feel that you need to go down certain paths that may be off the main course in order to do a proper review, the client may not want you to make that trip. They may be comfortable with what you have done so far, and they may wish you to stop there—and ultimately, the client's resources are being spent, so therefore you need to respect their wishes. It is important for the client to understand that not only are we working to protect their IP, but also that we will do so in the most efficient and effective way possible, by providing them with all the information they need to make the right choices with respect to resource allocation.

Challenging IP Situations

In many cases, companies do not develop their IP internally, but rather partner with outside sources to do so. Some of the most challenging situations in this practice area arise when the company you are representing purchases or licenses technology from outside inventors who are not employees of their company. It can also be challenging to represent smaller inventors who have licensed technology to a big company, because their needs have to be protected as well. Even though outside inventors may not believe they have a stake in the company to which they have licensed their technology, they certainly have a stake in both the technology and the product it is protecting, because generally the inventors receive payments based on the revenues derived from sales of that product. Consequently, it is important to make sure everyone is on the same page in these situations.

Therefore, if you are going to enforce a patent for a company that has obtained a license on technology from an outside inventor, it is essential to have the outside inventor on board with any litigation that may arise in the future with respect to that IP. In other words, the outside inventor must fully participate in the litigation on behalf of the client, even though it will take them away from their business or employment. Simply stated, they will have to be as committed to the litigation as the employees of the company.

The Role of Outside Experts

During IP litigation, we normally use technical experts and damages experts, although we do not usually bring these experts in at the outset of the case unless there is a need for an outside technical expert to assist with the infringement analysis at the front end of the litigation due to the complexity of the technology or the desire to obtain the best expert available and prevent your opponent from obtaining that expert. However, we generally bring these experts into the process fairly early on so they can develop an understanding of what the client's technology is all about and how the client views that technology. We also want to ensure that the experts agree with how the client views the technology, and understand how they can best assist me in promoting the client's interests.

Occasionally we will use outside legal experts if there is a matter of patent prosecution procedure at issue in the case, or a particular question about whether a patent is enforceable as a result of something someone did or did not do in connection with the prosecution of the patent. Courts are divided on the use of outside legal experts in patent cases, because most judges believe they understand what the law is in this area, and they feel confident that they can figure out a case without input from an outside legal expert. However, the area of patent prosecution can be arcane and full of regulations with which the general practitioner, or even a trial judge, is not familiar, and even people who do IP litigation on a regular basis may not be aware of or conversant with some of these regulations. Therefore, an outside legal expert can be of assistance in certain situations. For example, we have used people who have worked for the U.S. Patent and Trademark Office in some of our past cases, and they have been very helpful and persuasive in explaining the procedures that must be complied with to obtain a valid and enforceable patent.

Keith J. Grady is the chair of the intellectual property litigation practice group at Polsinelli Shalton Flanigan Suelthaus. He is also a shareholder in the commercial and business litigation practice group. He has more than eighteen years of combined experience in government and private law practice. In his general litigation practice, he has represented private companies, governmental entities, and municipalities and their employees on a variety of issues including enforcement of zoning regulations, employment matters, civil rights cases, and constitutional law.

In his intellectual property law practice, Mr. Grady has a wide range of experience, having appeared in courts throughout the country in every phase of intellectual property litigation, including preliminary injunction hearings, claim construction hearings, summary judgment hearings, jury trials, and appeals. He represents and has been involved in the representation of numerous companies and major manufacturers concerning a range of technologies in a variety of matters, including patent and trademark litigation, trade secret misappropriation, unfair competition, and trade dress infringement.

Mr. Grady is a member of the American Intellectual Property Law Association, the Bar Association of Metropolitan St. Louis, the Missouri Bar Association, and the American Bar Association. He is a regular speaker on his areas of expertise. He earned his B.A. from Tulane University and his J.D., cum laude, from Hamline University.

The Critical Role of Education between Lawyer and Client in the IP Space: Listen and Learn, Then Speak

Greg L. Berenstein

Partner

Barnes & Thornberg LLP

ASPATORE

Fortune cookie read last evening:
"Listen attentively. You will come out ahead."

As a transactional lawyer whose deals generally are driven by a focus on intellectual property (IP) rights, I counsel clients to develop, manage, strategize with, and use their IP assets. In fact, one of my most important contributions to the client lies in the ability to comprehensively identify a client's rights (and risks) with respect to their IP, and to identify how they can best exploit those rights as a commercial asset. However, with a practice that crosses industries—negotiating terms in a merger agreement for a pharmaceutical client in the morning, drafting a software license for a client in the technology space after lunch, and finishing the day counseling a marketing company on the best way to introduce a new marketing campaign—a critical dual counseling role becomes essential. First, this involves fully understanding each client, its business, and its industry, allowing us to then help the client understand how their IP assets can best be exploited for the company's near- and longer-term strategies. Second is educating the client about the essence of IP rights and their role, benefit, and risk in their business. To us, this sets up the necessary and beneficial mutual role of educating each other about essential, critical information—in the case of the client, regarding its businesses and planning, and in the case of us as legal counsel, regarding the nature of IP rights and their role in that business and planning.

For example, I recently had a matter for an information technology client where the merger between understanding their business, on my part, and the risk related to understanding the scope of IP risks, on their part, was never more evident. We were evaluating the nature of a proposed business expansion in the context of identifying, among other things, existing IP rights of the company and any potential risk of infringing upon third-party rights. This meant an evaluation of known risks and costs. Had I not fully understood their business and their strategies, near- and long-term, my role would have been materially impaired and less valuable. Had the client not fully understood the rights and risks related to IP (both their own as well as third-party rights), their assessment would have been materially impaired and less valuable. In this matter, after studying those strategies, we identified technology they had developed and how it is related to or, in some instances, was dependent upon other technology (proprietary to the company or to a third party). It then allowed them to evaluate their next steps, both from a strategic business and cost perspective, as well as a legal and risk-oriented one, and then they had the essential groundwork to optimize their business strategy.

Specifically, in identifying what we believed would be their next steps, they considered various commercialization options—a strategic alliance, a marketing or promotional relationship, or a license with another party. For this step, it was critical for the client to identify its IP rights in relation to a business commercialization venture, and this could only be done through an assessment of the client's opportunity relative to the value and position of its IP and relative to the market (i.e., what other companies are doing relative to their developing technologies and IP).

Simply put, you cannot understand the nature of how to successfully commercialize your IP rights in a vacuum. Therefore, one of our primary goals with any client in the IP arena is to allow our clients to fully understand the nature of the rights they own or the properties they want to develop so they can achieve an accurate representation of their IP rights.

Mistakes to Avoid

A big trouble spot for many clients in this practice area stems from not fully understanding what protections they may need in relation to the IP they are developing. Businesses that are not in business solely for the purpose of developing IP have the hardest time in this area. While a company such as IBM, Microsoft, or Sony is expected to understand how they should be developing their IP and what it means in the context of their product line, many other clients and industries do not. Simply, they do not have a strong enough understanding of what an IP right is relative to how they are going to commercialize it. For example, a client may believe that having a patent gives them all the IP protection they need, but having a patent does not mean you have a clear, unencumbered path with respect to how you move forward in terms of product development, marketing, and exploitation. If there are any IP rights that are related to your core technology and you have not developed them yourself, it is essential to acquire those rights (i.e., through a licensing arrangement or assignment) and/or develop some other form of IP that allows you to establish ownership or gives you the right to make use of your technology. For example, there may well be underlying IP rights that the patent holder does not own, but that are required to fully exploit the patented technology in the marketplace. More so, a patent is not a guarantee of the right to commercialize technology free and clear. A patent is subject to challenges such as a claim of invalidity or unenforceability. Therefore, often the biggest challenge we face in working with clients in this area is making sure they have a full and firm appreciation of what they need to do to develop their IP correctly.

Similarly, we often find that the client does not understand the importance or need of obtaining all of the rights surrounding the core technology they might be developing. For example, if the client is working with outside parties (either in a co-development or engaging an independent contractor) to develop a core technology, they need to make sure they have fully acquired all of the IP rights with respect to that technology generally with a proper assignment. Again, product development does not take place in a vacuum. Therefore, you need to fully understand what rights pertain to the technology you are developing, and how other rights that may already exist or need to be developed can be brought into that technology.

I believe every client with material IP in their business—not just the IBMs and Microsofts of this world—needs to create a program to help them deal with, protect, and monitor their IP portfolio. A comprehensive IP management program identifies how IP is being developed throughout a company, both from a contract standpoint as well as an internal management standpoint. If a company has people who are either developing technologies internally on a day-to-day basis, or who are working with outside companies to develop core technologies, it is important for those people to be fully aware of the IP issues that exist from both a management and a contractual standpoint. For example, we frequently find that management within a company often does not know what others within the same company are doing, often creating duplication, if not conflict, with each of their efforts. This is most troubling in the context of contractual commitments made with third parties that may, upon an internal audit, reveal that efforts in one initiative are thwarted by efforts in another—one group, for example, committing with a third party to license and market a product that another group within the company was simultaneously developing with another party. My biggest challenge can be helping clients in those areas to understand the nature of the commitments they are making on one path and how they affect concurrent development down another.

Trends in the IP Realm That Affect IP Counseling

A primary industry factor for our IP clients, especially in the pharmaceutical, medical devices, and biotech fields, is government regulation and industry self-regulation. Obviously, any business decisions and developments in these industries, when subject to a high level of government regulation and scrutiny, require that the client needs to fully understand that IP development is contingent upon this additional layer of consideration—ranging, for example, from regulatory approval for pharmaceutical drug development and clinical trials, to marketing, pricing, and trade practices, to privacy, to name just a few.

In addition, many industries internally or self-regulate their business practices. The nature of this self-regulation must be fully understood in order to manage IP successfully. For example, if we are representing a client in the food industry that wants to implement an aggressive direct mail marketing campaign to children—all business planning with IP concerns— it is critical that we understand how that industry is self-regulating itself in the privacy area and how applicable laws and regulations regarding privacy, promotion, and marketing will likely impact those plans (and to recognize that this area is constantly evolving in that regard).

Specifically, the biotech, pharmaceutical, and medical devices industries are probably the most rapidly evolving industries in my practice, and it is important to keep ahead of that curve. For example, legislation is evolving in the biotech space pertaining to the scope of permissible research in biotechnology development and genetics. Pharmaceutical industry regulations are always changing with respect to the development, manufacturing, marketing, and promotion of drugs, medical devices, cosmetics, and other Food and Drug Administration-regulated products. Therefore, an important note to IP lawyers it to not tread recklessly in the regulatory world—rely on experienced colleagues or other counsel to understand the regulatory landscape of your clients' businesses, and use them as the resources for monitoring IP trends.

Educating the Client and Yourself

Indeed, as noted above, education is a critical part of the IP attorney's role. Counseling the client's business and technical personnel in relation to IP issues is critical, because they are the people on the ground with respect to developing the client's IP rights. As an outside attorney, you aren't likely to be present to correct the client's mistakes or assist them in creating and instituting IP management programs, at least not on a daily basis.

Typically, we will work with the client's general counsel or staff attorney, as well as often the information technology, research and development, or business development personnel. And if we need to better understand how certain elements are put into play from a legal perspective, I will consult my own colleagues, including patent lawyers or trademark specialists, as well as the regulatory attorneys I referenced earlier. However, I always find it most helpful to draw upon the knowledge of the client's in-house experts first— their scientists, software programmers, the creative types, and business development people, because they more fully understand the client's business, technology, or innovation.

Importantly, throughout the education process, it is best to explain the client's IP issues in a way that makes them comprehendible—education in the abstract rarely serves much good purpose to a client. Use a tangible connection to how an issue applies directly to them—educating them after educating yourself. For example, recently we spent several hours with a client understanding a narrow, complex aspect of their technology business to better assess a possible claim of infringement against our client. Once we had a direct set of facts that addressed a potential problem, we then spent a considerable amount of time explaining the legal issues related to infringement, because they were now able to apply them directly, and narrowly, to their own world.

However, if the client chooses to pursue a different direction from one you have recommended, you need to remember they are the client, and they know their business better than you. Or at least, the decision is ultimately theirs. With that said, if the client is making mistakes in terms of how they are dealing with legal issues, that is a different matter, and you need to make sure the client knows the repercussions of the actions they are taking within the scope of your counsel. More so, if you are dealing with a subordinate who you think might be doing something that is not in the best interest of the company, you need to highlight the issues for the people at the senior management level. In the end, however, the client is the ultimate decision-maker, and even if you think they have not made the most prudent decision, it is their decision to make, as long as you have fully counseled them and provided them with all of the information they need to know.

Dealing with Cost and Risk

I feel IP management, maintenance, and infringement are the biggest issues in the IP area in terms of cost and risk. A well-managed, comprehensive IP program requires diligence and thoroughness, and that costs money. More so, infringement accusations can be very costly to defend or pursue—to say nothing of potential damages if found liable for infringement or misappropriation. Consequently, it is essential to ensure you have fully counseled your client with respect to how it is commercializing its products—balancing costs with benefit. To this point, the client needs to understand the importance of due diligence and monitoring its IP rights in relation to the outside world. As noted earlier, "ownership" of a certain IP property does not mean there is no risk related to claims of invalidity or unenforceability by a third party with respect to that property.

Another area of high cost and risk in the IP realm relates to the product development and research process. Product development is inherently expensive, especially if it turns out that the client's technology and the accompanying IP rights are not commercially valuable. Careful and prudent management, diligence, and scrutiny along the way, both by legal counsel and the business (often directed by legal counsel), goes a long way and often provides an insurance policy of sorts as the business charts its course.

Implementing and Reviewing Legal Compliance Practices and IP Assessments

Despite the costs discussed above, we always encourage clients to be very proactive about understanding their product development and other internal IP generation in relation to the patent and trademark area, as well as with regard to copyrights and trade secrets. The client needs to understand what rights it has, how it has developed those rights, and whether their rights in relation to patents and trademarks are superior to those of any outside party. Consequently, having a comprehensive program in place that provides for searches and mechanisms to evaluate your IP rights is very important. For example, on a very basic level, the company's personnel who deal with identifying new names for its products should be dealing with legal counsel to conduct trademark searches as a proactive effort to identify IP rights and limit risks of liability. Similarly, a constant diligence between scientist,, strategic development, research and development, and their legal counsel is critical to providing a necessary element—and protection—to the costly effort of product development and commercialization.

As part of this effort, it is important to work with your client to routinely and frequently review and assess who is doing what in relation to IP management within the company. The client should establish policies and procedures for ensuring its innovations are being catalogued in a way that ensures they are being properly protected and treated as IP assets. Ensure that what they are doing in the IP area meets the requirements of applicable law, and that their IP is being fully protected. This, in turn, will allow the client to know its IP portfolio is being commercially exploited to the fullest extent possible.

As noted earlier, one of the biggest challenges in this practice area is helping the client understand how the successful commercialization of a product is not singularly related to simply owning a patent. Indeed, there are a variety of other rights—some of which may need to be licensed from a third party—that may affect a client's ability to get a product into the marketplace. The client needs to fully understand what it means to develop a product that is largely proprietary, and what other rights may need to be considered in addition to any patent rights they have obtained.

Controlling Ongoing IP Management Costs

To control the client's costs in the IP area, it is important to understand the client's priorities and the complexities of the particular business, legal, and regulatory issues they are facing. More so, if a client does not appreciate the complexity of a certain IP issue, it is equally important to set out a comprehensive understanding of the issues this chapter has laid out. An ounce of prevention is worth a pound of cure. Understanding what makes an IP issue complex allows us to best monitor the process and explain that process to the client in advance, rather than after the fact.

Final Thoughts

Succeeding as an IP attorney is more than understanding the U.S. Patent and Trademark Office. It is more than drafting a good license. It is based on understanding your client's business and their priorities in the context of those skills. And it requires rolling up your sleeves, often stepping outside the expected "lawyer" role, and learning the client's business. Absent that, you may not be providing the optimal counsel your client needs—whether in IP counseling or other areas of legal concern. If you've done that, you have served your client well, often in a way they will never fully understand—unless you tell them, and maybe that should be part of your job, too.

Greg Berenstein is a member of Barnes & Thornberg's Life Sciences Health Industry Group, practicing in the area of transactions. Mr. Berenstein's practice includes the representation of pharmaceutical, medical devices, and biotechnology companies, retailers, manufacturers and food companies, as well as software developers, technology start-up companies, Internet and application service providers and consulting companies. In addition to providing general legal counsel to his clients, he specifically focuses on transactions that involve development, ownership or other rights related to intellectual property, such as licensing; joint ventures and strategic alliances; distribution agreements, pharmaceutical and medical device promotion and marketing agreements; technology development agreements; e-commerce and Internet-related agreements, Web site development and partnering agreements; systems integration and information technology consulting services; software development agreements; outsourcing; general intellectual property matters; and confidentiality and non-competition agreements.

Mr. Berenstein received his J.D. from the University of Iowa College of Law, in 1985 and his B.A. from the University of Iowa in 1982. He has published many articles and spoken at numerous programs in the areas of technology, e-commerce and licensing law. Mr. Berenstein served as an adjunct professor at the Kent College of Law, teaching in the area of intellectual property. He is a member of the Illinois Bar Association and the Iowa Bar Association.

Advising Clients in IP Matters from the Perspective of a Life Sciences Practitioner

Anne Brown, Ph.D.

Partner

Thompson Hine LLP

ASPATORE

The Patent Application Process

As a private practice biotechnology intellectual property (IP) attorney who was formerly an in-house counsel at a small biotechnology company, among many other matters, I prepare life sciences patent applications. Typically, I will receive an invention disclosure describing a discovery that could constitute a patentable invention. If the disclosure comes from a client with an established IP patent strategy (e.g., a large company with in-house counsel), the client has already determined a patent application should be filed. If, however, the client is smaller, a preliminary question is whether an application need be filed at all. If the client merely needs freedom to use the subject technology (i.e., does not want to be blocked in the case that another party later files on and obtains a patent to the subject technology, but does not necessarily wish to block others), a description of the invention can be published. If, however, the smaller client desires to prevent others from using the invention, an application should be filed.

Having passed the threshold question, the next step is to assess the discovery for patentability. This involves ascertaining whether, in fact, the discovery is novel. This requires searching scientific literature and patent databases to make sure the discovery has not been made already by another party or is not just an obvious version of another's prior discovery. If the discovery is new, writing the claims may be relatively straightforward. But if aspects of the invention are already in the scientific literature, claims must be carefully drafted to capture what is novel and non-obvious as broadly as possible, but avoiding the prior aspects. As an example, an inventor presented the discovery that if he introduced a certain type of DNA sequence into a cell, the cell would begin to produce certain clinically valuable proteins. In searching the scientific literature, I did indeed find an instance in which one subtype of that DNA sequence had been introduced into a cell, but in a context where it was not recognized that this method could be useful to produce clinically valuable proteins. The claims, therefore, were written to exclude that subtype. They captured the invention, therefore, as broadly as possible, without extending into an area that was already in the public domain. It is important to follow such a procedure in view of U.S. case law. *See Festo Corp. v. Shoketsu Kinzoku Kogyo Kabushiki Co.*, 535 U.S. 722 (U.S. 2002). This is because if that prior scientific literature had been discovered by a U.S. examiner rather than by me, and the claim had to be narrowed during examination, the broadest protection of the invention might not have been preserved. In fact, throughout the preparation of the application, various legal cases must be considered to make sure no valuable aspect of the invention might inadvertently be dedicated to the public. *See Johnson & Johnston Assocs. v. R.E. Serv. Co.*, 285 F.3d 1046 (Fed. Cir. 2002). Other areas include the description allowing the ordinary practitioner to make and use the invention as broadly as it is claimed, and the language in the claims being clear and unambiguous.

Another pitfall to avoid is not describing the way the inventors believe the invention may best be practiced. One must always clearly question the inventors on this point and make sure they understand it is critical to maintaining the validity of the patent that eventually issues.

Another critical aspect of the process involves determining who is an inventor. The material in the patent application is often published following the filing of the patent application. Scientists (inventors) often equate authorship on the publication with inventorship. But inventorship is a legal determination. For a party to be an inventor, generally they must have contributed to conception of the invention. Large amounts of work and position as laboratory head, for example, may be insufficient for inventorship. And inventorship must be determined in good faith or this may compromise the enforceability of the patent that eventually issues.

For determining inventorship, I speak independently to all parties associated with an invention and ask them to relate their perspective on the history of the discovery. Then I develop the inventorship determination. It is not uncommon that I am presented with two different stories from two different parties. As mentioned, a sensitive issue occurs when I have determined the head of the laboratory is not an inventor. In such cases, I explain that inventorship is a strictly legal determination. I explain that if they were to be designated as an inventor, the patent could be unenforceable. Therefore, it is important to teach the client the law of inventorship so they understand there are no personal factors involved.

During the search process, another basic issue that may need to be resolved is whether the client will have the freedom to use their own invention (or grant others the right to do so). Again, a larger client may have resolved this issue internally with its own inside counsel, but the issue may need to be discussed with the smaller client. An invention may be patentable in its own right, but if a genus of the invention is already patented, the invention, which is a species of the genus, cannot be practiced without infringing the broader claims in the genus patent. In such a case, the patent to the species may lack sufficient commercial value to justify the expense of the examination process. Therefore, to ensure the client is free to use the technology they wish to patent, I will often conduct a search of the patent literature to ascertain whether the technology they wish to patent falls under a broad claim in an unexpired patent. The search may be confined to the United States or extend to selected international territories. This will depend on where the client seeks to operate.

If blocking patents are discovered, one option is to conduct an analysis to assess the actual patentability of the patent to ascertain that the requirements of all the statutes pertaining to patentability have been met (i.e., ability to withstand a legal challenge of unpatentability). It is not uncommon that an examiner will issue a patent that, in fact, does not meet all of the requirements of patentability. I will also assess enforceability. For example, during the examination process, did the patent holder conduct themselves in such a manner that the public suffered an inequity in the issuance of the patent ("inequitable conduct")? This could occur, for example, if the patent holder intentionally proffered material misinformation or intentionally withheld, from the examiner, information material to patentability.

The formal examination process begins after the application is filed. Examination strategy is often based on further developments of the technology by the client company. For example, many aspects of the invention might have been described in the patent application, but some of them may assume a larger importance than others as the technology develops. For example, the application may have been directed to a compound that was thought to treat several diseases. Subsequent studies may show that the compound is effective for some diseases but not others, and particularly effective for one. In that case, the claims can be revised to better protect the further information. Or the client or another party may discover valuable aspects of the invention that were not even claimed but which could have been. In such a case, the claims can be revised to capture and protect the further aspect. The point is that, particularly with a small client, one should maintain a dialog with the client about further developments within the company and the industry to maximize protection for the invention. Thus, the examination process extends beyond simply responding to examiners in the formal examination process.

In this regard, another aspect, particularly relevant to small companies that may not have inside patent counsel, is to monitor the IP progress of potential competitors. With a small company, it may be desirable to monitor the IP of commercial competitors or potential competitors. This could involve regular review of their progress in prosecuting their patent applications in the various patent offices (which may provide this information to the public, such as the U.S. Patent and Trademark Office and the European Patent Office). Such a review is helpful in many ways. First, it provides insight into how examiners view the patentability of the technology and allows the client to develop solid rebuttal arguments (or claim amendments) in anticipation of examiner review of the client's similar or same technology. Second, it allows the client to police the examiner and make sure any mistakes are corrected. For example, if an examiner is unaware of an important prior reference and thus is about to erroneously grant a patent to a competitor, my client then has the opportunity to bring this reference to the attention of the examiner and, perhaps, delay or prevent grant.

Another issue to consider, for companies that are obtaining patents for therapeutic products that are subject to regulatory testing (e.g., therapeutic compounds) is to eliminate avoidable delays in responding the U.S. Patent and Trademark Office. Any such delay on the part of the client can reduce patent term extension that may be available to the client under U.S. law.

Major Regulatory Agencies in the Patent Realm

The U.S. Patent and Trademark Office examines U.S. patents and provides its binding opinion on whether a patent application meets patentability requirements (e.g., under 35 U.S.C. §§102 (novelty), 103 (non-obviousness), 112-1 (enablement, written description), and 112-2 (clarity)). If an examiner refuses to grant a patent, there is a further avenue of appeal, the Board of

Patent Appeals and Interferences, which is also a section of the U.S. Patent and Trademark Office. If the Board of Patent Appeals and Interferences refuses to grant, the matter can be appealed to a district court (D.C. District Court) and/or the Federal Circuit court established to decide patent cases (among others) and create uniformity in the patent case law, the Court of Appeals of the Federal Circuit.

There are various independent patent offices in many international territories with similar examination and appeal procedures. While there are some core similarities in patentability requirements (e.g., requirement for novelty), there are many differences and, ultimately, a local associate (e.g., European, Japanese, etc.) is consulted on many examination matters.

If international patent protection is sought, it often is cost-effective to file under the Patent Cooperation Treaty administered by the World Intellectual Property Organization in Geneva. This allows effective filing in all signatory territories and a search and examination for a modest fee. This strategy can serve a dual purpose. First, the examination may establish that the invention is not patentable (e.g., not novel). Then the applicant can decide to abandon the invention without having incurred the major expense of filing the application is many countries. Also, it provides an approximately two-year window to explore the technology and decide if the expense of patent protection is merited.

Other executive agencies decide matters related to IP. The Justice Department investigates antitrust issues with respect to IP ownership, and the International Trade Commission renders binding opinion on IP practices within the context of fair trade.

IP Legal Needs for Companies

Many of a client's legal needs, with respect to IP management from outside counsel, will depend on the stage, size, and type of client. For example, many of the needs of a start-up company (e.g., spin-off company developing university-originated technology) are different from the needs of an established company. The start-up generally relies on outside counsel for advice on every aspect of IP, including long-term strategy. Another distinction is whether the IP of the client is based on its own research and development (e.g., university, innovator companies, research institute) or is acquired or licensed from another party (e.g., patent holding company, manufacturer of generic products, development company). Priorities and strategies will vary, depending on the client's business model. Recent trends will also affect our strategies. For example, during the early development of the biotechnology industry, the focus of IP protection was on innovator companies. As the industry matured, generic companies began to exploit the discoveries of the innovators and there was a significant shift in focus to the IP needs of those generic companies.

Thus, the strategy with respect to a generic company might focus on seeking to invalidate an innovator's patent or finding ways to use the innovator's technology without technically infringing the innovator's claims, with less focus on protecting IP based on research and development. For a patent holding company that merely acquires others' patents and seeks to enforce them against, for example, large established companies, the focus might be on understanding the critical technologies used by an established company (which often use hundreds of important components or supporting research tools for their commercial products) and assessing the patent literature for patents that cover one or more such components/tools. The needs of a university or research institute might center on inventions made by university scientists. As these institutions are generally not in a position to develop (commercialize) the invention, the IP needs generally focus around licensing the invention to a third party who will develop it. In that case, my involvement would generally be limited to the patent application process. The strategy would be to obtain as broad claims as possible, as that would tend to create more value for the license.

There are some tasks that cut across the board for innovator technology-based companies:

1. *IP protection for platform technology.* This was discussed in detail above, and it relates to the patent application process and obtaining the broadest possible protection for the invention. Another way of saying this is that applications should be prepared so the scope of the client's technology is adequately protected (including, especially, its commercial products).

2. *Freedom to use critical supporting technology.* An ongoing need is opinion of counsel on freedom to use a specific technology (i.e., whether using a desired technology will infringe a valid U.S. patent to a non-company patentee). This has been touched on above in relation to whether an applicant has the freedom to use his or her own invention. But beyond this, most technology-based companies need to know if they have freedom to use specific technologies that are necessary to support research, development, and ultimate commercialization. The technology at issue may be fundamental to a proposed research and development direction for the company. Or it may be adjunctive technology to complement an existing program. It may involve research tools and reagents potentially critical to advancing a certain program. Such opinions can be a significant aspect of my practice. It is also one of the most interesting aspects, as it truly requires analyzing factual scientific and technical data with legal questions. And as mentioned above, if indeed there is a blocking patent, a further opinion is whether that patent is valid.

3. *Licensing.* In the case in which there is little or no freedom to use an important supporting technology, one task is to seek to obtain a license to the patented technology. In other cases, a client seeks to acquire relevant external IP to protect or complement its internally developed IP or technology. It may then also seek to license the technology. The terms of the license may depend upon the value of the IP. To that end, I will analyze the patents with respect to validity.

4. *Due diligence.* On the other hand, a client may seek to obtain ownership of third-party IP rather than take a license. If a client plans to acquire a company (or selected IP owned by a company), we will do an assessment of the other company's IP portfolio. If the IP is in active prosecution, I will review the claims and file histories (examination proceedings in one or more patent offices) to ascertain whether prosecution is proceeding (or even can proceed) with the correct scope. This also would involve a patentability analysis independent of any such analysis that may have been conducted by another party. An analysis would also be conducted to establish that the client would indeed have freedom to use that technology. If the IP has already issued as a patent, I

would assess the validity of the claims, and whether they confer the appropriate scope of protection to the invention. In either case, I would also examine chain of title to ascertain that the assignor of the patents to the company is entitled to do so.

Note that many companies are mixtures. A mature company may generate IP on technology derived from active internal research and development programs, but may also acquire protected technology by licensing IP from others to be used and developed. Or entire companies or parts of companies may be acquired to obtain new IP, and continue the research and develop new such technology/IP. The point is that the IP needs of any company will be based on its various business strategies.

Key Players in the IP Protection Process

This entirely depends on the nature of the client. Typically, I interact with several types of clients. In the life sciences, one type of client is a university or research institute. Typically, the contact is a senior party in the technology transfer office (which is generally responsible for licensing inventions that are made by scientists under contract to the university/institute). In this case, there may be little interaction with respect to how the IP relates to the business strategy of the client. With university-originated work, I may interact with the licensee of the technology, often a company. Another type of client is an established company with a significant legal department that includes one or more patent attorneys. In such a case, the interaction may be confined to one or more patent attorneys and, again, there may be minimal interaction regarding how the IP-related tasks (patent applications, opinions, due diligence) relate to the business strategy. In the case of the smaller company, and particularly one that does not have an in-house legal department and/or patent counsel, the interaction with key executives can be significant in terms of quality and quantity. In effect, I may serve as the de facto in-house patent counsel. In such a case, it is not uncommon to have direct and continuous interaction with the inventor/chief executive officer or other senior player, such as the chief security officer. This is the case particularly when a university professor (or the university itself) has created a spin-off company based on a particular university invention. In such a start-up company, the chief executive officer may be the actual inventor of the technology—they invented the technology when employed by the university, which has spun off their technology into a development entity. In that case, I may provide essentially all of the IP-related counsel and attend to virtually all of the projects. In such a case, I have the opportunity to understand the business objectives in detail and make sure IP supports those objectives and evolves as the business objectives evolve.

While not necessarily a company executive, a key player in the process of patent procurement, enforcement, and defense is the scientist (often the inventor). Interacting with the scientist/inventor provides understanding of the scientific aspects of an invention (the company's or a third party's), which is critical to obtaining the greatest possible protection for an invention during the application drafting and examination process, developing a legal theory in a litigation or supporting opinion, and altering the technology that is being used to avoid a third-party patent, to name a few.

Preliminary Client Meetings: Key Questions

When first meeting with a client in relation to an IP matter, it may be important to ask questions that provide understanding of the background, needs, and business goals of that client. There are going to be different questions depending on the type of client. But in a general sense, the first question is to understand why the client seeks IP counsel. What is the scope of the counsel they seek? Is there going to be a continued relationship or a short-term "one-shot" project? I let the potential client tell me why they have sought IP counsel. I also inquire about their past experience with counsel and, particularly, IP counsel. Were they satisfied? Why or why not? What do they seek from counsel? Do they currently have counsel? What is the scope of that counsel's responsibilities? Substantively, however, I seek to understand the long-term business goals that make the immediate IP issue important.

This applies even if the project is short-term and defined. The client may simply desire an opinion on patentability of an invention. Or they may simply desire to know about the validity of a patent. Or they may be interested in knowing whether they have freedom to use a specific technology. Or the client may need counsel to handle prosecution matters. I believe that to provide the best service, it is almost always helpful, if not necessary, to understand the context of the project. Taking the first project (above) as an example, why is patentability of the invention important? Are they going to use the invention? How? Do they plan to form a company around it? In that case, what are the other IP needs of the company? What supporting technology will they need? Is any of that already patented? Will, or can, they obtain the necessary licenses? Do they have freedom to use the invention? Where will the company operate? In summary, I ask about the context: the technology and the business plan around that technology so the appropriate scope of protection is obtained with respect to the application itself, and the goals of the company.

Other questions could be appropriate. Do they make a product or provide a service? If the client is a service company, who is going to be using their service? Do they have the freedom to operate with respect to all of the essential components that are needed to perform that service? Do they have competition in their area of operations, and if so, what does their competition consist of? Do they need to take a license in a specific technology, and is their company based on that technology? It is important to ensure that whatever IP the client has licensed will cover the technology they expect to develop. Do they need to take out a license for certain forms of IP, or can they trade technologies? That might mean cross-licensing technologies where, for example, two distinct patented technologies are owned by two different companies, but each of the companies needs both technologies. In such a case, the companies might license to each other. Ultimately, I need to know what the client plans to do in the future in order to determine what IP protection they will need to achieve that goal.

Due diligence comes into play often in the context of a merger or acquisition. Again, IP tasks depend upon the client's ultimate business objective. As an example, a company may acquire another company simply to obtain ownership of potentially competing IP so it can prevent the competition. There may be no intention of commercializing the technology. In this case, rather than assess the strength of the patents as one normally would, the major due diligence effort might be limited to simply validating the right to assign ownership of the IP to the client (although the price of the transaction certainly could depend on the strength and breadth of the IP).

Patent Protection Recommendations

Ownership

As an adjunct to substantive patent protection, however, the issue of ownership is also critical to protecting platform technology (and, as discussed below, is critical in any enforcement or transfer of IP rights). A review of all assignments is mandatory. This includes all assignments from all the original inventors, as well as any subsequent assignments from any party to whom the inventors have assigned. These should have been duly recorded with the appropriate patent offices. With respect to future IP from the company (if the client has plans to develop IP internally), have they put employment contracts in place to ensure any employee (or contractor) is under an obligation to assign their rights to inventions? Ownership issues may not be so straightforward. For example, an inventor may refuse to assign ownership to the client. In such cases, it is important to determine if there is any type of contractual obligation (e.g., employment contract).

Practical Protectability

The IP a client seeks to protect may be patentable but may not be enforceable, in a practical sense. One reason could be that the territory does not have adequate enforcement provisions based on lack of personnel or government commitment or policy (e.g., Brazil has ignored patents directed to drugs for treating life-threatening diseases such as AIDS). Or the invention may be directed to a research tool that can be used in any territory to make a product that is then imported into a desired market. To protect such an invention, one would have to file in virtually every territory where the tool can be used. Obviously this is hardly possible, particularly for the small client. Accordingly, except for an enormously valuable research tool, I might recommend that a particular patentable technology is not practically protectable. A well-known example involves patentable disease-related gene sequences that are screened against compounds to find a compound that inhibits that gene (and thus is a candidate for a therapeutic drug). The ultimate commercial value is in the compound. But screening could be done virtually anywhere. So unless one filed in every territory where screening could be done, the gene sequence, while patentable, is essentially not protectable.

Considerations in Determining Protection

There is no "one size fits all" patent protection plan—it all depends on the client's business plan and their intangible goals (e.g., their "mission," both short-term and long-term). To determine what IP protection a company needs, determine what is most important to that company and create an IP strategy to achieve it. Some key issues are as follows. Some of these are discussed in more detail above.

- If the IP is developed externally and licensed in, are they complying with all terms of the license?
- What IP does the client need to acquire to operate? (Assess whether they can acquire that IP if they do not already have it. If the client is unable to license or acquire the IP, assess the validity of the other party's IP.)
- Do the patent claims fully cover the client's product?
- Have all the technical and material disclosure requirements for patent procurement been met?

The chief objective in this initial IP analysis is to ensure the client can operate within their space, that they are free from any potentially infringing activities, and that they have protected the IP they need to protect.

Legal Review Questions

In summary, key questions to consider in a legal review of the client's IP issues include:

1. Is the IP portfolio and strategy consistent with the business objectives?
2. Has the client adequately protected the platform technology? Are all of its patents of sufficient scope to cover the technology of the client's current or future commercial embodiments, or the technology it needs to use to achieve its goals? Are all ownership issues resolved? Is inventorship determined? Are all fees paid?
3. Where does the client's technology and IP stand in relation to a potential competitor's IP? Can claims be broadened to cover a competitor's technology?

145

4. Does the client have freedom to use its key technology and any critical adjunctive technology? If not, is the client able to acquire the freedom to use it through licensing, acquisition, or invalidating a blocking patent? Are all non-infringement opinions in place?

Financial and Legal IP Risks for Small and Large Companies

There are various legal risks a company faces with respect to its IP use and strategies. Legal risks often have financial consequences. The major risks are (1) losing as a defendant in an infringement suit and being enjoined from using patented IP (with attendant cessation of business operations around that IP), and (2) losing as a plaintiff in an infringement suit where the defendant (and any other competitor) will be able to use the patented invention. Obviously, a larger company financially is better able to conduct litigation than a smaller one is. The cost is prohibitive for a small company and, unless there is a partner to subsidize the litigation, there may be little a small company can do if one of its patents is infringed. Accordingly, it may be only very commercially valuable patents that are the subject of prolonged litigation. To prepare for an allegation of infringement (if there is any question that the activity is an infringing activity) and avoid attorneys' fees and higher damages in a suit, however, a small company may have non-infringement opinions in place. All too often, a management team will dispense with obtaining the opinions or the analysis that needs to be done, simply because they do not have (or want to spend) the necessary funds. Therefore, it is extremely important for a small company to raise sufficient funds to perform the necessary analysis to ensure they have freedom to operate in their arena.

The flip side is that a small company may not have the resources to enforce its own IP. One thing that can be done, however, is to stand in the shoes of an alleged infringer and perform the exercise of thoroughly trying to invalidate one's own patent (which the alleged infringer will try to do). That way there will be a legal theory in place and at least one will have the comfort of relative certainty that the patent can withstand challenge.

Another risk for any company is that of losing in an interference proceeding. Interference means the client and an unrelated party invented the same thing independently. Resolving an interference is a matter of sorting out which party invented first. However, a small company may not be able to provide the funds for interference litigation and may be forced into a settlement because it is financially vulnerable.

Naturally, the financial aspect is not so critical for a large company. Yet the legal (and financial) consequences of being on the losing side of an infringement or interference proceeding could be severe. As an example, the largest biotechnology company in the world (Amgen) was party to a three-way interference over the gene sequence for an anti-anemia drug, erythropoietin. Amgen was found to be the first party to invent. Based on this success (and the therapeutic efficacy of this one drug), the company proceeded to become the leading biotechnology company in the world. On the other hand, Amgen also may have lost its huge revenue from erythropoietin if it had not prevailed in an infringement litigation conducted in the late 1990s. With the vast commercial market for erythropoietin, others sought to enter the erythropoietin market by developing technologies to produce erythropoietin that they asserted were not covered by Amgen's patents. Although the other party was ultimately found to infringe, even a large company such as Amgen was under considerable legal (and financial) risk.

With respect to larger companies, there have been certain recent potentially adverse developments with the advent of patent holding companies. These companies simply own patents and enforce them against companies that are commercially successful. For example, an electronic product may have numerous components that are necessary for the product to operate. A holding company may own patents to one or more of such components and seek to enforce that patent. Therefore, large companies face a significant financial challenge in terms of licensing all of the components they use. And if they do not obtain those licenses, they face the possibility of being forced to stop marketing the product if another other party is able to obtain a court directive stipulating that they can no longer use the patented component in their product.

Aside from the patent holding company, certain competitors may seek to enforce their patents to gain an injunction. Indeed, the threat of an injunction is probably the biggest legal issue for a large company. Unfortunately, large companies that use a lot of different technologies face a higher prospect of being sued for infringement, simply because it is believed that they have the financial resources to take out licenses, and that they have important products they cannot afford to stop marketing. It has been suggested that the goal of the holding company is not to shut the "infringer" down, but to effect a lucrative settlement.

Monitoring IP Trends: The Importance of Following Case Law

I recommend monitoring the case law. It is easy to back-burner this aspect of our practice because there is no "deadline" involved. But IP strategy is based in many instances on decisions from the Court of Appeals for the Federal Circuit and the Supreme Court. Therefore, to provide the best advice to my clients, I strive to be current on court decisions, especially in my technical area. There are several IP legal blogs that provide case law summaries, analysis, and interactive commentaries. There are also some newsletters that are very helpful, such as *IP Strategy and Management* and *Intellectual Property Today*. These cover IP issues and discuss how case law applies to the industry. The American Intellectual Property Law Association and the American Bar Association frequently have meetings that have IP sections. In addition, one can follow Court of Appeals for the Federal Circuit decisions on the court's Web site, which provides current cases and is updated daily. Holding group discussions of important cases is also very helpful.

An example is a recent case from the Supreme Court on the issue of obviousness. *See KSR Int'l Co. v. Teleflex Inc.*, 127 S. Ct. 1727 (U.S. 2007). This case has changed the way patent applications are written. Prior to this decision, an applicant often explained how the industry was deficient and how the invention solved that deficiency. Now that may be considered an "admission" of obviousness, so a patent application should no longer contain such explanation.

With respect to other industry trends, the area of drug development is an example. In the 1990s, there was a major effort to discover gene targets that were implicated in certain diseases. Therefore, a significant amount of financing and research centered on the patenting of gene sequences. Four major players were involved. And there was significant controversy, extending from the U.S. Patent and Trademark Office to the U.S. executive branch, about the patentability of these sequences. This area is not controversial today, partly because the industry has matured. Many gene targets were discovered, and those targets were used in the drug discovery process (as I have discussed above) to screen for therapeutic compounds. Thus, the focus of IP protection began to be on those compounds. Many compounds entered the market and thus led to the further development of the generic drug industry. Now the generic drug industry is beginning to innovate.

Another reason for the decreasing focus on IP around gene sequences was the obstacle discussed above in the section on protectability. The Court of Appeals for the Federal Circuit rendered a decision that affected, detrimentally, the patenting of gene sequences for purposes of drug discovery. In the early 1990s, Congress amended the patent law relating to infringement. The law stated that if a product was made by a process that was patented in the United States, it would be an act of infringement to import that product into the United States if it was made by that process outside the United States. The question then arose of whether a drug discovered using a patented gene sequence was a product "made" by that process. The Court of Appeals for the Federal Circuit said such a drug was not "made" by the process. *See Bayer AG v. Housey Pharms. Inc.*, 386 F. Supp. 2d 578 (D. Del. 2005). That decision eviscerated the value of claims to drug discovery processes with gene sequences—which started a trend in the IP realm whereby those particular claims, and in fact genes themselves, became much less valuable.

Final Thoughts

To serve clients successfully in this practice area, I recommend having a clear idea of the company's mission and business plan (i.e., what it values and how it expects to bring in revenue). And ascertain what the company has already done and what it needs further to do to achieve that plan. Keep apprised of its research and development. Only then can one ask the right questions that help determine how IP fits into achieving the client's particular goals.

Anne Brown, Ph.D., is a partner with Thompson Hine LLP. She is an intellectual property lawyer and registered patent agent. She has extensive experience in domestic and foreign patent (biotechnical) practice, including genomics, stem cells, clinical diagnostics, therapeutics, molecular biology, genetic engineering, pharmaceuticals, and polymer product technology. She was the head legal counsel at a biotechnology company for seven years, and spent ten years in private practice focusing on patent prosecution, opinion, due diligence, client counseling, competitive intelligence, and intellectual property strategy and management. She was a U.S. Patent and Trademark Office biotechnology patent examiner.

Ms. Brown earned her B.S. in biological sciences, her M.S. in genetics, and her Ph.D. in molecular genetics all from Florida State University. She earned her J.D. from the University of Maryland School of Law. She is a member of the American Intellectual Property Law Association, the American Bar Association, the Cleveland Intellectual Property Law Association, the District of Columbia Bar, and the North Carolina Bar.

Understanding Your Client's Trademark and Other IP Needs

John Arado

Partner

Wildman, Harrold, Allen & Dixon LLP

ASPATORE

Approaching a New IP Client

Before the initial meeting with a potential new intellectual property (IP) client, the attorney must do all he or she can to find out about the company. If it is a company the law firm is currently representing or has represented before, the attorney may be able to obtain substantial information from colleagues who have done work for the company. If not, the attorney should examine the company's Web site and avail himself or herself of all the resources of the Internet. One can obtain financial statements, press releases, news articles, and other source material. In addition, the attorney can search the U.S. Patent and Trademark Office databases to find out what trademarks and patents the potential client has.

IP Audits

If a trademark attorney is speaking with a client or potential client for the first time, he or she may want to recommend an IP audit, which is an investigation of all of the IP assets the client has, and how it is protecting its IP assets. This is an expensive process, and not every client will be interested in taking it on, but an IP audit gives the IP lawyer the best possible look at what the client's situation is, what problems there are, and what the attorney can do from a prophylactic standpoint to avoid having problems down the road.

If the client approves the undertaking of an IP audit, the initial task is to talk with the company's general counsel or chief financial officer and find out their perception of what IP assets the company has, and what issues they may be aware of.

Armed with a list of registered trademarks, the attorney should do a thorough examination of the company's Web site to see whether the company is using its marks properly on the site. Trademarks should be used as adjectives, not as nouns. The attorney wants to make sure the client is using its trademarks as adjectives so the client avoids the possibility of a trademark becoming a generic word that all others could use as well to describe the goods. This would prevent the trademark from continuing to function as a source identifier, and would result in a loss of rights in the trademark. It is not uncommon for the attorney to find out when he or she examines the Web sites and/or talks to people at the company that the client is using more trademarks than the ones that are registered. Chances are that the client is using these unregistered marks without even recognizing they are trademarks. The attorney will want to make sure the marks are being used correctly, that they are cleared, and that they do not infringe any third-party rights. All unregistered trademarks should be brought to the attention of the client so they can be cleared and perhaps registered.

Another source of trademark use is the company's marketing materials—how the client goes to market and what it is saying to the consuming public. Once again, the attorney should look for correct use of trademarks and the existence of unregistered trademarks to be cleared. With regard to patents, the attorney should find out if the company is working on any ideas that could lead to patents, whether the client is enforcing its patents, and whether anyone has accused the company of infringement. The attorney should also ascertain the identity of the person who has oversight responsibility for the company's patents.

When looking at the company's Web site, the attorney should determine whether the company is doing business on its Web site (i.e., selling goods and/or services over the Internet). The attorney should also ascertain whether personal and private information is collected from visitors to the Web site. If a company is doing business on the Web, there are mail order regulations that must be followed, and the company must comply with state and federal privacy and security laws that protect the confidentiality and integrity of confidential information given to the company. This is currently one of the hottest issues in the IP world. If there is a breach, at the very least the company needs to say it was in compliance with all of the privacy and security requirements of the various laws to which the client is subject.

The attorney should interview the appropriate person at the company to determine what sort of confidential information of its own the company maintains, and how it is being protected, if at all. Generally, trade secret laws require that if confidential information is claimed as a trade secret, it must be treated as such by the company and maintained in a manner where only selected persons have access to it. Procedures should be in place to maintain the security of the confidential information, and if a company does not do that, the law will not treat the confidential information as a trade secret, because—at least theoretically—the company itself is not treating the confidential information as a trade secret.

The attorney should also look at contracts to which the company is a party. The attorney should make sure the company is complying with whatever obligations it has undertaken with respect to a third party's IP. For example, if the contract is a license and the client is the licensee, there are no doubt obligations in the license with respect to how and on what products the mark may be used. Also in contracts with consultants and other vendors where ownership of the copyright in the contracted work is an issue, the attorney should determine whether the provisions of the contract are sufficient to vest copyright ownership in the client. If not, the wording of standard contracts should be changed, and perhaps consultants/vendors should be approached in an attempt to persuade them to assign the relevant copyrights to the client. Similarly, the attorney should examine the employee manuals and determine whether the agreements and policies contained therein require the employees to honor the trade secrets of the company and make the work product of the employees in the course of their employment the property (including copyright) of the employer.

In addition to looking at marketing materials to see whether trademarks are being used properly, the attorney should also concern himself or herself with false advertising issues. Marketing people will need to be interviewed, and the attorney will need to determine whether the company has substantiation for the claims it is making, and if so, whether that substantiation existed at the time the marketing materials were first promulgated. False advertising is a claim that can be very serious in terms of damages, reputation, and the downtime of employees. It can involve both federal and state regulation, and can embroil a company in litigation with consumers or its competitors, and so the attorney should make sure someone is looking at the ads before they go to market, and the ultimate oversight should be in the hands of an attorney. In addition, both marketing materials and the Web site should be examined to make sure the company is not infringing the copyrights of any third parties. Copyright is a federal right, and it is directed to protecting the copyright owner in its manner of original expression. The expression can be a sculpture, book, design, song, movie, just printed words. If a third party has access to the copyrighted work and copies something in which someone else owns the copyright, this constitutes copyright infringement. For example, one is not permitted to download something off someone else's Web site and use it without permission.

Advantages of IP Audits

One of the advantages of an IP audit is that it allows the attorney and client to be proactive. One of the best things an attorney can do for a client is to solve a problem before it becomes a problem. If the attorney sees something during an audit that he or she thinks is a time bomb waiting to go off, he or she can take care of that matter before it "goes off" and becomes a problem. One of the reasons for doing an audit is to not only figure out what the client has, but to put the client on a course so it will hopefully follow recommendations that will avoid problems in the future. Attorneys try to get clients to agree to an IP audit based on those kinds of considerations.

Once an audit is complete, a report should be generated. Depending upon the length of the report, it is also advisable to draft an executive summary for upper management and/or the board of directors. The attorney should try to receive the opportunity to deliver the report in person to emphasize certain points and answer questions.

The Use of Trademarks

A trademark is a word, symbol, phrase, logo, or design that identifies a particular party's goods or services, and enables a consumer to identify the source of the goods or services they are purchasing, and enables a consumer to realize expectations about the quality of those goods or services. In this respect, a trademark really exists for the benefit of the consuming public, even though the mark is owned by a third-party company and may constitute a substantial portion of the total value of that company. If you go into a McDonald's in El Paso, you expect the burger to taste the same as it would at a McDonald's in New York, and it usually does. A trademark tells a member of the consuming public that the item they are purchasing comes from the same source as the last item they bought bearing that same trademark, and they can expect the quality of the purchase to be consistent with the quality of the prior purchase.

Recommendations for IP Protection

With respect to trademarks, a company should search its trademarks and clear them before it starts using those marks, and then use them correctly. If someone is infringing a mark the company owns, the company needs to do something about it. If a company is aware of trademark infringements and ignores them, someone can claim—and the courts will uphold this under certain circumstances—that the company has allowed infringements without policing them. This means the public can no longer rely on the trademark in question to designate source, and may result in the trademark owner losing its rights in the trademark.

When clients inform a trademark lawyer that they want to adopt a new trademark, the clearance process should begin. First, the attorney should conduct a relatively preliminary search. He or she searches the databases of the U.S. Patent and Trademark Office and the state trademark offices in the United States. This search is referred to as a "kick-out" search, because the attorney is trying to find a mark already out there that will preclude the client from using the mark it is considering. If that occurs, the client is advised to go back to the drawing board. If the search does not find such a mark, the attorney orders a full trademark search by a national search firm and receives a report that is often the size of a suburban phonebook. The lawyer reviews the full search to see whether there is a problem with a particular reference or trademark the client wants to use. The clearance process also involves Internet research that is normally done by paralegals to reduce the cost to the client. There may be a particular problematic reference, and so the paralegal will then find out if the mark is still being used. The paralegal may call up the owner or search the owner's Web site to seek additional information about the mark in question. At the end of the process, when the search has been reviewed and analyzed by the attorney, he or she renders an opinion to the client. This can be a frustrating process. I once did sixteen full searches for a client before finding a mark that could be used. When the client gets frustrated, the attorney must try to convince the client that it is better to be frustrated now rather than adopt a mark where there is an unacceptable risk of receiving a cease-and-desist letter six months down the road, because that is a much more expensive and difficult situation. Once the attorney clears the mark, they will often recommend that the mark be registered. That process takes place at the U.S. Patent and Trademark Office and can, in part, be expedited by paralegals.

Financial and Legal Risks

If a party is infringing someone else's trademark, the damages can be substantial because they can include the profits the infringer earned because of infringing the other trademark, as well as the lost profits of the trademark owner. In the majority of instances where someone is accused of trademark infringement in a claim or in a lawsuit, the allegations relate not to using the exact same mark, but to using a mark that is too close to the trademark owner's mark and is likely to cause confusion. The standard in a trademark infringement action is likelihood of confusion—if the consumer is likely to be confused by the infringer's mark and is likely to think it is the claimant's mark and that the consumer is getting goods or services from the same source that provided the goods and services sold under the claimant's mark. In that event, liability is established. An infringer may be able to generate a great number of sales because of this confusing trademark, because people associate it with the claimant's mark and the claimant's goodwill. If the claimant can prove the infringer had substantial sales because of using the infringing trademark (which sales were really due to the goodwill the first trademark owner had built up over perhaps many years), the infringer may have to disgorge the profits the infringer earned. These profits can be very substantial if the infringement has been going on for some time. In addition, if the claimant can prove it lost sales because of the infringement, the claimant may be awarded its own profits, assuming there is no duplication there. In addition, the court has the discretion to apply a multiplier if it thinks there is bad faith involved and the trademark infringer deliberately infringed, and in that event, the infringer may wind up paying a multiple of the amount of actual damages.

In the United States, we have the federal trademark law, known as the Lanham Act, which is the law that sets up the mechanism for registering trademarks and provides remedies for infringement of trademarks. The Lanham Act also prohibits false advertising, so you look to that statute to ascertain a party's obligations under the law. The Patent Law, the Copyright Law, the various state laws that regulate unfair trade practices, the laws that provide for privacy and security, and the Federal Trade Commission Act are other major laws involved in the enforcement of IP rights.

Counterfeiting is slightly different from trademark infringement. Using a trademark that is confusingly similar to someone else's trademark so the public will likely be confused constitutes trademark infringement. Counterfeiting is using the same trademark on the same goods, such as some of the watches and handbags that come into this country from other places. The counterfeiter purports to sell the exact same item someone else is selling, but usually at a much lower price and of inferior quality. Most importantly, the counterfeiter is selling an item that does not come from the owner of the trademark. Counterfeiting is also prohibited by the Lanham Act.

Learning and Listening to the Legal Needs of Clients

To understand the legal needs of one's client, the attorney has to know the law. In addition to their experience, one accomplishes this by reading cases and treatises. There are reporters that circulate through the law firms in all of the various areas of practice, as well as periodicals that report on cases of interest that have been decided throughout the country. A particular publication might come across the attorney's desk with a blurb he or she should read before crossing their name off the list and sending it on. If something is of interest, one should get hold of the case and read the entire opinion. IP attorneys develop various interests and start focusing on specifics when they begin practicing law.

When working with a client, the attorney should listen and find out everything they can. IP is a fact-intensive practice like most practices, so the attorney has to find out what is going on, what the problem is, what the client has, and what someone is saying the client did. The manner of fact gathering depends on why the attorney is at the client's office. If the attorney is there because of a specific problem, he or she wants to get all of the facts possible from the client's standpoint about what the problem is and why it occurred, and then talk to individual members of the company who are involved to get their perspective. The attorney has to present himself or herself as someone who is trying to help. He or she cannot be threatening, because the attorney will not get anywhere that way. Perhaps there was a mistake or an omission, and so the attorney approaches people as an ally. He or she is trying to solve the problem, and that is how he or she should present himself or herself. After getting all the facts, the attorney should sit down and apply their legal thinking to the problem. Is there really a problem? What defenses does the client have? What theory of defense should the client use? What is the best way for the client to minimize the problem? The clients want to put these things behind them. And if an attorney goes to the client talking about how they are going to try the lawsuit, they will likely not get very far, because the last thing the client wants is to go to court. Clients want the problem solved and have it put behind them, so the lawyers should come up with a strategy so the problem no longer exists.

Conclusion

We want to make sure our clients are clearing their trademarks and registering them, which gives a particular trademark a layer of protection. If a mark is not registered, we call it a "common law mark" and the trademark owner still has rights if it adopts a mark and starts using it first, even if a third party comes along later and registers the same trademark. The prior user cannot be stopped from using the mark in whatever geographical area it was using the mark before the registration. Still, we recommend that a company register all of its important marks. Trademark registration lasts for ten years, and after you submit a statutory affidavit of use that has to be filed between the fifth and sixth year after registration, you may renew the registration after ten years if you are still using the mark. Thereafter, the trademark owner can renew the registration every ten years for as long as it continues to use the trademark.

As far as compliance is concerned, compliance with privacy and security laws, and compliance with advertising laws contained in the Lanham Act and the Federal Trade Commission Act are critical. The Federal Trade Commission tends to take a less specific and more global approach to these advertising issues and has developed certain regulations (e.g., when you can use the word "free" or the words "made in the U.S.A."). From a trademark and patent perspective, it is a matter of using your trademarks and patents correctly and enforcing and policing your rights. From a patent perspective, it is making sure you are enforcing your patents and not infringing the rights of others. From a copyright perspective, one does not have an obligation to police one's copyrights, because copyright is a different kind of right and protects the copyright holder, not the general public. Thus, there can be ten copyright infringers, and the copyright holder may decide to only go after one or two or none at all, and it will not affect the rights of the copyright owner.

We have a computerized docket, and all of the trademarks of all of the clients we represent are on the docket, along with all of the deadlines. Each of the attorneys receives an automatic reminder from the docket as he or she gets closer to a filing deadline, so no deadlines will be missed. We have a patent docket that operates in a similar fashion. Internet searching is a wonderful tool, and you are able to find a great deal of information about what people and companies are doing. If a client gets a claim from someone accusing the client of infringing a trademark, you can find out if third parties are also using the same trademark, which can be a helpful defense. We have circulating reporters and monthly periodicals that some lawyers subscribe to independently. We attend seminars to stay abreast of issues. We try to keep our clients apprised of any developments by either writing specific letters or general group mailings that go out to all of our clients when something has happened that we think is germane to their businesses. The most important thing you can do for your client is to get the client to ask questions and seek legal reviews before the client does something, not afterwards.

John Arado is a partner in the intellectual property department of Wildman Harrold. A skilled trademark and copyright lawyer, he counsels clients in all aspects of trademark law, including clearance and registration, licensing agreements and quality control, claims of infringement, dilution and unfair competition, prosecution of trademark applications and inter partes *proceedings in the U.S. Patent and Trademark Office, and litigation in federal courts. He is also called upon to conduct due diligence reviews for clients considering mergers or acquisitions in order to identify all intellectual property and any associated risks or issues. He represents clients engaged in publishing, real estate, entertainment, and specialty food retailing. He also represents a large regional agricultural cooperative. He also serves as an arbitrator in intellectual property and commercial cases through the American Arbitration Association.*

Mr. Arado is a member of the American Bar Association, the Illinois State Bar Association, the Chicago Bar Association, the International Trademark Association, Beta Gamma Sigma, and the American Arbitration Association. He earned his B.B.A. from the University of Notre Dame and his J.D. from the University of Michigan.

Creating Long-Term Value

Paul D. Ackerman

Partner

Dorsey & Whitney LLP

ASPATORE

IP Legal Needs and Trends

The major categories of intellectual property (IP) include patent, trademark, copyright, and trade secret protection. How a particular client addresses its needs for proper IP protection and management, however, depends on the nature of the client's business. Many businesses will require each form of IP, while others may rely mainly on one form of protection to protect their competitive advantage. For example, pharmaceutical companies, which typically make substantial investments in research and development and look to market exclusivity to recover this significant investment, rely heavily on the limited monopoly provided by patent law. Retailers and other companies that rely primarily on brand name recognition to differentiate themselves from competitors are often more focused on trademark protection. Publishers of printed works or musical compositions tend to rely on copyright protection to ensure their rights are protected. Understanding the benefits and limitations of each type of protection, and how to apply those considerations to a particular business, are key to effective IP management.

In general, in the United States, IP rights are protected by a body of federal copyright, patent, and trademark laws. This is controlled by federal statutes as well as regulations promulgated by the U.S. Patent and Trademark Office. In addition, certain forms of IP, such as trade secrets and trademarks, are also protectable under state law. Further, through international treaties, clients in the United States also have the ability to secure international protection for patents, trademarks, and copyrights. International organizations, such as the World Intellectual PropertyOrganization ("WIPO"), work to create a standardized mechanism for protecting IP throughout the world.

Prioritizing IP needs starts with an understanding of the client's current and future business climate. What does the client consider its most valuable assets? Is it technology, brand awareness, generation of creative content such as writing or graphical works, or a combination of these creative efforts? What is the timeline needed for adequate protection? Patents and trade secrets are generally mutually exclusive, although a client can protect different aspects of a business with these two forms of protection. Patents can take several years to mature from application to issued patent, and they require public disclosure of an invention, which may give short-term advantage to a client's competitors. Further, the process of preparing and prosecuting a patent application to an issued patent can be expensive. As a result, if a product or service is expected to have a useful market life of less than five years, patent protection may not be attractive. To the contrary, trade secrets provide both immediate and long-term protection, but can be destroyed through public disclosure and offer no protection if the IP can be uncovered through independent research or reverse engineering of publicly available products or information. Trademarks, which are intended to identify source or sponsorship of goods or services, are essential when branding, marketing, and brand awareness are key assets of a company. Copyrights can offer valuable protection, not only to traditional written and artistic works, but also to certain aspects of technology, such as computer source code, graphical user interface arrangements, and display configurations. Copyright protection tends to be relatively narrow in scope, but can often be used to complement patent protection to prevent copying of a work by a competitor.

A common thread running throughout IP law is that IP law is the vehicle for protecting a company's creativity and increasing the return on investment for the company's creative efforts. One way to identify a client's IP needs is to understand where the company makes its internal and external creative business investments. Does the company have a significant marketing department and budget? Does the company invest in a large engineering department? Although very different at first blush, each of these corporate functions have a common element—creativity—which is the engine that drives the development of new IP assets.

Although the emphasis of one category of IP protection over another fluctuates over time, the fundamental categories of IP protection have not changed significantly over the last several years. With that being said, there has been a recent trend in the courts that patent practitioners recognize as being somewhat hostile to patent rights. This recent trend should be recognized, as it may affect a client's decision about whether to invest the time and capital required to obtain patents in the future.

One significant aspect in the trend affecting patent rights is that the scope of what is being considered "patentable subject matter" is being restricted.

Recently, the Federal Circuit, the appellate court that oversees appeals in patent cases, addressed the question of whether certain computer-related inventions satisfy the requirements for patentable subject matter. In *In re Comiskey*, ___ F.3d ___ (Fed. Cir. 2007), the Federal Circuit distinguished between methods that may be performed on a computer or microprocessor, from those that explicitly require performance of the method by a computer, and held that the former category did not represent patentable subject matter. This decision has been viewed by some as restricting the availability of so-called "business method patents." Additional cases addressing the scope of patentable subject matter remain pending before the Federal Circuit and may continue to shape what can be patented as we look to the future.

More significantly, the standard for obtaining a patent (and protecting the validity of the patent once issued) for all technical areas has been made more difficult by a recent Supreme Court case, *KSR v. Teleflex*, 550 U.S. ___, 127 S. Ct. 1727 (2007). In *KSR*, the Supreme Court reviewed the use of what had become known as the "teaching, suggestion, motivation test" that was formulated by the Federal Circuit for evaluating whether the subject matter being claimed in a patent or patent application is "obvious" when compared to the prior art and therefore not patentable. In the test, to invalidate a patent claim, not only would the elements for which patent protection was sought need to be identified in the prior art, but the party seeking to invalidate the claim (either the patent office or a party in a lawsuit) was required to identify a suggestion in the prior art for combining the elements and a motivation for a person in the field to make the asserted combination. Since it is not uncommon for innovations to be made by combining known elements (*e.g.*, a clock was a combination of known gears and springs), the extra requirement of identifying a teaching, suggestion, and motivation was considered a vehicle to prevent the application of hindsight in rejecting patent claims. The test also made obviousness a fairly challenging standard to meet. In *KSR*, without expressly rejecting the teaching, suggestion, motivation test, the Supreme Court did reject a formalistic approach to using this test. The Supreme Court noted that a motivation to combine known elements may be found in the nature of the problem to be solved, by similar problems being solved in different technical areas, and even by the common sense of a person of ordinary skill in the art. By allowing a patent claim to be rejected without requiring an express teaching, suggestion, or motivation to combine elements known in the prior art, the Supreme Court raised the bar to obtaining and sustaining a valid patent.

If a patent applicant can overcome these new challenges, obtain a patent, and successfully assert the patent at trial, the successful patent infringement plaintiff now faces higher hurdles in obtaining an injunction to prevent future infringing conduct. Until recently, a patent owner that was successful at trial in enforcing its patent was nearly guaranteed that the court would issue an injunction to prevent the defendant from continuing the infringing activity. The rationale was that "irreparable harm" to the patent owner was presumed when its patent right, which is a right to exclude others, was found to be violated. In *eBay v. MercExchange*, 544 U.S. 388 (2006), the Supreme Court disagreed and now requires patent owners to make the same showing to obtain an injunction that is required in non-patent cases, including an affirmative showing of irreparable harm. This heightened standard makes it more difficult for a patent owner to obtain injunctive relief against an infringer, and reduces some of the risks associated with an unfavorable outcome in a patent infringement lawsuit. Indeed, under *eBay*, a patent owner may find itself with a court-imposed "compulsory license" that allows the infringer to continue its activity indefinitely.

Another example of the recent trend eroding the value of U.S. patent rights is the Federal Circuit's recent decision in *In re Seagate Technology LLC*, 497 F.3d 1360 (2007), which significantly redefined the law of willful patent infringement. When a party is found to be a willful infringer of a patent, the court may increase damages by up to three times the amount of actual damages and award attorneys' fees. See 35 U.S. C. §§284, 285. With patent damages often reaching into the millions and tens of millions of dollars, the threat of such treble damages is daunting. Prior to the recent *Seagate* decision, when a party had notice of a potential infringement claim, it was charged with an affirmative duty of due care to avoid infringing the patent, and in most cases was required to obtain an opinion from competent patent counsel to meet this burden. Because parties had an affirmative duty of due care, a patent owner could establish willful infringement by showing that the defendant did not meet this duty. This was not a difficult standard to satisfy, and a significant portion of defendants who were found to infringe a patent were also found to be infringing the patent willfully. The *Seagate* decision rejected the affirmative duty of care and the associated affirmative obligation to obtain an opinion of counsel to successfully defend against an accusation of willful infringement. In place of an affirmative duty on the defendant, *Seagate* established a new standard, where the patent owner seeking to prove "willfullness" must establish that the defendant had notice of the patent rights and then acted in a manner that was "objectively reckless." This is a far more difficult standard to satisfy, and it significantly reduces the risk that a finding of patent infringement will also be found to be willful.

Collectively, the changes to patent law that flow from these court decisions may alter the economics of obtaining and attempting to enforce a patent. This is a consideration that may affect a client's desire to invest in a significant patent portfolio and its ultimate decision to seek patent protection.

It is often said that information is power. This is certainly true in the field of IP law. To understand trends in the development of IP law, it is necessary to stay informed. Fortunately, there is a vast array of readily available information. Of the various sources of information for identifying IP trends, as an IP professional, the following sources have consistently proven to be most valuable:

1. Supreme Court and appellate court decisions
2. U.S. Patent and Trademark Office Web site and notices
3. Copyright Office Web site
4. Industry groups such as the Intellectual Property Owners Organization and the American Intellectual Property Law Association
5. General media coverage of IP issues

As a lawyer, it is absolutely critical to follow the decisions of the applicable appellate courts and the Supreme Court. For patent law, there is a single appellate court, the Federal Circuit, and all the decisions from this court should be reviewed as they come down. By regularly following both the holdings and tone of the dicta of these legal decisions, not only can the current state of the law be understood, but hints at future trends can be seen as well.

The U.S. Patent and Trademark Office Web site is a valuable resource that provides news on developments in that office and proposed rules changes for patent and trademark practitioners. Prior to making significant rule changes, the U.S. Patent and Trademark Office generally publishes the proposed rules for public comment. Both the proposed rules and the nature of the comments on those proposals provide insight into possible changes and trends. This Web site also includes searching capabilities that allow individuals to search for issued patents, published patent applications, registered trademarks, and pending trademark applications. This can be a very useful tool for identifying a client's IP, as well as that which may be owned by competitors.

Industry groups such as the American Intellectual Property Law Association, the Intellectual Property Owners Organization (www.ipo.org), the International Trademark Association, and the IP sections of the American Bar Association and state bar associations also provide a wealth of useful information on IP trends in the legislature and recent court decisions. These organizations have diverse membership and often have valuable information presenting critical and competing views of recent developments in IP law.

Industry trends shape IP trends, so it is important to read not only legal periodicals, but also articles in industry-specific periodicals for insights on how a particular industry is viewing the importance of various IP to the industry. For example, industry news articles often describe recently obtained patents and discuss significant patent infringement litigation in the industry. Online news services such as Yahoo! news deliver stories by e-mail based on selected keywords and are useful for staying informed about industry trends.

The law is constantly changing. Sometimes change occurs in small increments, and other times in much larger ways. Without a solid understanding of the current law, a practitioner cannot effectively advise clients. As the courts interpret the statutory and regulatory framework in which IP rights are created and shaped, different approaches to obtaining appropriate IP protection emerge. Knowing when changes to the regulations are being proposed allows you to become proactive and engage clients in lobbying efforts for or against provisions that may affect their industry.

For example, over the last two years there have been a number of proposals directed at what is referred to as "patent reform," which are aimed at curbing what is perceived as an increase in predatory patent enforcement efforts by investors and holding companies that acquire under-exploited patents with the objective of engaging in enforcement efforts. These proposals touch on a broad range of issues and are endorsed by certain industries and challenged by others. For example, changes have been proposed in Congress to the Patent Act (35 U.S.C. §1 et. seq.) that could affect who could obtain a patent, where that patent could be enforced, and what measure of damages would apply to the successful patent owner in litigation. The division between support and opposition is usually drawn based on whether the industry benefits from a strong patent system. In general, industries such a biotechnology and pharmaceutical companies that depend on a strong patent system tend to oppose efforts to weaken the patent system. In contrast, technology companies, such as software companies that have products with numerous features and a relatively short product life cycle, tend to consider the threat of patents to be more significant than the benefits they derive from them and are in favor of various measures at patent reform. These proposals have been the subject of extensive debate and lobbying over the last two years, and it is still unclear whether any of the changes will make it through Congress. A practitioner who understands the economics of their client's business and what factors drive success in that business sector is required to advise the client on whether to encourage representatives in Congress to support or reject such measures.

Working with Clients

In IP law, it is common to work not only with a client's legal personnel, but the marketing and technical employees of the company as well. These individuals do not view the world as lawyers do, and they bring a different perspective to the issues at hand. In many cases, these individuals are not sensitive to the legal issues that underlie the proper development and protection of IP rights. This presents both an opportunity for the IP lawyer, as well as a challenge. The opportunity is to learn the workings of the client from the creative side of the company, not just the legal and business side. The challenge is in educating non-legal employees in complex areas of law in a way that is meaningful to them and arms them with the knowledge required to help them help you protect the company's valuable IP assets.

It is important to ask questions that allow the client to explain its business to you, especially all of the creative aspects of the business. The best questions are open-ended questions that allow the client to provide explanations. Most responses to these questions lead to follow-up questions, which lead to a better understanding of the client's needs. Such questions include:

- What are your short-term business objectives?
- What are your long-term business objectives?
- What creative activities is your company engaged in?
- How do these creative activities help differentiate your company in the marketplace?
- Who are involved in these creative activities?
- When are new products being released?
- Is there a new marketing campaign associated with the product release?
- Is there a new branding initiative associated with the new product release?
- How are you planning on competing in the marketplace over the next five years?
- Do you expect the product or service to change over the next five years? What about the next ten years?
- How will it change?
- How do you expect to respond to that change?
- Have you dedicated any of your creative talents toward addressing these expected changes?
- Do you expect your research and development budget to increase, decrease, or stay the same over the next five years? Why?
- Do you expect your marketing budget to increase, decrease, or stay the same over the next five years? Why?

These questions probe into what is important to the client as well as the nature of IP protection that is most applicable to a given business. For example, if a company invests heavily in new product development and perceives itself as an innovator, patent protection will likely be important to that company. Based on this information, a more detailed IP audit can commence that focuses on the creative aspects of the client's product development team. In a sales and marketing-centric operation, branding may be viewed as being pivotal to success, and the company will likely require guidance regarding trademark issues. The key is understanding the client's business needs and applying the right legal solution to advance those needs. For example, in one case, when asked whether the marketing budget was expected to increase or decrease over the next five years, we learned that the client expected a significant short-term increase in its marketing costs over the coming year. The natural follow-up question is "Why?" The answer was that the company had recently decided to engage in a significant global re-branding effort. From this one answer, it was apparent that this client had significant needs in clearing the brand in each country it intended to operate in, registering the new trademarks associated with the re-branding, and ensuring the new content of its Web site would be adequately protected under applicable copyright law. This information allowed us to work proactively with the client and ensure a smooth and successful rollout of the new brand.

Once the client's needs are understood and it is decided to obtain a specific form of IP protection, certain information (e.g., when a trademark was used, when an invention was disclosed, who the author of a creative work was) must be carefully verified to ensure the IP that is sought is available and will be valid. This is of particular concern in the area of patent law, where patent rights can be lost forever if steps are not taken to protect the invention before the invention is disclosed to the public or sold. For example, in the United States, an inventor has a one-year grace period to file a patent application after the invention is first made available to the public. In Europe and other parts of the world, however, no such grace period is provided. To avoid inadvertently moving valuable IP into the public domain, it is important to coordinate the legal activities needed to protect the IP with the business processes of the client that are generating and distributing the IP.

Although the needs of each client are very specific, standard checklists can sometimes be used once a particular form of IP protection is decided upon. For example, some clients use checklists internally to gather relevant information and ensure the requirements for obtaining the selected form of IP protection are satisfied. In the case of patent protection, for example, many clients use checklists in an invention disclosure form to collect relevant information regarding details of conception of an invention, reduction to practice, the identity of all inventors, publication information, and the like. These forms can serve as a helpful reminder to everyone involved in the process of what information is important.

Of the major categories of IP protection—patent, trademark, copyright, and trade secret—each may be applicable in some way to a particular business. The nature of the goods and services of the client, as well as the current state of the client's industry, will dictate the specific IP protection needed in each situation. Some factors that help guide this inquiry include:

- What type of financing is the industry receiving?
- Is the client's industry emerging from a period of research and moving into a commercialization phase (such as biotech and nanotech)?
- Is the client working in an established industry, or is the entire industry in a start-up phase?
- Is the client in a highly competitive market that is focusing on branding and marketing as a differentiator?

Following general and industry-specific news and current events is important in identifying the factors mentioned above. Reviewing the company Web site, company literature, and annual statements (when available), are all helpful in gaining insight into the company. Asking the client which industry-specific trade literature they read, and reviewing copies of this material, is often helpful. Internet research can often be helpful to understand how people outside the company perceive the client. After some preliminary research, conducting interviews with company officers and managers is critical to fully understand the client's immediate and long-term needs.

From time to time, it is valuable to a client to undertake a review of its IP portfolio. This may be done for new clients, to understand what steps the client has taken to identify and protect its IP assets. It may also be done when the client needs to assess and evaluate its IP portfolio, such as in connection with a due diligence investigation associated with a merger or acquisition. In either case, the steps to follow when performing a formal or informal legal review of a client's IP portfolio and IP protection strategies can generally be summarized as:

1. Conducting a public records search to identify existing patents, trademarks, and copyrights
2. Assembling and reviewing documents the client holds regarding IP protection
3. Reviewing employment agreements and contracts
4. Interviewing officers and managers regarding the client's standard IP practices, if any
5. Reviewing existing creative initiatives to identify potential IP

The purpose of the public records search is to obtain a baseline understanding of a client's IP assets and compare this baseline to other records of the company to ensure all rights are perfected and properly assigned. The review of public records is generally straightforward, if the client has taken reasonable steps to have IP assets applied for in the name of the company or properly assigned to the company. This task is somewhat more challenging if the company has undergone corporate changes such as name changes, mergers, acquisitions, or divestitures. It can also be more complicated if the client operates under multiple operating divisions, each having its own IP policies. If a company has been through several name changes, or has not properly assigned IP rights from individuals to the company, identifying the assets in the portfolio generally requires more information and cooperation from the client.

Reviewing applicable internal documents of the client varies in complexity, depending on whether the company has an established IP policy in place and personnel in-house to manage IP-related materials. The documents of interest include such things as invention disclosure documents, written IP policies, contracts, employment agreements, assignments, license agreements, files related to patent applications, files related to trademark applications, and correspondence to and from third parties discussing IP issues (ownership and accusations of infringement). When a company has a policy in place and follows that policy, the internal document review is usually straightforward. In those cases where each creative employee is the custodian of his or her own documents that may relate to IP rights, the task is far more difficult, in that each employee must be contacted to assemble the relevant documents. In this case, it is difficult to confirm that all documents have been collected. Ideally, rather than being distributed throughout the company, these documents should reside with a particular custodian in the company for easy reference.

The internal documents of a client will generally identify the lawyers who were or are involved in protecting the various IP assets in the past. If the internal client documents are not complete and well maintained, it will often be necessary to review the files of outside IP counsel to get a completed overview of the client's portfolio.

The employment agreements used by a company can be critical to ensuring the client obtains proper title to inventions and patents, and has taken reasonable steps to protect trade secrets. The key provisions of these agreements include assignment of inventions to the company, reasonable non-compete provisions, and confidentiality restrictions. The specific language of these agreements must be reviewed to ensure the client has all rights in the IP being created by its employees. Employee agreements are contracts governed by state law, so the provision of the applicable state law should be reviewed to ensure the agreement is enforceable.

With a baseline of information collected from public and in-house documents, interviews with the managers or officers who are responsible for creative development and IP rights allow the practitioner to determine if additional IP rights exist within the company that need to be perfected. It is also important to identify what steps the company uses to identify new IP, protect developing IP, and make the informed decision regarding whether to invest in the emerging IP.

Reviewing various creative initiatives allows the client to identify IP rights as they are developing. By interviewing engineers, Web site developers, marketing managers, and the like, the IP practitioner can determine if the work in progress at a company may include burgeoning IP rights, and take steps early on to capture and perfect those rights. In certain cases, such as with patent rights, steps must be taken prior to any public use, offer, or sale of goods or services that may embody the invention, or rights can be lost. Early review of ongoing initiatives allows the client to prevent the unintended loss of rights and make reasonable decisions regarding which IP rights to pursue. In certain cases, such as public disclosure of inventions or trade secrets, the loss of rights often cannot be cured. Preventing the loss of valuable IP generally requires generating written company policies that govern the identification and protection of IP, educating employees about those policies, and routinely taking steps to enforce compliance with the policies. The rewards of these efforts, however, can be significant, as engineering and marketing costs can be converted into valuable long-term assets of the company.

Paul D. Ackerman is a partner in Dorsey & Whitney LLP's intellectual property group. His practice involves all aspects of intellectual property law, with an emphasis on patent litigation and trial. He has been involved in a number of contested proceedings before the U.S. Patent and Trademark Office, including appeals and interference practice. He has litigated cases involving various technology, including Internet technology, semiconductor fabrication and testing, biotechnology, and mechanical devices.

Mr. Ackerman earned his B.S.E.E., cum laude, from the New York Institute of Technology and his J.D., summa cum laude, from the Touro College Jacob D. Fuchsberg Law Center.

Appendices

Appendix A: Domain Name and Trademark Transfer Agreement   178

Appendix B: Trade Secrets and Confidential Information Checklist   186

Appendix C: Copyright Checklist   189

Appendix D: Patent Checklist   190

Appendix E: Trademark Checklist   192

Appendix F: Intellectual Property Audit Outline   194

Appendix G: Invention Disclosure Outline   211

Appendix H: Intellectual Property Checklist   215

Appendix I: *Edward H. Phillips V. AWH Corporation,
Hopeman Brothers, Inc., and Lofton Corporation*   220

Appendix J: *In Re Seagate Technology, LLC*   258

Appendix K: *KSR International Co., Petitioner V. Teleflex Inc. Et Al.*   289

APPENDIX A

DOMAIN NAME AND TRADEMARK TRANSFER AGREEMENT

This DOMAIN NAME AND TRADEMARK TRANSFER AGREEMENT (this "Agreement") is entered into as of this 21st day of March, 2008, by and between ABC, a Delaware corporation, with a business address at _____ ("ABC"), and ABC Corporation, an _____ corporation, with an address of _____. ("Registrant").

RECITALS

WHEREAS, Registrant is the registered owner of the domain names ABC.COM and ABC.ORG (the "Domain Names"); and the trademark ABC as used in connection with business consulting services for practical risk management, process improvement, performance measurement, and software projects together with U.S. Registration No. 2,800,373 therefor (the "Trademark");

WHEREAS, ABC desires to obtain both Domain Names and the Trademark, and Registrant is willing to transfer them to ABC and to relinquish any and all claims to any right, title, or interest in the Domain Names and the Trademark.

NOW, THEREFORE, in consideration of the foregoing and other good and valuable consideration, the receipt and sufficiency of which is hereby acknowledged, the parties hereby agree as follows:

1.   <u>Assignment of Domain Names and Trademark</u>. Registrant hereby irrevocably transfers and assigns to ABC all right, title and interest worldwide in and to the Domain Names, and the Trademark, together with any goodwill and all intellectual property or other rights associated therewith that Registrant (or any company or entity related or associated with Registrant) has, may have, or claims to have had in the Domain Names and the Trademark; and the right to recover damages for past acts of infringement of the Trademark.

2.   <u>Transfer of Domain Names and Trademark</u>. Registrant hereby agrees to undertake any and all actions necessary or desirable in good faith to effectuate the recordation of the transfer and assignment of the Domain Names to ABC through use of the domain name transfer procedures provided by the Registrar (defined below), including, without limitation, executing any documents and sending or responding to any email messages that may be necessary to accomplish the transfer of the Domain Names to ABC. Immediately upon execution of this Agreement, Registrant will also verify that the primary contact email address listed in the WHOIS record for the Domain Names is correct and up-to-date and that neither of the Domain Names has a "locked" status or any other status that would prevent the successful transfer of the Domain Names to ABC. Without limiting the foregoing, (a) promptly following the full execution of this Agreement, ABC will contact the registrar of the Domain Names, Network Solutions, LLC (the "Registrar"), and request a transfer of the Domain Names from Registrant to ABC and notify Registrant that such request has been made and (b) within two (2) business days thereafter (or at such time that the Registrar allows, whichever is later), Registrant will affirmatively consent to the transfer of the Domain Names to ABC by notifying the Registrar of Registrant's desire to transfer the Domain Names to ABC through the domain name transfer procedures provided by the Registrar. Registrant shall execute and deliver to ABC the Assignment of Registered Mark which is Exhibit A hereto.

3.   <u>Compensation</u>. In consideration for Registrant's agreement to transfer the Domain Names and Trademark to ABC, ABC hereby agrees that within five (5) business days following the updating of the Registrar's WHOIS records to reflect ABC as the registrant of the Domain Names using the new WHOIS information shown on attached Exhibit B, ABC shall pay Registrant a one-time buyout payment of _____ by wire transfer to Registrant's account at the following banking institution and account information:

_____

_____

_____

By making the above payment, ABC does not assume or acquire any liabilities, known or unknown, arising out of Registrant's use, ownership or administration of the Domain Names or Trademark. For the avoidance of doubt, Registrant shall not be entitled to any other compensation as a result of ABC's exercise of its rights under this Agreement or ABC's ownership or use of the Domain Names and Trademark.

4.   Registrant's Representations and Warranties. Registrant represents and warrants that (a) it is the valid owner of the Domain Names and Trademark and has the full right, power and authority to execute, deliver and perform this Agreement and to transfer the Domain Names and Trademark to ABC; (b) to the best of Registrant's knowledge, there are no claims outstanding relating to the Domain Names and Trademark or its ownership, registration or use thereof; (c) all payments due to the Registrar or any other domain name registrar for the maintenance of the Domain Names have been made and will continue to be made by Registrant until the transfer of the Domain Names to ABC is complete; (d) neither Registrant nor any third party associated with or related to Registrant has registered or used any other domain names or trademark embodying in whole or in part the name "ABC," any confusingly similar term or any intentional misspelling of ABC; (e) neither Registrant nor any third party associated with or related to Registrant will at any time now or in the future use or register, or cause any third party to use or register, any other domain names or trademark embodying in whole or in part the name "ABC," any confusingly similar term or any intentional misspelling of ABC; and (f) Registrant will not publicly disclose the amount ABC paid for the Domain Names and Trademark pursuant to this Agreement unless required to do so as a matter of law.

5.   ABC's Representations and Warranties. ABC represents and warrants that it is duly authorized to execute, deliver and perform this Agreement.

6.   Release. Upon the successful transfer of the Domain Names to ABC, ABC hereby releases and forever discharges Registrant and its successors and assigns from any and all causes of action, suits, liabilities, debts, damages, controversies, agreements, trespasses, judgments, executions, demands and claims of any nature whatsoever, whether in law

or in equity, whether known or unknown, whether matured or unmatured, and any and all rights, duties, liabilities and obligations, whether presently enforceable or enforceable in the future, by reason of any matter or cause regarding or in any way relating to its registration and use of the Domain Names from the beginning of time to the date of the execution of this Agreement.]

7.   Governing Law; Venue. This Agreement shall be governed by and construed under the laws of the state of Tennessee, without regard to such state's conflicts of laws rules and, if applicable, United States federal laws. The sole and exclusive venue for resolution of all disputes hereunder shall be in federal and state courts located in Shelby County, Tennessee. The parties expressly consent to personal jurisdiction in Tennessee and waive any challenges to exclusive venue in courts located in Shelby County, Tennessee.

8.   Miscellaneous. This Agreement shall be binding upon and inure to the benefit of the parties' respective successors and assigns. This Agreement constitutes the entire agreement between the parties with respect to the Domain Names and Trademark and supersedes all prior negotiations and agreements, whether written or oral, relating to this subject matter. This Agreement may not be modified in any respect except by an instrument in writing expressly referring to this Agreement and executed by authorized representatives of each party to be charged.

9.   Counterparts. This Agreement may be executed in counterparts, each of which shall constitute an original and all of which together constitute one Agreement. A facsimile signature on this Agreement will be treated with the same force and effect as the original.

IN WITNESS WHEREOF the parties have caused this Agreement to be executed as of the date first above written by their duly authorized representatives.

ABC   ABC CORPORATION,
                                       REGISTRANT

By: _____   By: _____

Name: _____   Name: _____

Title: _____   Title: _____

Date: _____   Date: _____

Exhibit A

Assignment of Registered Mark

WHEREAS, ABC Corporation, an Oregon corporation, having its principal office at _____ (hereinafter "Assignor"), has adopted and is using the trademark ABC in connection with business consulting services for practical risk management, process improvement, performance measurement, and software projects and owns U.S. Registration No. 0,000,000 therefor (the "Trademark"); and

WHEREAS, ABC, a Delaware corporation, having its principal place of business at _____ (hereinafter "Assignee"), is desirous of acquiring the Trademark and the above registration therefor;

NOW, THEREFORE, for good and valuable consideration, the receipt and sufficiency of which are hereby acknowledged, Assignor does hereby assign and transfer to Assignee all of its right, title, and interest in and to the Trademark, together with the goodwill of the business symbolized by the Trademark, U. S. registration No. 0,000,000 therefor, and the right to sue for damages for past acts of trademark infringement.

ABC CORPORATION,
an Oregon corporation

By: _____

Name: _____

Title: _____

Date: _____

STATE OF OREGON
COUNTY OF _____

Before me, _____, a Notary Public in and for the State and County aforesaid, personally appeared _____, with whom I am personally acquainted (or proved to me on the basis of satisfactory evidence), and who, upon oath, acknowledged himself (or herself) to be the _____ of ABC CORPORATION, the within named bargainer, a corporation, and that _he as such _____, being duly authorized so to do, executed the foregoing instrument for the purposes therein contained, by signing the name of the corporation by ___self as such _____.

WITNESS my hand and seal at office, on this the _____ day of _____, 2008.

_____
Notary Public

The Marks

Registered United States Trademarks

Mark	Image	Goods/Services	Reg. No.	Reg. Date

Courtesy of Grady M. Garrison and John R. Branson,
Baker Donelson, Bearman, Caldwell & Berkowitz PC

APPENDIX B

TRADE SECRETS AND
CONFIDENTIAL INFORMATION CHECKLIST

1) Does the Company have a written policy telling all employees that confidential information of the Company is to be treated in confidence?

2) Does the Company have a written policy telling all employees that confidential information of outsiders held by the Company is to be treated in confidence?

3) Does the Company have a written policy against employees using or disclosing confidential information or trade secrets of others (especially former employers) while employed with the Company?

4) Do all employees of the Company sign a non-disclosure and trade secret assignment agreement?

5) Does the Company mark all confidential documents and items with an appropriate confidentiality notice?

Example:

THIS DOCUMENT CONTAINS CONFIDENTIAL AND TRADE SECRET INFORMATION OF [COMPANY]. THE RECEIPT OR POSSESSION OF THIS DOCUMENT DOES NOT CONVEY ANY RIGHTS TO REPRODUCE OR DISCLOSE ITS CONTENTS, OR TO MANUFACTURE, USE, OR SELL ANYTHING THAT IT MAY DESCRIBE, IN WHOLE OR IN PART, WITHOUT THE SPECIFIC WRITTEN AUTHORIZATION OF [COMPANY].

6) Is confidential information kept in a restricted access area?

7) Are restricted access areas appropriately marked?

8) Does the Company maintain a visitor's log?

9) Does the Company require that all visitors to the Company be identified by a badge or a similar indication?

10) Does the Company require that all visitors be escorted when in restricted access areas?

11) Are discarded confidential documents and items shredded on the Company's premises or by a trustworthy vendor who has signed a confidentiality agreement?

12) Does the Company use technological measures to restrict access to areas containing confidential information?

      Example: electronic card keys.

13) Are written non-disclosure agreements obtained from all non-employee recipients of confidential information before the confidential information is disclosed?

14) Are written agreements obtained from all outside parties that requires compensation to the Company if one of the Company's ideas is used by a recipient?

15) Does the Company obtain review of counsel of any non-disclosure agreements of outside entities that the Company is requested to sign?

16) Does the Company have a written agreement with all employees prohibiting competitive planning while employed by the Company?

17) Does the Company have a written agreement with all employees prohibiting solicitation of customers after termination?

18) Does the Company have a written agreement with all employees prohibiting solicitation of other employees after termination?

19) Does the Company conduct termination interviews with departing employees regarding invention and trade secret rights of the Company?

— Is the employee leaving to join a competitor?

— Does the Company confirm that the employee is not taking, nor retains in his/her possession, any confidential or proprietary information or documents?

Examples: Documents; Code on Hard Drive or Floppies at Home;

— Does the departing employee understands he/she is not to use Proprietary Information

— Does the Company document the exit interview if possible?

— Does the Company make sure that any departing employee who is a named inventor on patent applications has signed an assignment to the company?

For startup companies in particular:

20) Does the Company make sure that its founders have taken steps to avoiding conflict with the rights of their former employers?

— Did they take proprietary materials when they left?

— While still at their former employer, did they use company resources or time to develop the technology they are using in their new Company? (California Labor Code §2870 is not as broad as employees often think)

— Did they leave their former employer on good terms?

Courtesy of Michael Barclay, Wilson Sonsini Goodrich & Rosati

APPENDIX C

COPYRIGHT CHECKLIST

1) Does the Company mark its important copyrightable documents with a copyright notice?

2) Are the copyright notices placed in such a manner and location so they give reasonable notice of the claim to copyright?

> Examples: Title page of book or manual; first screen of computer program output; labels on computer disks.

3) Does the Company use a proper copyright notice?

> Examples:
> Copyright 2008 Company, Inc.
> © 2008 Company, Inc.
> COPR. 2008 Company, Inc.
> Recommended edition: "All rights reserved."

4) When a work is revised, does the Company use in its copyright notices both the first year of publication, and the year the most recent version was published?

5) Does the Company register its copyright in its most important works?

6) Does the Company retain archive copies of the materials deposited with the copyright office?

7) Does the Company obtain a written contractual assignment of copyright from vendors and independent contractors at the outset of a project to assign all copyrightable works to the Company?

8) Does the Company have a written policy against copyright infringement by its employees?

Courtesy of Michael Barclay, Wilson Sonsini Goodrich & Rosati

APPENDIX D

PATENT CHECKLIST

1) Does the Company mark the relevant patent numbers of its issued and unexpired patents on its products and on marketing materials for the products?

2) Does the Company require all licensees of its patents to mark the Company's patent numbers on the licensed products?

3) Does the Company calendar the payment dates for its patent maintenance fees?

4) Does the Company actively solicit patent disclosures from the Company's employees?

5) Does the Company have a patent committee that regularly evaluates patent disclosures from the Company's employees?

6) If feasible in the particular industry, does the Company obtain a patent clearance search before starting a new development project?

7) Does the Company seek non-infringement opinions from patent counsel when emulating or designing around a competitor's patented product?

8) Does the Company have a procedure for handling incoming notices of alleged infringement? When appropriate, does the Company seek non-infringement or invalidity opinions from patent counsel when the Company is accused of infringement?

9) Does the Company generally obtain written representations of non-infringement from its suppliers relating to the suppliers' products?

10) Does the Company obtain written invention assignment agreements from all employees at the beginning of employment?

11) Does the Company obtain written invention assignment agreements from all outside developers and consultants at the beginning of a relationship?

12) Do the patent filings name the correct inventors? That is, are all the named inventors really true inventors, and are there any unnamed inventors left off the application?

13) Are there possible claims of ownership of the company's patents by third parties? These could include former employers, universities, outside consultants.

14) If there have been foreign filings of a US patent, has all of the foreign cited prior art also been cited in related US applications?

Courtesy of Michael Barclay, Wilson Sonsini Goodrich & Rosati

APPENDIX E

TRADEMARK CHECKLIST

1) Does the Company consistently use its trademarks and service marks in a proper manner, that is, as adjectives instead of as a noun?

2) Does the Company use each registered mark in the form that the mark was registered?

3) Does the Company consistently use an ® with its federally registered trademarks and service marks?

4) Does the Company use a TM or an SM symbol for trademarks or service marks that are not federally registered?

5) Does the Company have written guidelines for its employees for the proper use of its trademarks, service marks and trade name?

6) Does the Company seek to protect the non-functional design aspects of its products as trademarks?

7) Does the Company calendar the dates of all required renewal payments and affidavit of use requirements?

8) Does the Company conduct availability searches when adopting a new trademark, service mark, or trade name?

9) When marks are assigned to the Company, does the Company obtain written assignments of the good will accompanying the marks?

10) Does the Company keep records of first use and first interstate use for each of its trademarks and service marks?

11) Does the Company register its trademarks and service marks in foreign countries before marketing abroad?

12) Does the Company maintain quality control rights for the products and services of any licensees of the Company's trademarks or service marks?

13) Does the Company obtain a written hold harmless or indemnity against product liability claims from all licensees and authorized users of its trademarks and service marks?

14) Does the Company use a trademark watch service to detect unauthorized use and registration applications of its marks by others?

15) Does the Company promptly give a written warning notice to infringers of the Company's marks or trade name?

16) Does the Company record its federally registered trademarks with U.S. Customs to prevent importation of counterfeit or gray market goods bearing the marks?

17) Does the Company register to do business under its trade name in each state in which the Company has offices or employees?

18) Does the Company have a fictitious business name statement on file, if appropriate?

Courtesy of Michael Barclay, Wilson Sonsini Goodrich & Rosati

APPENDIX F

INTELLECTUAL PROPERTY AUDIT OUTLINE

Ownership

Inbound licenses

What to collect:

Copies of licenses for intellectual property from other entities. Examples include software licenses from third parties that are utilized in Company products.

Scope of Review:

Determine what IP is covered by the license.

Determine the scope of license.

Is the license equivalent to an assignment?

Does it contain a right to enforce?

Are after-developed inventions mentioned?

Examine change of control provisions to determine the effect of an IPO or sale of the relevant business.

Determine whether or not the license is assignable.

Determine the royalty obligations under the license.

Outbound Licenses

What to collect:

Copies of licenses for intellectual property to other entities. Examples include software licenses to third parties using Company products.

Scope of Review:

For each license:

Determine what IP is covered by the license.

Determine the scope of license.

Determine whether the license is exclusive.

Determine whether Company has any ongoing obligations.

Development Agreements

What to collect:

Copies of agreements with employees, contractors, and 3rd parties. Examples include contracts with application developers working on specific products.

Scope of Review:

For each agreement:

Examine provisions of the agreement affecting IP rights, including, for example, confidentiality clauses, duty of assignment clauses, etc.

Determine ongoing obligations of each party to the agreement.

Source Code Escrow Agreement

What to collect:

Copies of the source code escrow agreement and any agreements requiring the source code escrow.

Scope of Review:

For each agreement:

Examine provisions of the agreements requiring the source code escrow.

Determine requirements for release of source code.

UCC Filings

What to collect:

Copies of any UCC filings that affect Company IP rights (e.g., Bank of America).

Scope of Review:

> For each filing, determine effect on IP rights.
>
> Perform a search of UCC filings to determine whether a security interest has been perfected that may encumber patent rights.

Warranties

What to collect:

> Copies of warranties in any agreements to or from third parties.

Scope of Review:

> Examine agreements for the following warranties:
>
> Third party has ownership of inbound licensed IP.
>
> The licensed IP is free of encumbrance.
>
> Not pledged as collateral.
>
> No third-party liens.
>
> Any licensed patents valid and enforceable.
>
> > Or, at a minimum, warrantor knows of no reason why they are not.
> >
> > No third party claims of infringement.
> >
> > No violation of third party patent rights.
> >
> > Indemnification.

Or, at a minimum, no knowledge of violation.

No patent litigations.

Consider warranty that patents rights cover technology.

Patent

Existing Patents and Patent Applications

What to collect:

List of existing issued patents and pending patent applications in the U.S. and foreign countries (you sent us a list, we just need to confirm that the list is complete.

List may come from internal and outside counsel docket. Will also search external databases (USPTO web site, delphion, etc.).

A list of subsidiaries and acquisitions so that we can conduct a database search for IP owned by the subsidiaries.

Scope of Review:

Prepare a list of U.S. Patents, including:

Patent Number

Issue Date

Inventors

Title

Dates on which the maintenance fees were paid and the identity of the parties paying the maintenance fees.

Obtain a copy of each listed U.S. patent, reissue patent and reexamination certificate.

Prepare a list of U.S. Patent Applications, including:

Application number

Filing date

Inventors

Title

Determine whether the information on the face of the patents is correct, including:

Serial No.

Patent No.

Filing date.

Issue date.

Inventors

Full names

Declarations signed

Title - does it match the technology claimed.

Are references cited on the face of the patent?

Ownership

Perform an independent title survey in U.S. Patent and Trademark Office for each listed patent to ensure that title of record is in Company. (35 U.S.C. 261 imposes BFP rule if assignment is not recorded in PTO within 3 months from its date or before subsequent purchase.) Check for collateral assignments and other conveyances.

Are assignments executed and recorded?

Have any interferences been initiated?

Do any UCC filings affect the ownership of the patents?

Enforceability

Have maintenance fees and annuities been paid?

Further Possible Tasks:

Perform a substantive review.

Validity analysis.

Prior art search.

Obtain and review the prosecution history of each U.S. Patent (all correspondence between applicant and the Patent and Trademark Office during pendency of the application for each patent).

Obtain a copy of the prosecution history of each application to date. Review the history to ensure, among other things, that claims are being prosecuted the way your client believes they should be in order to obtain maximum commercial exclusivity for the product.

Obtain and review all correspondence between Company and patent lawyers regarding its patents. This may shed light on statutory bar issues and inventorship issues, among others, which accused infringers may raise in the future.

Perform a competitive patent/freedom to operate analysis.

Perform a thorough enforceability analysis, examining:

Prior litigation.

Prosecution history.

Comprehensive list of references disclosed versus references available. If patent exclusivity is significant to the Company, consider conducting an independent invalidity search for prior patents or publications which may not have been found by the Company or the Patent and Trademark Office and therefore which could affect scope or validity of the patent rights.

Past opinion letters.

Past cease and desist letters.

Perform laches analysis.

Potential Patentable Inventions.

What to collect:

A list of key personnel to contact. Any invention disclosure material for non-patented inventions, if any such material exists. The existing patent policy, if such a policy exists.

Scope of Review:

Interview key employees regarding innovation.

Obtain and review each invention development memorandum (which recites details about patentable inventions for review by Company's patent lawyer and which could tell about areas the Company has chosen not to patent).

Determine whether any potentially patentable innovations exist.

Trademark

Existing Trademarks

What to collect:

List of existing registered trademarks and pending trademark applications. List may come from internal and outside counsel docket. May also search external databases (USPTO web site, etc.).

Advertising, brochures, packaging and other materials.

Scope of Review:

Examine the registration to ensure it is correct.

Determine the status of issued and pending trademarks.

Whether any cancellation or opposition proceedings are pending.

Determine whether use of existing trademarks is consistent with registration.

For third party trademarks:

Examine purchase agreement.

Determine whether assignments been executed.

Examine advertising, brochures, packaging and other materials which may disclose, inter alia:

Style and secondary marks that are protectable or which may infringe third party uses.

Slogans that are protectable or which may infringe third party uses.

Misuse of marks (e.g., use as generic terms; misuse of ®; failure to use ®).

Proper marking of packaging.

Potential Trademarks

What to collect:

A list of key personnel to contact.

Scope of Review:

Interview key employees regarding trademarks.

Determine whether any potential trademarks exist.

Copyright

Existing Copyrights

What to collect:

List of existing registered copyrights and pending copyright registrations. List may come from internal and outside counsel docket. May also search external databases (Copyright Office web site, etc.).

List of unregistered copyrights.

Scope of Review:

Examine the registration to ensure it is correct.

Determine the status of registered and unregistered copyrights.

Obtain and review the copyright registrations and files listed for each registration.

For third party copyrights:

Examine purchase agreement.

Determine whether assignments been executed.

Analyze license agreements in light of copyrights.

Potential Copyrights

What to collect:

A list of key personnel to contact.

Scope of Review:

Obtain a list of all relevant non-registered works (which are nevertheless protected via copyright) which have ever been offered for license, use or sale by Company, including:

Name and version of work

Release date

List of previous versions and their release dates

Creation Date

Name and current address of each person who participated in creation of the work from whom a written assignment has been obtained.

Name and current address of each person who participated in creation of the work from whom a written assignment has not been obtained.

Trade Secret

What to collect:

List of trade secrets.

Employee and contractor agreements (confidentiality clauses).

Non-disclosure agreements with third parties.

Company Internet policy, laptop policy, e-mail destruction policy, and computer system backup policy.

Company facilities security policy.

List of key personnel to interview.

Scope of Review:

Determine whether employees and contractors subject to confidentiality agreements.

Determine whether trade secrets have been disclosed.

If so, under non-disclosure agreements?

Ascertain whether any key employees have left the Company that had access to trade secrets and if so, what measures were taken to protect trade secrets.

Determine where the Company's trade secrets are stored and what protections are in place to protect them.

Review Company Internet policy, laptop policy, e-mail destruction policy, and computer system backup policy.

Review Company facilities security policy.

Determine where Company's key employees came from and whether they were privy to another's trade secrets.

Determine whether Company's key employees were screened for limitations based on agreements with former employees.

Determine how source code is protected.

Internet

What to collect:

List of Domain names.

Website operation or development agreements.

Scope of Review:

Determine whether any third parties have trademark rights that could affect any of Company's domain names.

Examine operation or development agreements to determine IP ownership.

Examine websites to determine if any issues exist concerning the content on the website.

Examine websites to determine if any issues exist with linking or framing.

Other Confidential Information

What to collect:

List of any additional confidential information disclosed to third parties.

Scope of Review:

Examine agreements associated with the disclosure.

Litigation

Pending threats/notices regarding IP

What to collect:

Copies of the received threats, notices, and complaints.

Scope of Review:

Examine the threats/notices.

Subsidiaries and Affiliated Companies

What to collect:

List of subsidiaries and affiliated companies.

Scope of Review:

Use list of subsidiaries and affiliated companies in performing searches for various types of IP.

Courtesy of John Alemanni, Kilpatrick Stockton LLP

APPENDIX G

INVENTION DISCLOSURE OUTLINE

1.   Invention Background

   A)   Without referring to your invention, describe the problem addressed by the invention.

   B)   Again, without referring to your invention, describe how others attempted to solve the problem.

   C)   Again, without describing your invention, what are the disadvantages of other attempts to solve the problem; i.e., why have the past attempts failed to work?

2.   Summary: 3-minute-drill

   A)   Technical - In 3 minutes, describe your invention to a new technical hire, someone with some very basic knowledge, but no experience or knowledge of systems in your organization.

      i)   Think of an elevator ride.

      ii)   The person must be able to go away and make or use the invention without access to you or your documentation; i.e., without asking any questions.

      iii) Keep the description technical, not a description of why the invention is good or better than past attempts.

   B)   Funding - In 3 minutes, explain to a capital provider why they should fund this invention.

      i)   What is good?

           (1)   Revenue generation

           (2)   Efficiency/Cost-cutting

      ii)   What are the competitive advantages?

3.   Detailed Description

    A)   Tell us how your invention should be made and used:

      i)   Start with system/hardware in the system.

      ii)   Steps the system carries out.

      iii)   Detail the documentation given in the disclosure

    B)   Describe features that are new; how is your invention different than the conventional?

      i)   Provide a system diagram for context.

      ii)   Provide flowcharts described in terms of the system.

    C)   What is the closest invention to your invention?

      i)   Created prior to you conceiving of your invention?

      ii)   What aspects of your invention differentiate it over the closest prior invention?

D)   Market

     i)   Who are the primary competitors in the target market?

     ii)   What aspects of your invention do you want to protect, stop others from doing and/or receive payment for?

4.   Additional Material

A)   Documents

B)   Web Sites

5.   Public Use/On Sale Bar

A)   Has the invention been disclosed or used publicly?

B)   If so when?

     i)   First developed/tested

     ii)   First public use, knowledge, publication, etc.

C)   Disclosed outside of the company?

D)   Was the disclosure under a development or non-disclosure agreement?

E)   Any plans to disclose or implement in the future/if so when?

6.   Anyone involved in the patenting process has an ongoing duty to disclose any information that may be material to patentability; when in doubt, disclose. The duty extends to the inventor and attorney.

7.   Inventorship

     A)   All those who conceived of the claimed invention.

     B)   Ensure you provide ALL inventor names, citizenships and home and e-mail addresses.

Courtesy of John Alemanni, Kilpatrick Stockton LLP

APPENDIX H

INTELLECTUAL PROPERTY CHECKLIST

Patents

- Patents the company owns

    - Subject matter

    - Assigned properly

    - Continuations in place

    - Maintenance paid

    - Identify any possible infringers

- Patents the company licenses from others

    - Scope of license

    - Royalties paid

- Patents the company licenses to others

    - Scope of license

    - Royalties paid

- Patents the company should seek

    - Identify key technology and innovations

    - Work with patent counsel on applications

- Inventor's agreements with all employees in place

- Locate and determine rights under any joint development or similar agreements

- Competitors' patents

    - Issued patents

        - Scope

        - Validity

        - Analysis of any possible infringement by the company

    - Patents applied for

        - Scope

        - Validity

        - Analysis of any possible infringement by the company

            - Design around or license

- Document the company's prior invention and methods to be used in defense against infringement claims, if need be

Trademarks

- Trademarks the company owns

  - Company name

  - Product names

  - Assigned properly

  - Registrations in place

    - State

    - Federal

  - Identify any possible infringers

- Trademarks the company licenses from others

  - Scope of license

  - Registrations in place

  - Proper assignments to licensor

  - Fees paid

- Trademarks the company licenses to others

  - Scope of license

  - Registrations in place

  - Registrations in place

  - Royalties paid

- Competitors' Trademarks

    - Analysis of any possible infringement by the company

    - Trademarks applied for

        - Scope

        - Validity

        - Analysis of any possible infringement by the company

        - Determine whether there are grounds to challenge

Trade Secrets/Confidential Information

- Identify the company's trade secrets

    - Technology, processes formulas, customer and competitive information

- Trade Secrets licensed from others

    - Conform to confidentiality provisions

    - Fees/royalties paid

- Formulate a program to protect trade secrets

    - Confidentiality agreements/non-competition agreements with employees

    - Non-disclosure/confidentiality agreements with suppliers, joint developers, etc.

    - Procedures to keep information secret

- Determine obligations regarding the trade secrets/confidential information of others

    - Non-competition agreements of employees with former employers

    - Non-disclosure/confidentiality agreement with suppliers, joint developers, etc.

Copyrights

- Identify any copyright registrations owned by the company

    - Assignments properly done

- Identify any works that should be registered and register

- Assure that all independent contractors assign rights to copyrightable material to the company

Courtesy of David A. Allgeyer, Lindquist & Vennum PLLP

APPENDIX I

EDWARD H. PHILLIPS V. AWH CORPORATION, HOPEMAN BROTHERS, INC., AND LOFTON CORPORATION

United States Court of Appeals for the Federal Circuit

EDWARD H. PHILLIPS,
Plaintiff-Appellant,

v.

AWH CORPORATION,
HOPEMAN BROTHERS, INC., and LOFTON CORPORATION,
Defendants-Cross Appellants.

LOURIE, Circuit Judge, concurring in part and dissenting in part, with whom NEWMAN, Circuit Judge, joins.

I fully join the portion of the court's opinion resolving the relative weights of specification and dictionaries in interpreting patent claims, in favor of the specification. I could elaborate more expansively on that topic, but Judge Bryson's opinion for the majority says it so well, there is little reason for me to repeat its truths. I also agree with the court that claims need not necessarily be limited to specific or preferred embodiments in the specification, although they are limited to what is contained in the overall disclosure of the specification.

However, I do dissent from the court's decision to reverse and remand the district court's decision. The original panel decision of this court, which implicitly decided the case based on the priorities that the en banc court has now reaffirmed, interpreted the claims in light of the specification and found that the defendant did not infringe the claims. We affirmed the district court, which had arrived at a similar conclusion. The dissent from the panel decision relied on the "dictionaries first" procedure, which the court now has decided not to follow. Thus, while the claim construction issue had to be decided by the en banc court, I see no reason for the court, having reaffirmed the principle on which the district judge and the panel originally decided the case, to send it back for further review.

The court premises its reverse-and-remand decision on the concept of claim differentiation and the reasoning that the contested term "baffle" need not fulfill all of the functions set out for it in the specification. Reasonable people can differ on those points. However, the court did not take this case en banc because the full court differed with the panel majority on those disputable criteria. It did so to resolve the claim construction issue, which it has now done so well. Having done so, I believe that it should simply affirm the district court's decision on the merits, consistently with that court's rationale and that of the panel that affirmed the district court, which it now adopts.

I will not critique in detail particular statements the majority makes in rationalizing its reversal of the district court's decision, such as "that a person of skill in the art would not interpret the disclosure and claims of the '798 patent to mean that a structure extending inward from one of the wall faces is a 'baffle' if it is at an acute or obtuse angle, but is not a 'baffle' if it is disposed at a right angle," or that "the patent does not require that the inward extending structures always be capable of performing that function [deflecting projectiles]" in order to be considered 'baffles'.

I will simply point out that the specification contains no disclosure of baffles at right angles. Moreover, as the majority correctly states, a patent specification is intended to describe one's invention, and it is essential to read a specification in order to interpret the meaning of the claims. This specification makes clear that the "baffles" in this invention are angled. There is no reference to baffles that show them to be other than angled. The abstract refers to "bullet deflecting . . . baffles." Only angled baffles can deflect. It then mentions "internal baffles at angles for deflecting bullets." That could not be clearer. The specification then refers several times to baffles, often to figures in the drawings, all of which are to angled baffles. A compelling point is that the only numbered references to baffles (15, 16, 26, 27, 30, and 31) all show angled baffles.

The specification further states that steel panels "form the internal baffles at angles for deflecting bullets." It states that the baffles are "disposed at such angles that bullets which might penetrate the outer steel panels are deflected." It explains that if bullets "were to penetrate the outer steel wall, the baffles are disposed at angles which tend to deflect the bullets." There is no specific reference in this patent to a baffle that is not angled at other than 90°.

While, as the majority states, the specification indicates that multiple objectives are achieved by the invention, none of the other objectives is dependent upon whether the baffles are at other than a 90° angle, whereas the constantly stated objective of deflection of bullets is dependent upon such an angle.

Finally, even though claim construction is a question of law, reviewable by this court without formal deference, I do believe that we ought to lean toward affirmance of a claim construction in the absence of a strong conviction of error. I do not have such a conviction in this case, after considering the district court's opinion and the patent specification.

For these reasons, while I wholeheartedly join the majority opinion in its discussion and resolution of the "specification v. dictionaries" issue, I would affirm the decision below.

United States Court of Appeals for the Federal Circuit

EDWARD H. PHILLIPS,
Plaintiff-Appellant,

v.

AWH CORPORATION,
HOPEMAN BROTHERS, INC., and LOFTON CORPORATION,
Defendants-Cross Appellants.

MAYER, Circuit Judge, with whom NEWMAN, Circuit Judge,
joins, dissenting.

Now more than ever I am convinced of the futility, indeed the absurdity, of this court's persistence in adhering to the falsehood that claim construction is a matter of law devoid of any factual component. Because any attempt to fashion a coherent standard under this regime is pointless, as illustrated by our many failed attempts to do so, I dissent.

This court was created for the purpose of bringing consistency to the patent field. See H.R. Rep. No. 312, 97th Cong., 1st Sess. 20-23 (1981). Instead, we have taken this noble mandate, to reinvigorate the patent and introduce predictability to the field, and focused inappropriate power in this court. In our quest to elevate our importance, we have, however, disregarded our role as an appellate court; the resulting mayhem has seriously undermined the legitimacy of the process, if not the integrity of the institution.

In the name of uniformity, Cybor Corp. v. FAS Technologies, Inc., 138 F.3d 1448 (Fed. Cir. 1998) (en banc), held that claim construction does not involve subsidiary or underlying questions of fact and that we are, therefore, unbridled by either the expertise or efforts of the district court.[1] What we have wrought, instead, is the substitution of a black box, as it so pejoratively has been said of the jury, with the black hole of this court. Out of this void

---

[1] The Supreme Court did not suggest in affirming Markman v. Westview Instruments, Inc., 52 F.3d 967 (1995) (en banc), that claim construction is a purely legal question. 517 U.S. 370 (1996). It held only that, as a policy matter, the judge, as opposed to the jury, should determine the meaning of a patent claim. See Cybor, 138 F.3d at 1464 (Mayer, C.J., dissenting) (explaining that "the [Supreme] Court chose not to accept our formulation of claim construction: as a pure question of law to be decided de novo in all cases on appeal").

we emit "legal" pronouncements by way of "interpretive necromancy"[2]; these rulings resemble reality, if at all, only by chance. Regardless, and with a blind eye to the consequences, we continue to struggle under this irrational and reckless regime, trying every alternative—dictionaries first, dictionaries second, never dictionaries, etc., etc., etc.

Again today we vainly attempt to establish standards by which this court will interpret claims. But after proposing no fewer than seven questions, receiving more than thirty amici curiae briefs, and whipping the bar into a frenzy of expectation, we say nothing new, but merely restate what has become the practice over the last ten years—that we will decide cases according to whatever mode or method results in the outcome we desire, or at least allows us a seemingly plausible way out of the case. I am not surprised by this. Indeed, there can be no workable standards by which this court will interpret claims so long as we are blind to the factual component of the task. See Cooter & Gell v. Hartmarx Corp., 496 U.S. 384, 405 (1990) ("Fact-bound resolutions cannot be made uniform through appellate review, de novo or otherwise." (quoting Mars Steel Corp. v. Cont'l Bank N.A., 880 F.2d 928, 936 (7th Cir.1989))).[3]

Federal Rule of Civil Procedure 52(a) states that "[f]indings of fact . . . shall not be set aside unless clearly erroneous, and due regard shall be given to the opportunity of the trial court to judge of the credibility of witnesses." According to the Supreme Court, this "[r]ule means what it says"—that findings of fact, even "those described as 'ultimate facts' because they may determine the outcome of litigation," are to be reviewed deferentially on appeal.[4] Bose Corp. v. Consumers Union of United States, 456 U.S. 273,

---

[2] See The Holmes Group, Inc. v. Vornado Air Circulation Sys., Inc., 535 U.S. 826, 833 (2002).

[3] The question asked but not answered by the court which might have allowed it to cure its self-inflicted wound was: "Question 7. Consistent with the Supreme Court's decision in Markman v. Westview Instruments, Inc., 517 U.S. 370 (1996) and our en banc decision in Cybor Corp. v. FAS Technologies, Inc., 138 F.3d 1448 (Fed. Cir. 1998), is it appropriate for this court to accord any deference to any aspect of trial court claim construction rulings? If so, on what aspects, in what circumstances, and to what extent?"

[4] Because some facts are so intertwined with a constitutional standard the Supreme Court has held that de novo review is appropriate. For example, whether a defendant has acted with actual malice in a defamation suit is reviewed de novo because, among other

287 (1982) ("Rule 52(a) broadly requires that findings of fact not be set aside unless clearly erroneous."); 466 U.S. 485, 498 & 501 (1984); see also Anderson v. Bessemer City, 470 U.S. 564, 575 (1985) ("[R]eview of factual findings under the clearly-erroneous standard—with its deference to the trier of fact—is the rule, not the exception."); Pullman-Standard v. United Steel Workers of Am.United States v. United States Gypsum Co., 333 U.S. 364, 394 (1948). Even those findings of fact based entirely on documentary evidence are entitled to deference. Anderson, 470 U.S. at 574 ("That [Rule 52(a)] goes on to emphasize the special deference to be paid credibility determinations does not alter its clear command: Rule 52(a) 'does not make exceptions or purport to exclude certain categories of factual findings from the obligation of a court of appeals to accept a district court's findings unless clearly erroneous.'" (quoting Pullman-Standard, 456 U.S. at 287)). In short, we are obligated by Rule 52(a) to review the factual findings of the district court that underlie the determination of claim construction for clear error.

While this court may persist in the delusion that claim construction is a purely legal determination, unaffected by underlying facts, it is plainly not the case. Claim construction is, or should be, made in context: a claim

---

reasons, the scope of the First Amendment is shaped and applied by reference to such factual determinations. Bose, 466 U.S. at 502 ("[T]he content of the rule is not revealed simply by its literal text, but rather is given meaning through the evolutionary process of common-law adjudication."). Similarly, whether there is reasonable suspicion to conduct an investigatory stop or probable cause to perform a search under the Fourth Amendment are reviewed without deference. Ornelas v. United States, 517 U.S. 690, 696 (1996) (holding that the protections afforded by the Fourth Amendment are "fluid concepts that take their substantive content from the particular contexts in which the standards are being assessed"). The reasoning behind these limited exceptions surely does not apply to claim construction. While appearing from the perspective of this court's limited sphere of influence to be dreadfully important, claim construction does not implicate a constitutional value. Cf. Bose, 466 U.S. at 502 ("[T]he constitutional values protected by the rule make it imperative that judges—and in some cases judges of [the Supreme] Court—make sure that it is correctly applied."). This is illustrated by the fact that the outcome of a patent case, unlike a defamation or illegal search case, has little impact on how future cases are decided or on how future parties behave. at 501 n.17 ("Regarding certain largely factual questions in some areas of the law, the stakes—in terms of impact on future cases and future conduct—are too great to entrust them finally to the judgment of the trier of fact."). Even if claim construction did implicate a constitutional value, it, unlike the decisions underlying the First and Fourth Amendments, could readily be reduced, when distinguished from its factual underpinnings, to "a neat set of legal rules." , 517 U.S. at 695-96 (quoting , 462 U.S. 213, 232 (1983)). Cf. id. OrnelasIll. v. Gates

should be interpreted both from the perspective of one of ordinary skill in the art and in view of the state of the art at the time of invention. See Multiform Desiccants, Inc. v. Medzam, Ltd., 133 F.3d 1473, 1477 (Fed. Cir. 1998) ("It is the person of ordinary skill in the field of the invention through whose eyes the claims are construed."). These questions, which are critical to the correct interpretation of a claim, are inherently factual. They are hotly contested by the parties, not by resort to case law as one would expect for legal issues, but based on testimony and documentary evidence.[5] During so called Markman "hearings," which are often longer than jury trials, parties battle over experts offering conflicting evidence regarding who qualifies as one of ordinary skill in the art; the meaning of patent terms to that person; the state of the art at the time of the invention; contradictory dictionary definitions and which would be consulted by the skilled artisan; the scope of specialized terms; the problem a patent was solving; what is related or pertinent art; whether a construction was disallowed during prosecution; how one of skill in the art would understand statements during prosecution; and on and on. In order to reconcile the parties' inconsistent submissions and arrive at a sound interpretation, the district court is required to sift through and weigh volumes of evidence. While this court treats the district court as an intake clerk, whose only role is to collect, shuffle and collate evidence, the reality, as revealed by conventional practice, is far different.

Even if the procedures employed by the district court did not show that it is engaging in fact finding, the nature of the questions underlying claim construction illustrate that they are factual and should be reviewed in accordance with Rule 52(a). For each patent, for example, who qualifies as one of ordinary skill in the art will differ, just as the state of the art at the time of invention will differ. These subsidiary determinations are specific, multifarious and not susceptible to generalization; as such their resolution in one case will bear very little, if at all, on the resolution of subsequent cases. See Ornelas, 517 U.S. at 703 ("Law clarification requires generalization, and some issues lend themselves to generalization much

---

[5] That most of the cases now appealed to this court are "summary judgments" is irrelevant. We have artificially renamed findings of fact as legal conclusions; the district courts have dutifully conformed to our fictional characterization, but this does not change the inherent nature of the inquiry. Of course, if the parties do not dispute the material facts, summary judgment is appropriate.

more than others."); Pierce v. Underwood, 487 U.S. 552, 561-62 (1988) ("Many questions that arise in litigation are not amenable to regulation by rule because they involve multifarious, fleeting, special, narrow facts that utterly resist generalization." (quoting Maurice Rosenberg, Judicial Discretion of the Trial Court, Viewed from Above, 22 Syracuse L. Rev. 635, 662 (1971))); Icicle Seafoods, Inc. v. Worthington, 475 U.S. 709, 714 (1986) (rejecting de novo review of factual questions, even when outcome determinative). That the determination of the meaning of a particular term in one patent will not necessarily bear on the interpretation of the same term in a subsequent patent illustrates this point; while the term is the same, the underlying factual context is different. It further proves that these questions (e.g., who qualifies as one of ordinary skill in the art and what was the state of the art at the time of invention, among others) are implicitly being determined in each case; because we refuse to acknowledge either their existence or importance, however, the manner of their resolution is never elucidated. Finally, that claim construction is dependent on underlying factual determinations has been verified by our experience, which shows that reviewing these questions de novo has not clarified the law, but has instead "distort[ed] the appellate process," causing confusion among the district courts and bar. See Cooter, 496 U.S. at 404 (quoting Pierce, 487 U.S. at 561); see also Koon v. United States, 518 U.S. 81, 99 (1996).

Our purely de novo review of claim interpretation also cannot be reconciled with the Supreme Court's instructions regarding obviousness. While ultimately a question of law, obviousness depends on several underlying factual inquiries. Graham v. John Deere Co., 383 U.S. 1, 17 (1966); see also Dennison Mfg. Co. v. Panduit Corp., 475 U.S. 809, 811 (1986) (holding that Rule 52(a) requires that the district court's subsidiary factual determinations should be reviewed for clear error); cf. Graver Tank & Mfg. Co. v. Linde Air Prods. Co., 336 U.S. 271, 275 (1949) (holding that validity, while ultimately a question of law, is founded on factual determinations that are entitled to deference). "Under [section] 103, the scope and content of the prior art are to be determined; differences between the prior art and the claims at issue are to be ascertained; and the level of ordinary skill in the pertinent art resolved." Graham, 383 U.S. at 17.

To a significant degree, each of these factual inquiries is also necessary to claim construction. Before beginning claim construction, "the scope and content of the prior art [should] be determined," id., to establish context. The "differences between the prior art and the claims at issue [should] be ascertained," id., to better define what the inventor holds out as the invention. And, the foundation for both the obviousness and claim construction determinations is "the level of ordinary skill in the pertinent art." Id.; see Multiform, 133 F.3d at 1477. These underlying factual considerations receive the level of deference due under Rule 52(a) when considering obviousness, but they are scrutinized de novo in the claim construction context. As directed by the Supreme Court, however, it is especially important in the patent field, "where so much depends upon familiarity with specific scientific problems and principles not usually contained in the general storehouse of knowledge and experience," to give deference to the district court's findings of fact. Graver Tank & Mfg. Co. v. Linde Air Prods. Co., 339 U.S. 605, 609-10 (1950).

While the court flails about in an attempt to solve the claim construction "conundrum," the solution to our plight is straightforward. We simply must follow the example of every other appellate court, which, regarding the vast majority of factual questions, reviews the trial court for clear error.[6] This equilibrium did not come about as the result of chance or permissive appellate personalities, but because two centuries of experience has shown that the trial court's factfinding ability is "unchallenged." Salve Regina Coll. v. Russell, 499 U.S. 225, 233 (1991); Inwood, 456 U.S. at 856 ("Determining the weight and credibility of the evidence is the special province of the trier of fact."). Time has similarly revealed that it is more economical for the district court to find facts. Pierce, 487 U.S. at 560 ("Moreover, even where the district judge's full knowledge of the factual setting can be acquired by the appellate court, that acquisition will often come at unusual expense, requiring the court to undertake the unaccustomed task of reviewing the entire record . . . .").

Therefore, not only is it more efficient for the trial court to construct the record, the trial court is better, that is, more accurate, by way of both

---

[6] While jurisprudentially sound, the bar also supports this proposition, as evident by the many amici curiae briefs urging adherence to Rule 52(a).

position and practice, at finding facts than appellate judges. Anderson, 470 U.S. at 574 ("The rationale for deference to the original finder of fact is not limited to the superiority of the trial judge's position to make determinations of credibility. The trial judge's major role is the determination of fact, and with experience on fulfilling that role comes expertise."); Zenith Radio Corp. v. Hazeltine Research, Inc., 395 U.S. 100, 123 (1969). Our rejection of this fundamental premise has resulted, not surprisingly, in several serious problems, including increased litigation costs, needless consumption of judicial resources, and uncertainty, as well as diminished respect for the court and less "decisional accuracy." Salve, 499 U.S. at 233. We should abandon this unsound course.[7]

If we persist in deciding the subsidiary factual components of claim construction without deference, there is no reason why litigants should be required to parade their evidence before the district courts or for district courts to waste time and resources evaluating such evidence. It is excessive to require parties, who "have already been forced to concentrate their energies and resources on persuading the trial judge that their account of the facts is the correct one," to "persuade three more judges at the appellate level." Anderson, 470 U.S. at 575. If the proceedings before the district court are merely a "tryout on the road," id. (quoting Wainwright v. Sykes, 433 U.S. 72, 90 (1977)), as they are under our current regimen, it is wasteful to require such proceedings at all. Instead, all patent cases could be filed in this court; we would determine whether claim construction is necessary, and, if so, the meaning of the claims. Those few cases in which claim construction is not dispositive can be remanded to the district court for trial. In this way, we would at least eliminate the time and expense of the charade currently played out before the district court.

Eloquent words can mask much mischief. The court's opinion today is akin to rearranging the deck chairs on the Titanic—the orchestra is playing as if nothing is amiss, but the ship is still heading for Davey Jones' locker.

---

[7] There are some scenarios where it is difficult to weed facts from law, see Pullman-Standard, 456 U.S. at 288, but claim construction is not one of them.

United States Court of Appeals for the Federal Circuit

EDWARD H. PHILLIPS,
Plaintiff-Appellant,

v.

AWH CORPORATION,
HOPEMAN BROTHERS, INC., and LOFTON CORPORATION,
Defendants-Cross Appellants.

DECIDED: July 12, 2005

Before MICHEL, Chief Judge, NEWMAN, MAYER, LOURIE,
CLEVENGER, RADER, SCHALL, BRYSON, GAJARSA, LINN, DYK,
and PROST, Circuit Judges.

Opinion for the court filed by Circuit Judge BRYSON, in which Chief
Judge MICHEL and Circuit Judges CLEVENGER, RADER, SCHALL,
GAJARSA, LINN, DYK, and PROST join; and in which Circuit Judge
LOURIE joins with respect to parts I, II, III, V, and VI; and in which
Circuit Judge NEWMAN joins with respect to parts I, II, III, and V.
Opinion concurring in part and dissenting in part filed by Circuit Judge
LOURIE, in which Circuit Judge NEWMAN joins. Dissenting opinion
filed by Circuit Judge MAYER, in which Circuit Judge NEWMAN joins.

BRYSON, Circuit Judge.

Edward H. Phillips invented modular, steel-shell panels that can be welded
together to form vandalism-resistant walls. The panels are especially useful
in building prisons because they are load-bearing and impact-resistant, while
also insulating against fire and noise. Mr. Phillips obtained a patent on the
invention, U.S. Patent No. 4,677,798 ("the '798 patent"), and he
subsequently entered into an arrangement with AWH Corporation,
Hopeman Brothers, Inc., and Lofton Corporation (collectively "AWH") to
market and sell the panels. That arrangement ended in 1990. In 1991,
however, Mr. Phillips received a sales brochure from AWH that suggested
to him that AWH was continuing to use his trade secrets and patented
technology without his consent. In a series of letters in 1991 and 1992, Mr.
Phillips accused AWH of patent infringement and trade secret

misappropriation. Correspondence between the parties regarding the matter ceased after that time.

In February 1997, Mr. Phillips brought suit in the United States District Court for the District of Colorado charging AWH with misappropriation of trade secrets and infringement of claims 1, 21, 22, 24, 25, and 26 of the '798 patent. Phillips v. AWH Corp., No. 97-N-212 (D. Colo.). The district court dismissed the trade secret misappropriation claim as barred by Colorado's three-year statute of limitations.

With regard to the patent infringement issue, the district court focused on the language of claim 1, which recites "further means disposed inside the shell for increasing its load bearing capacity comprising internal steel baffles extending inwardly from the steel shell walls." The court interpreted that language as "a means . . . for performing a specified function," subject to 35 U.S.C. § 112, paragraph 6, which provides that such a claim "shall be construed to cover the corresponding structure, material, or acts described in the specification and equivalents thereof." Looking to the specification of the '798 patent, the court noted that "every textual reference in the Specification and its diagrams show baffle deployment at an angle other than 90° to the wall faces" and that "placement of the baffles at such angles creates an intermediate interlocking, but not solid, internal barrier." The district court therefore ruled that, for purposes of the '798 patent, a baffle must "extend inward from the steel shell walls at an oblique or acute angle to the wall face" and must form part of an interlocking barrier in the interior of the wall module. Because Mr. Phillips could not prove infringement under that claim construction, the district court granted summary judgment of noninfringement.

Mr. Phillips appealed with respect to both the trade secret and patent infringement claims. A panel of this court affirmed on both issues. Phillips v. AWH Corp., 363 F.3d 1207 (Fed. Cir. 2004). As to the trade secret claim, the panel unanimously upheld the district court's ruling that the claim was barred by the applicable statute of limitations. Id. at 1215. As to the patent infringement claims, the panel was divided. The majority sustained the district court's summary judgment of noninfringement, although on different grounds. The dissenting judge would have reversed the summary judgment of noninfringement.

The panel first determined that because the asserted claims of the '798 patent contain a sufficient recitation of structure, the district court erred by construing the term "baffles" to invoke the "means-plus-function" claim format authorized by section 112, paragraph 6. Id. at 1212. Nonetheless, the panel concluded that the patent uses the term "baffles" in a restrictive manner. Based on the patent's written description, the panel held that the claim term "baffles" excludes structures that extend at a 90 degree angle from the walls. The panel noted that the specification repeatedly refers to the ability of the claimed baffles to deflect projectiles and that it describes the baffles as being "disposed at such angles that bullets which might penetrate the outer steel panels are deflected." '798 patent, col. 2, ll. 13-15; see also id. at col. 5, ll. 17-19 (baffles are "disposed at angles which tend to deflect the bullets"). In addition, the panel observed that nowhere in the patent is there any disclosure of a baffle projecting from the wall at a right angle and that baffles oriented at 90 degrees to the wall were found in the prior art. Based on "the specification's explicit descriptions," the panel concluded "that the patentee regarded his invention as panels providing impact or projectile resistance and that the baffles must be oriented at angles other than 90°." Phillips, 363 F.3d at 1213. The panel added that the patent specification "is intended to support and inform the claims, and here it makes it unmistakably clear that the invention involves baffles angled at other than 90°." Id. at 1214. The panel therefore upheld the district court's summary judgment of noninfringement.

The dissenting judge argued that the panel had improperly limited the claims to the particular embodiment of the invention disclosed in the specification, rather than adopting the "plain meaning" of the term "baffles." The dissenting judge noted that the parties had stipulated that "baffles" are a "means for obstructing, impeding, or checking the flow of something," and that the panel majority had agreed that the ordinary meaning of baffles is "something for deflecting, checking, or otherwise regulating flow." Phillips, 363 F.3d at 1216-17. In the dissent's view, nothing in the specification redefined the term "baffles" or constituted a disclaimer specifically limiting the term to less than the full scope of its ordinary meaning. Instead, the dissenting judge contended, the specification "merely identifies impact resistance as one of several objectives of the invention." Id. at 1217. In sum, the dissent concluded that "there is no reason to supplement the plain meaning of the claim language with a limitation from the preferred embodiment." Id. at 1218. Consequently, the dissenting judge argued that the court should have adopted the general purpose dictionary definition of the term baffle, i.e., "something for deflecting, checking, or otherwise regulating flow," id., and therefore should have reversed the summary judgment of noninfringement.

This court agreed to rehear the appeal en banc and vacated the judgment of the panel. Phillips v. AWH Corp., 376 F.3d 1382 (Fed. Cir. 2004). We now affirm the portion of the district court's judgment addressed to the trade secret misappropriation claims. However, we reverse the portion of the court's judgment addressed to the issue of infringement.

I

Claim 1 of the '798 patent is representative of the asserted claims with respect to the use of the term "baffles." It recites:

Building modules adapted to fit together for construction of fire, sound and impact resistant security barriers and rooms for use in securing records and persons, comprising in combination, an outer shell . . . , sealant means . . . and further means disposed inside the shell for increasing its load bearing capacity comprising internal steel baffles extending inwardly from the steel shell walls.

As a preliminary matter, we agree with the panel that the term "baffles" is not means-plus-function language that invokes 35 U.S.C. § 112, paragraph 6. To be sure, the claim refers to "means disposed inside the shell for increasing its load bearing capacity," a formulation that would ordinarily be regarded as invoking the means-plus-function claim format. However, the claim specifically identifies "internal steel baffles" as structure that performs the recited function of increasing the shell's load-bearing capacity. In contrast to the "load bearing means" limitation, the reference to "baffles" does not use the word "means," and we have held that the absence of that term creates a rebuttable presumption that section 112, paragraph 6, does not apply. See Personalized Media Communications, LLC v. Int'l Trade Comm'n, 161 F.3d 696, 703-04 (Fed. Cir. 1998).

Means-plus-function claiming applies only to purely functional limitations that do not provide the structure that performs the recited function. See

Watts v. XL Sys., Inc., 232 F.3d 877, 880-81 (Fed. Cir. 2000). While the baffles in the '798 patent are clearly intended to perform several functions, the term "baffles" is nonetheless structural; it is not a purely functional placeholder in which structure is filled in by the specification. See TurboCare Div. of Demag Delaval Turbomachinery Corp. v. Gen. Elec. Co., 264 F.3d 1111, 1121 (Fed. Cir. 2001) (reasoning that nothing in the specification or prosecution history suggests that the patentee used the term "compressed spring" to denote any structure that is capable of performing the specified function); Greenberg v. Ethicon Endo-Surgery, Inc., 91 F.3d 1580, 1583 (Fed. Cir. 1996) (construing the term "detent mechanism" to refer to particular structure, even though the term has functional connotations). The claims and the specification unmistakably establish that the "steel baffles" refer to particular physical apparatus. The claim characterizes the baffles as "extend[ing] inwardly" from the steel shell walls, which plainly implies that the baffles are structures. The specification likewise makes clear that the term "steel baffles" refers to particular internal wall structures and is not simply a general description of any structure that will perform a particular function. See, e.g., '798 patent, col. 4, ll. 25-26 ("the load bearing baffles 16 are optionally used with longer panels"); id., col. 4, ll. 49-50 (opposing panels are "compressed between the flange 35 and the baffle 26"). Because the term "baffles" is not subject to section 112, paragraph 6, we agree with the panel that the district court erred by limiting the term to corresponding structures disclosed in the specification and their equivalents. Accordingly, we must determine the correct construction of the structural term "baffles," as used in the '798 patent.

II

The first paragraph of section 112 of the Patent Act, 35 U.S.C. § 112, states that the specification shall contain a written description of the invention, and of the manner and process of making and using it, in such full, clear, concise, and exact terms as to enable any person skilled in the art to which it pertains . . . to make and use the same . . . .

The second paragraph of section 112 provides that the specification shall conclude with one or more claims particularly pointing out and distinctly claiming the subject matter which the applicant regards as his invention.

Those two paragraphs of section 112 frame the issue of claim interpretation for us. The second paragraph requires us to look to the language of the claims to determine what "the applicant regards as his invention." On the other hand, the first paragraph requires that the specification describe the invention set forth in the claims. The principal question that this case presents to us is the extent to which we should resort to and rely on a patent's specification in seeking to ascertain the proper scope of its claims.

This is hardly a new question. The role of the specification in claim construction has been an issue in patent law decisions in this country for nearly two centuries. We addressed the relationship between the specification and the claims at some length in our en banc opinion in Markman v. Westview Instruments, Inc., 52 F.3d 967, 979-81 (Fed. Cir. 1995) (en banc), aff'd, 517 U.S. 370 (1996). We again summarized the applicable principles in Vitronics Corp. v. Conceptronic, Inc., 90 F.3d 1576 (Fed. Cir. 1996), and more recently in Innova/Pure Water, Inc. v. Safari Water Filtration Systems, Inc., 381 F.3d 1111 (Fed. Cir. 2004). What we said in those cases bears restating, for the basic principles of claim construction outlined there are still applicable, and we reaffirm them today. We have also previously considered the use of dictionaries in claim construction. What we have said in that regard requires clarification.

A

It is a "bedrock principle" of patent law that "the claims of a patent define the invention to which the patentee is entitled the right to exclude." Innova, 381 F.3d at 1115; see also Vitronics, 90 F.3d at 1582 ("we look to the words of the claims themselves . . . to define the scope of the patented invention"); Markman, 52 F.3d at 980 ("The written description part of the specification itself does not delimit the right to exclude. That is the function and purpose of claims."). That principle has been recognized since at least 1836, when Congress first required that the specification include a portion in which the inventor "shall particularly specify and point out the part, improvement, or combination, which he claims as his own invention or discovery." Act of July 4, 1836, ch. 357, § 6, 5 Stat. 117, 119. In the following years, the Supreme Court made clear that the claims are "of primary importance, in the effort to ascertain precisely what it is that is patented." Merrill v. Yeomans, 94 U.S. 568, 570 (1876). Because the patentee is required to "define precisely what his invention is," the Court explained, it is "unjust to the public, as well as an evasion of the law, to construe it in a manner different from the plain import of its terms." White v. Dunbar, 119 U.S. 47, 52 (1886); see also Cont'l Paper Bag Co. v. E. Paper Bag Co., 210 U.S. 405, 419 (1908) ("the claims measure the invention"); McCarty v. Lehigh Valley R.R. Co., 160 U.S. 110, 116 (1895) ("if we once begin to include elements not mentioned in the claim, in order to limit such claim . . . , we should never know where to stop"); Aro Mfg. Co. v. Convertible Top Replacement Co., 365 U.S. 336, 339 (1961) ("the claims made in the patent are the sole measure of the grant").

We have frequently stated that the words of a claim "are generally given their ordinary and customary meaning." Vitronics, 90 F.3d at 1582; see also Toro Co. v. White Consol. Indus., Inc., 199 F.3d 1295, 1299 (Fed. Cir. 1999); Renishaw PLC v. Marposs Societa' per Azioni, 158 F.3d 1243, 1249 (Fed. Cir. 1998). We have made clear, moreover, that the ordinary and customary meaning of a claim term is the meaning that the term would have to a person of ordinary skill in the art in question at the time of the invention, i.e., as of the effective filing date of the patent application. See Innova, 381 F.3d at 1116 ("A court construing a patent claim seeks to accord a claim the meaning it would have to a person of ordinary skill in the art at the time of the invention."); Home Diagnostics, Inc. v. LifeScan, Inc., 381 F.3d 1352, 1358 (Fed. Cir. 2004) ("customary meaning" refers to the "customary meaning in [the] art field"); Ferguson Beauregard/Logic Controls v. Mega Sys., LLC, 350 F.3d 1327, 1338 (Fed. Cir. 2003) (claim terms "are examined through the viewing glass of a person skilled in the art"); see also PC Connector Solutions LLC v. SmartDisk Corp., 406 F.3d 1359, 1363 (Fed. Cir. 2005) (meaning of claim "must be interpreted as of [the] effective filing date" of the patent application); Schering Corp. v. Amgen Inc., 222 F.3d 1347, 1353 (Fed. Cir. 2000) (same).

The inquiry into how a person of ordinary skill in the art understands a claim term provides an objective baseline from which to begin claim interpretation. See Innova, 381 F.3d at 1116. That starting point is based on the well-settled understanding that inventors are typically persons skilled in the field of the invention and that patents are addressed to and intended to be read by others of skill in the pertinent art. See Verve, LLC v. Crane Cams, Inc., 311 F.3d 1116, 1119 (Fed. Cir. 2002) (patent documents are meant to be "a concise statement for persons in the field"); In re Nelson,

280 F.2d 172, 181 (CCPA 1960) ("The descriptions in patents are not addressed to the public generally, to lawyers or to judges, but, as section 112 says, to those skilled in the art to which the invention pertains or with which it is most nearly connected.").

Importantly, the person of ordinary skill in the art is deemed to read the claim term not only in the context of the particular claim in which the disputed term appears, but in the context of the entire patent, including the specification. This court explained that point well in Multiform Desiccants, Inc. v. Medzam, Ltd., 133 F.3d 1473, 1477 (Fed. Cir. 1998):

It is the person of ordinary skill in the field of the invention through whose eyes the claims are construed. Such person is deemed to read the words used in the patent documents with an understanding of their meaning in the field, and to have knowledge of any special meaning and usage in the field. The inventor's words that are used to describe the invention—the inventor's lexicography—must be understood and interpreted by the court as they would be understood and interpreted by a person in that field of technology. Thus the court starts the decisionmaking process by reviewing the same resources as would that person, viz., the patent specification and the prosecution history.

See also Medrad, Inc. v. MRI Devices Corp., 401 F.3d 1313, 1319 (Fed. Cir. 2005) ("We cannot look at the ordinary meaning of the term . . . in a vacuum. Rather, we must look at the ordinary meaning in the context of the written description and the prosecution history."); V-Formation, Inc. v. Benetton Group SpA, 401 F.3d 1307, 1310 (Fed. Cir. 2005) (intrinsic record "usually provides the technological and temporal context to enable the court to ascertain the meaning of the claim to one of ordinary skill in the art at the time of the invention"); Unitherm Food Sys., Inc. v. Swift-Eckrich, Inc., 375 F.3d 1341, 1351 (Fed. Cir. 2004) (proper definition is the "definition that one of ordinary skill in the art could ascertain from the intrinsic evidence in the record").

B

In some cases, the ordinary meaning of claim language as understood by a person of skill in the art may be readily apparent even to lay judges, and claim construction in such cases involves little more than the application of the widely accepted meaning of commonly understood words. See Brown v. 3M, 265 F.3d 1349, 1352 (Fed Cir. 2001) (holding that the claims did "not require elaborate interpretation"). In such circumstances, general purpose dictionaries may be helpful. In many cases that give rise to litigation, however, determining the ordinary and customary meaning of the claim requires examination of terms that have a particular meaning in a field of art. Because the meaning of a claim term as understood by persons of skill in the art is often not immediately apparent, and because patentees frequently use terms idiosyncratically, the court looks to "those sources available to the public that show what a person of skill in the art would have understood disputed claim language to mean." Innova, 381 F.3d at 1116. Those sources include "the words of the claims themselves, the remainder of the specification, the prosecution history, and extrinsic evidence concerning relevant scientific principles, the meaning of technical terms, and the state of the art." Id.; see also Gemstar-TV Guide Int'l, Inc. v. Int'l Trade Comm'n, 383 F.3d 1352, 1364 (Fed. Cir. 2004); Vitronics, 90 F.3d at 1582-83; Markman, 52 F.3d at 979-80.

1

Quite apart from the written description and the prosecution history, the claims themselves provide substantial guidance as to the meaning of particular claim terms. See Vitronics, 90 F.3d at 1582; see also ACTV, Inc. v. Walt Disney Co., 346 F.3d 1082, 1088 (Fed. Cir. 2003) ("the context of the surrounding words of the claim also must be considered in determining the ordinary and customary meaning of those terms").

To begin with, the context in which a term is used in the asserted claim can be highly instructive. To take a simple example, the claim in this case refers to "steel baffles," which strongly implies that the term "baffles" does not inherently mean objects made of steel. This court's cases provide numerous similar examples in which the use of a term within the claim provides a firm basis for construing the term. See, e.g., Mars, Inc. v. H.J. Heinz Co., 377 F.3d 1369, 1374 (Fed. Cir. 2004) (claim term "ingredients" construed in light of the use of the term "mixture" in the same claim phrase); Process Control Corp. v. HydReclaim Corp., 190 F.3d 1350, 1356 (Fed. Cir. 1999) (claim term "discharge rate" construed in light of the use of the same term in another limitation of the same claim).

Other claims of the patent in question, both asserted and unasserted, can also be valuable sources of enlightenment as to the meaning of a claim term. Vitronics, 90 F.3d at 1582. Because claim terms are normally used consistently throughout the patent, the usage of a term in one claim can often illuminate the meaning of the same term in other claims. See Rexnord Corp. v. Laitram Corp., 274 F.3d 1336, 1342 (Fed. Cir. 2001); CVI/Beta Ventures, Inc. v. Tura LP, 112 F.3d 1146, 1159 (Fed. Cir. 1997). Differences among claims can also be a useful guide in understanding the meaning of particular claim terms. See Laitram Corp. v. Rexnord, Inc., 939 F.2d 1533, 1538 (Fed. Cir. 1991). For example, the presence of a dependent claim that adds a particular limitation gives rise to a presumption that the limitation in question is not present in the independent claim. See Liebel-Flarsheim Co. v. Medrad, Inc., 358 F.3d 898, 910 (Fed. Cir. 2004).

2

The claims, of course, do not stand alone. Rather, they are part of "a fully integrated written instrument," Markman, 52 F.3d at 978, consisting principally of a specification that concludes with the claims. For that reason, claims "must be read in view of the specification, of which they are a part." Id. at 979. As we stated in Vitronics, the specification "is always highly relevant to the claim construction analysis. Usually, it is dispositive; it is the single best guide to the meaning of a disputed term." 90 F.3d at 1582.

This court and its predecessors have long emphasized the importance of the specification in claim construction. In Autogiro Co. of America v. United States, 384 F.2d 391, 397-98 (Ct. Cl. 1967), the Court of Claims characterized the specification as "a concordance for the claims," based on the statutory requirement that the specification "describe the manner and process of making and using" the patented invention. The Court of Customs and Patent Appeals made a similar point. See In re Fout, 675 F.2d 297, 300 (CCPA 1982) ("Claims must always be read in light of the specification. Here, the specification makes plain what the appellants did and did not invent . . . .").

Shortly after the creation of this court, Judge Rich wrote that "[t]he descriptive part of the specification aids in ascertaining the scope and meaning of the claims inasmuch as the words of the claims must be based on the description. The specification is, thus, the primary basis for construing the claims." Standard Oil Co. v. Am. Cyanamid Co., 774 F.2d 448, 452 (Fed. Cir. 1985). On numerous occasions since then, we have reaffirmed that point, stating that "[t]he best source for understanding a technical term is the specification from which it arose, informed, as needed, by the prosecution history." Multiform Dessicants, 133 F.3d at 1478; Metabolite Labs., Inc. v. Lab. Corp. of Am. Holdings, 370 F.3d 1354, 1360 (Fed. Cir. 2004) ("In most cases, the best source for discerning the proper context of claim terms is the patent specification wherein the patent applicant describes the invention."); see also, e.g., Kinik Co. v. Int'l Trade Comm'n, 362 F.3d 1359, 1365 (Fed. Cir. 2004) ("The words of patent claims have the meaning and scope with which they are used in the specification and the prosecution history."); Moba, B.V. v. Diamond Automation, Inc., 325 F.3d 1306, 1315 (Fed. Cir. 2003) ("[T]he best indicator of claim meaning is its usage in context as understood by one of skill in the art at the time of invention.").

That principle has a long pedigree in Supreme Court decisions as well. See Hogg v. Emerson, 47 U.S. (6 How.) 437, 482 (1848) (the specification is a "component part of the patent" and "is as much to be considered with the [letters patent] in construing them, as any paper referred to in a deed or other contract"); Bates v. Coe, 98 U.S. 31, 38 (1878) ("in case of doubt or ambiguity it is proper in all cases to refer back to the descriptive portions of the specification to aid in solving the doubt or in ascertaining the true intent and meaning of the language employed in the claims"); White v. Dunbar, 119 U.S. 47, 51 (1886) (specification is appropriately resorted to "for the purpose of better understanding the meaning of the claim"); Schriber-Schroth Co. v. Cleveland Trust Co., 311 U.S. 211, 217 (1940) ("The claims of a patent are always to be read or interpreted in light of its specifications."); United States v. Adams, 383 U.S. 39, 49 (1966) ("[I]t is fundamental that claims are to be construed in the light of the specifications and both are to be read with a view to ascertaining the invention.").

The importance of the specification in claim construction derives from its statutory role. The close kinship between the written description and the claims is enforced by the statutory requirement that the specification describe the claimed invention in "full, clear, concise, and exact terms." 35 U.S.C. § 112, para. 1; see Netword, LLC v. Centraal Corp., 242 F.3d 1347, 1352 (Fed. Cir. 2001) ("The claims are directed to the invention that is described in the specification; they do not have meaning removed from the context from which they arose."); see also Markman v. Westview Instruments, Inc., 517 U.S. 370, 389 (1996) ("[A claim] term can be defined only in a way that comports with the instrument as a whole."). In light of the statutory directive that the inventor provide a "full" and "exact" description of the claimed invention, the specification necessarily informs the proper construction of the claims. See Merck & Co. v. Teva Pharms. USA, Inc., 347 F.3d 1367, 1371 (Fed. Cir. 2003) ("A fundamental rule of claim construction is that terms in a patent document are construed with the meaning with which they are presented in the patent document. Thus claims must be construed so as to be consistent with the specification, of which they are a part.") (citations omitted). In Renishaw, this court summarized that point succinctly:

Ultimately, the interpretation to be given a term can only be determined and confirmed with a full understanding of what the inventors actually invented and intended to envelop with the claim. The construction that stays true to the claim language and most naturally aligns with the patent's description of the invention will be, in the end, the correct construction. 158 F.3d at 1250 (citations omitted).

Consistent with that general principle, our cases recognize that the specification may reveal a special definition given to a claim term by the patentee that differs from the meaning it would otherwise possess. In such cases, the inventor's lexicography governs. See CCS Fitness, Inc. v. Brunswick Corp., 288 F.3d 1359, 1366 (Fed. Cir. 2002). In other cases, the specification may reveal an intentional disclaimer, or disavowal, of claim scope by the inventor. In that instance as well, the inventor has dictated the correct claim scope, and the inventor's intention, as expressed in the specification, is regarded as dispositive. See SciMed Life Sys., Inc. v. Advanced Cardiovascular Sys., Inc., 242 F.3d 1337, 1343-44 (Fed. Cir. 2001).

The pertinence of the specification to claim construction is reinforced by the manner in which a patent is issued. The Patent and Trademark Office ("PTO") determines the scope of claims in patent applications not solely on the basis of the claim language, but upon giving claims their broadest reasonable construction "in light of the specification as it would be interpreted by one of ordinary skill in the art." In re Am. Acad. of Sci.

Tech. Ctr., 367 F.3d 1359, 1364 (Fed. Cir. 2004). Indeed, the rules of the PTO require that application claims must "conform to the invention as set forth in the remainder of the specification and the terms and phrases used in the claims must find clear support or antecedent basis in the description so that the meaning of the terms in the claims may be ascertainable by reference to the description." 37 C.F.R. § 1.75(d)(1). It is therefore entirely appropriate for a court, when conducting claim construction, to rely heavily on the written description for guidance as to the meaning of the claims.

3

In addition to consulting the specification, we have held that a court "should also consider the patent's prosecution history, if it is in evidence." Markman, 52 F.3d at 980; see also Graham v. John Deere Co., 383 U.S. 1, 33 (1966) ("[A]n invention is construed not only in the light of the claims, but also with reference to the file wrapper or prosecution history in the Patent Office."). The prosecution history, which we have designated as part of the "intrinsic evidence," consists of the complete record of the proceedings before the PTO and includes the prior art cited during the examination of the patent. Autogiro, 384 F.2d at 399. Like the specification, the prosecution history provides evidence of how the PTO and the inventor understood the patent. See Lemelson v. Gen. Mills, Inc., 968 F.2d 1202, 1206 (Fed. Cir. 1992). Furthermore, like the specification, the prosecution history was created by the patentee in attempting to explain and obtain the patent. Yet because the prosecution history represents an ongoing negotiation between the PTO and the applicant, rather than the final product of that negotiation, it often lacks the clarity of the specification and thus is less useful for claim construction purposes. See Inverness Med. Switz. GmbH v. Warner Lambert Co., 309 F.3d 1373, 1380-82 (Fed. Cir. 2002) (the ambiguity of the prosecution history made it less relevant to claim construction); Athletic Alternatives, Inc. v. Prince Mfg., Inc., 73 F.3d 1573, 1580 (Fed. Cir. 1996) (the ambiguity of the prosecution history made it "unhelpful as an interpretive resource" for claim construction). Nonetheless, the prosecution history can often inform the meaning of the claim language by demonstrating how the inventor understood the invention and whether the inventor limited the invention in the course of prosecution, making the claim scope narrower than 402 F.3d 1371, 1384 (Fed. Cir. 2005) ("The purpose of consulting the prosecution history in construing a claim is to 'exclude any interpretation that was disclaimed during prosecution.'"), , 844 F.2d 1576, 1580 (Fed. Cir. 1988); , 54 F.3d 1570, 1576 (Fed. Cir. 1995). it would otherwise be. Vitronics, 90 F.3d at 1582-83; see also Chimie v. PPG Indus., Inc.quoting ZMI Corp. v. Cardiac Resuscitator Corp.Southwall Techs., Inc. v. Cardinal IG Co.

C

Although we have emphasized the importance of intrinsic evidence in claim construction, we have also authorized district courts to rely on extrinsic evidence, which "consists of all evidence external to the patent and prosecution history, including expert and inventor testimony, dictionaries, and learned treatises." Markman, 52 F.3d at 980, citing Seymour v. Osborne, 78 U.S. (11 Wall.) 516, 546 (1870); see also Vitronics, 90 F.3d at 1583. However, while extrinsic evidence "can shed useful light on the relevant art," we have explained that it is "less significant than the intrinsic record in determining 'the legally operative meaning of claim language.'" C.R. Bard, Inc. v. U.S. Surgical Corp., 388 F.3d 858, 862 (Fed. Cir. 2004), quoting Vanderlande Indus. Nederland BV v. Int'l Trade Comm'n, 366 F.3d 1311, 1318 (Fed. Cir. 2004); see also Astrazeneca AB v. Mutual Pharm. Co., 384 F.3d 1333, 1337 (Fed. Cir. 2004).

Within the class of extrinsic evidence, the court has observed that dictionaries and treatises can be useful in claim construction. See Renishaw, 158 F.3d at 1250; Rexnord, 274 F.3d at 1344. We have especially noted the help that technical dictionaries may provide to a court "to better understand the underlying technology" and the way in which one of skill in the art might use the claim terms. Vitronics, 90 F.3d at 1584 n.6. Because dictionaries, and especially technical dictionaries, endeavor to collect the accepted meanings of terms used in various fields of science and technology, those resources have been properly recognized as among the many tools that can assist the court in determining the meaning of particular terminology to those of skill in the art of the invention. See Teleflex, Inc. v. Ficosa N. Am. Corp., 299 F.3d 1313, 1325 (Fed. Cir. 2002). Such evidence, we have held, may be considered if the court deems it helpful in determining "the true meaning of language used in the patent claims." Markman, 52 F.3d at 980.

We have also held that extrinsic evidence in the form of expert testimony can be useful to a court for a variety of purposes, such as to provide background on the technology at issue, to explain how an invention works, to ensure that the court's understanding of the technical aspects of the patent is consistent with that of a person of skill in the art, or to establish that a particular term in the patent or the prior art has a particular meaning in the pertinent field. See Pitney Bowes, Inc. v. Hewlett-Packard Co., 182 F.3d 1298, 1308-09 (Fed. Cir. 1999); Key Pharms. v. Hercon Labs. Corp., 161 F.3d 709, 716 (Fed. Cir. 1998). However, conclusory, unsupported assertions by experts as to the definition of a claim term are not useful to a court. Similarly, a court should discount any expert testimony "that is clearly at odds with the claim construction mandated by the claims themselves, the written description, and the prosecution history, in other words, with the written record of the patent." Key Pharms., 161 F.3d at 716.

We have viewed extrinsic evidence in general as less reliable than the patent and its prosecution history in determining how to read claim terms, for several reasons. First, extrinsic evidence by definition is not part of the patent and does not have the specification's virtue of being created at the time of patent prosecution for the purpose of explaining the patent's scope and meaning. Second, while claims are construed as they would be understood by a hypothetical person of skill in the art, extrinsic publications may not be written by or for skilled artisans and therefore may not reflect the understanding of a skilled artisan in the field of the patent. Third, extrinsic evidence consisting of expert reports and testimony is generated at the time of and for the purpose of litigation and thus can suffer from bias that is not present in intrinsic evidence. The effect of that bias can be exacerbated if the expert is not one of skill in the relevant art or if the expert's opinion is offered in a form that is not subject to cross-examination. See Senmed, Inc. v. Richard-Allan Med. Indus., Inc., 888 F.2d 815, 819 n.8 (Fed. Cir. 1989). Fourth, there is a virtually unbounded universe of potential extrinsic evidence of some marginal relevance that could be brought to bear on any claim construction question. In the course of litigation, each party will naturally choose the pieces of extrinsic evidence most favorable to its cause, leaving the court with the considerable task of filtering the useful extrinsic evidence from the fluff. See Daubert v. Merrell Dow Pharms., Inc., 509 U.S. 579, 595 (1993) ("Expert evidence can be both powerful and quite misleading because of the difficulty in evaluating it."). Finally, undue reliance on extrinsic evidence poses the risk that it will be used to change the meaning of claims in derogation of the "indisputable public records consisting of the claims, the specification and the prosecution history," thereby undermining the public notice function of patents. Southwall Techs., 54 F.3d at 1578.

In sum, extrinsic evidence may be useful to the court, but it is unlikely to result in a reliable interpretation of patent claim scope unless considered in the context of the intrinsic evidence. Nonetheless, because extrinsic evidence can help educate the court regarding the field of the invention and can help the court determine what a person of ordinary skill in the art would understand claim terms to mean, it is permissible for the district court in its sound discretion to admit and use such evidence. In exercising that discretion, and in weighing all the evidence bearing on claim construction, the court should keep in mind the flaws inherent in each type of evidence and assess that evidence accordingly.

III

Although the principles outlined above have been articulated on numerous occasions, some of this court's cases have suggested a somewhat different approach to claim construction, in which the court has given greater emphasis to dictionary definitions of claim terms and has assigned a less prominent role to the specification and the prosecution history. The leading case in this line is Texas Digital Systems, Inc. v. Telegenix, Inc., 308 F.3d 1193 (Fed. Cir. 2002).

A

In Texas Digital, the court noted that "dictionaries, encyclopedias and treatises are particularly useful resources to assist the court in determining the ordinary and customary meanings of claim terms." 308 F.3d at 1202. Those texts, the court explained, are "objective resources that serve as reliable sources of information on the established meanings that would have been attributed to the terms of the claims by those of skill in the art," and they "deserve no less fealty in the context of claim construction" than in any other area of law. Id. at 1203. The court added that because words often have multiple dictionary meanings, the intrinsic record must be consulted to determine which of the different possible dictionary meanings is most consistent with the use of the term in question by the inventor. If more than one dictionary definition is consistent with the use of the words in the intrinsic record, the court stated, "the claim terms may be construed to encompass all such consistent meanings." Id.

The Texas Digital court further explained that the patent's specification and prosecution history must be consulted to determine if the patentee has used "the words [of the claim] in a manner clearly inconsistent with the ordinary meaning reflected, for example, in a dictionary definition." 308 F.3d at 1204. The court identified two circumstances in which such an inconsistency may be found. First, the court stated, "the presumption in favor of a dictionary definition will be overcome where the patentee, acting as his or her own lexicographer, has clearly set forth an explicit definition of the term different from its ordinary meaning." Id. Second, "the presumption also will be rebutted if the inventor has disavowed or disclaimed scope of coverage, by using words or expressions of manifest exclusion or restriction, representing a clear disavowal of claim scope." Id.

The Texas Digital court explained that it advanced the methodology set forth in that opinion in an effort to combat what this court has termed "one of the cardinal sins of patent law—reading a limitation from the written description into the claims," SciMed Life Sys., 242 F.3d at 1340. The court concluded that it is improper to consult "the written description and prosecution history as a threshold step in the claim construction process, before any effort is made to discern the ordinary and customary meanings attributed to the words themselves." Texas Digital, 308 F.3d at 1204. To do so, the court reasoned, "invites a violation of our precedent counseling against importing limitations into the claims." Id. Summarizing its analysis, the Texas Digital court stated:

By examining relevant dictionaries, encyclopedias, and treatises to ascertain possible meanings that would have been attributed to the words of the claims by those skilled in the art, and by further utilizing the intrinsic record to select from those possible meanings the one or ones most consistent with the use of the words by the inventor, the full breadth of the limitations intended by the inventor will be more accurately determined and the improper importation of unintended limitations from the written description into the claims will be more easily avoided. Id. at 1205.

B

Although the concern expressed by the court in Texas Digital was valid, the methodology it adopted placed too much reliance on extrinsic sources such as dictionaries, treatises, and encyclopedias and too little on intrinsic sources, in particular the specification and prosecution history. While the court noted that the specification must be consulted in every case, it suggested a methodology for claim interpretation in which the specification should be consulted only after a determination is made, whether based on a dictionary, treatise, or other source, as to the ordinary meaning or meanings of the claim term in dispute. Even then, recourse to the specification is limited to determining whether the specification excludes one of the meanings derived from the dictionary, whether the presumption in favor of the dictionary definition of the claim term has been overcome by "an explicit definition of the term different from its ordinary meaning," or whether the inventor "has disavowed or disclaimed scope of coverage, by using words or expressions of manifest exclusion or restriction, representing a clear disavowal of claim scope." 308 F.3d at 1204. In effect, the Texas Digital approach limits the role of the specification in claim construction to serving as a check on the dictionary meaning of a claim term if the specification requires the court to conclude that fewer than all the dictionary definitions apply, or if the specification contains a sufficiently specific alternative definition or disavowal. See, e.g., Texas Digital, 308 F.3d at 1202 ("unless compelled otherwise, a court will give a claim term the full range of its ordinary meaning"); Nystrom v. TREX Co., 374 F.3d 1105, 1111-13 (Fed. Cir. 2004) (ascertaining the "full range" of the ordinary meaning of the term "board" through a collection of dictionary definitions, and stating that those candidate definitions should be removed from consideration only if they were "disclaimed" in the written description or prosecution history); Inverness Med. Switz., 309 F.3d at 1379 (claim should be construed to encompass multiple dictionary meanings unless "the specification or prosecution history clearly demonstrates that only one of the multiple meanings was intended"). That approach, in our view, improperly restricts the role of the specification in claim construction.

Assigning such a limited role to the specification, and in particular requiring that any definition of claim language in the specification be express, is inconsistent with our rulings that the specification is "the single best guide to the meaning of a disputed term," and that the specification "acts as a dictionary when it expressly defines terms used in the claims or when it defines terms by implication." Vitronics, 90 F.3d at 1582; Irdeto Access, Inc. v. Echostar Satellite Corp., 383 F.3d 1295, 1300 (Fed. Cir. 2004) ("Even when guidance is not provided in explicit definitional format, the specification may define claim terms by implication such that the meaning may be found in or ascertained by a reading of the patent documents.") (citations omitted); Novartis Pharms. Corp. v. Abbott Labs., 375 F.3d 1328, 1334-35 (Fed. Cir. 2004) (same); Bell Atl. Network Servs., Inc. v. Covad Communications Group, Inc., 262 F.3d 1258, 1268 (Fed. Cir. 2001) ("[A] claim term may be clearly redefined without an explicit statement of redefinition.").

The main problem with elevating the dictionary to such prominence is that it focuses the inquiry on the abstract meaning of words rather than on the meaning of claim terms within the context of the patent. Properly viewed, the "ordinary meaning" of a claim term is its meaning to the ordinary artisan after reading the entire patent. Yet heavy reliance on the dictionary divorced from the intrinsic evidence risks transforming the meaning of the claim term to the artisan into the meaning of the term in the abstract, out of its particular context, which is the specification. The patent system is based on the proposition that claims cover only the invented subject matter. As the Supreme Court has stated, "[i]t seems to us that nothing can be more just and fair, both to the patentee and the public, than that the former should understand, and correctly describe, just what he has invented, and for what he claims a patent." Merrill v. Yeomans, 94 U.S. at 573-74. The use of a dictionary definition can conflict with that directive because the patent applicant did not create the dictionary to describe the invention. Thus, there may be a disconnect between the patentee's responsibility to describe and claim his invention, and the dictionary editors' objective of aggregating all possible definitions for particular words.

Although the Texas Digital line of cases permit the dictionary definition to be narrowed in some circumstances even when there is not an explicit disclaimer or redefinition in the specification, too often that line of cases has been improperly relied upon to condone the adoption of a dictionary definition entirely divorced from the context of the written description. The problem is that if the district court starts with the broad dictionary definition in every case and fails to fully appreciate how the specification implicitly limits that definition, the error will systematically cause the construction of the claim to be unduly expansive. The risk of systematic overbreadth is greatly reduced if the court instead focuses at the outset on how the patentee used the claim term in the claims, specification, and prosecution history, rather than starting with a broad definition and whittling it down.

Dictionaries, by their nature, provide an expansive array of definitions. General dictionaries, in particular, strive to collect all uses of particular words, from the common to the obscure. By design, general dictionaries collect the definitions of a term as used not only in a particular art field, but in many different settings. In such circumstances, it is inevitable that the multiple dictionary definitions for a term will extend beyond the "construction of the patent [that] is confirmed by the avowed understanding of the patentee, expressed by him, or on his behalf, when his application for the original patent was pending." Goodyear Dental Vulcanite Co. v. Davis, 102 U.S. 222, 227 (1880). Thus, the use of the dictionary may extend patent protection beyond what should properly be afforded by the inventor's patent. See Smith v. Snow, 294 U.S. 1, 14 (1935) ("if the claim were fairly susceptible of two constructions, that should be adopted which will secure to the patentee his actual invention") (emphasis added). For that reason, we have stated that "a general-usage dictionary cannot overcome art-specific evidence of the meaning" of a claim term. Vanderlande Indus. Nederland, 366 F.3d at 1321; see also Renishaw, 158 F.3d at 1250, quoting Liebscher v. Boothroyd, 258 F.2d 948, 951 (CCPA 1958) ("Indiscriminate reliance on definitions found in dictionaries can often produce absurd results. . . . One need not arbitrarily pick and choose from the various accepted definitions of a word to decide which meaning was intended as the word is used in a given claim. The subject matter, the context, etc., will more often than not lead to the correct conclusion.").

Even technical dictionaries or treatises, under certain circumstances, may suffer from some of these deficiencies. There is no guarantee that a term is used in the same way in a treatise as it would be by the patentee. In fact, discrepancies between the patent and treatises are apt to be common because the patent by its nature describes something novel. See Autogiro, 384 F.2d at 397 ("Often the invention is novel and words do not exist to describe it. The dictionary does not always keep abreast of the inventor. It cannot.").

Moreover, different dictionaries may contain somewhat different sets of definitions for the same words. A claim should not rise or fall based upon the preferences of a particular dictionary editor, or the court's independent decision, uninformed by the specification, to rely on one dictionary rather than another. Finally, the authors of dictionaries or treatises may simplify ideas to communicate them most effectively to the public and may thus choose a meaning that is not pertinent to the understanding of particular claim language. See generally Ellen P. Aprill, The Law of the Word: Dictionary Shopping in the Supreme Court, 30 Ariz. St. L.J. 275, 293-314 (1998). The resulting definitions therefore do not necessarily reflect the inventor's goal of distinctly setting forth his invention as a person of ordinary skill in that particular art would understand it.

As we have noted above, however, we do not intend to preclude the appropriate use of dictionaries. Dictionaries or comparable sources are often useful to assist in understanding the commonly understood meaning of words and have been used both by our court and the Supreme Court in claim interpretation. See Exhibit Supply Co. v. Ace Patents Corp., 315 U.S. 126, 134 (1942) (relying on dictionaries to construe the claim term "embedded"); Weber Elec. Co. v. E.H. Freeman Elec. Co., 256 U.S. 668, 678 (1921) (approving circuit court's use of dictionary definitions to define claim terms); Renishaw, 158 F.3d at 1247-53 (approving the use of dictionaries with proper respect for the role of intrinsic evidence). A dictionary definition has the value of being an unbiased source "accessible to the public in advance of litigation." Vitronics, 90 F.3d at 1585. As we said in Vitronics, judges are free to consult dictionaries and technical treatises at any time in order to better understand the underlying technology and may also rely on dictionary definitions when construing claim terms, so long as the dictionary definition does contradict any definition found in or ascertained by a reading of the patent documents. Id. at 1584 n.6.

We also acknowledge that the purpose underlying the Texas Digital line of cases—to avoid the danger of reading limitations from the specification into the claim—is sound. Moreover, we recognize that the distinction between using the specification to interpret the meaning of a claim and importing limitations from the specification into the claim can be a difficult one to apply in practice. See Comark Communications, Inc. v. Harris Corp., 156 F.3d 1182, 1186-87 (Fed. Cir. 1998) ("there is sometimes a fine line between reading a claim in light of the specification, and reading a limitation into the claim from the specification"). However, the line between construing terms and importing limitations can be discerned with reasonable certainty and predictability if the court's focus remains on understanding how a person of ordinary skill in the art would understand the claim terms. For instance, although the specification often describes very specific embodiments of the invention, we have repeatedly warned against confining the claims to those embodiments. See, e.g., Nazomi Communications, Inc. v. ARM Holdings, PLC, 403 F.3d 1364, 1369 (Fed. Cir. 2005) (claims may embrace "different subject matter than is illustrated in the specific embodiments in the specification"); Liebel-Flarsheim, 358 F.3d at 906-08; Teleflex, 299 F.3d at 1327; SRI Int'l v. Matsushita Elec. Corp. of Am., 775 F.2d 1107, 1121 (Fed. Cir. 1985). In particular, we have expressly rejected the contention that if a patent describes only a single embodiment, the claims of the patent must be construed as being limited to that embodiment. Gemstar-TV Guide, 383 F.3d at 1366. That is not just because section 112 of the Patent Act requires that the claims themselves set forth the limits of the patent grant, but also because persons of ordinary skill in the art rarely would confine their definitions of terms to the exact representations depicted in the embodiments.

To avoid importing limitations from the specification into the claims, it is important to keep in mind that the purposes of the specification are to teach and enable those of skill in the art to make and use the invention and to provide a best mode for doing so. See Spectra-Physics, Inc. v. Coherent, Inc., 827 F.2d 1524, 1533 (Fed. Cir. 1987). One of the best ways to teach a person of ordinary skill in the art how to make and use the invention is to provide an example of how to practice the invention in a particular case. Much of the time, upon reading the specification in that context, it will become clear whether the patentee is setting out specific examples of the invention to accomplish those goals, or whether the patentee instead intends for the claims and the embodiments in the specification to be strictly coextensive. See SciMed Life Sys., 242 F.3d at 1341. The manner in which the patentee uses a term within the specification and claims usually will make the distinction apparent. See Snow v. Lake Shore & M.S. Ry. Co., 121 U.S. 617, 630 (1887) (it was clear from the specification that there was "nothing in the context to indicate that the patentee contemplated any alternative" embodiment to the one presented).

In the end, there will still remain some cases in which it will be hard to determine whether a person of skill in the art would understand the embodiments to define the outer limits of the claim term or merely to be exemplary in nature. While that task may present difficulties in some cases, we nonetheless believe that attempting to resolve that problem in the context of the particular patent is likely to capture the scope of the actual invention more accurately than either strictly limiting the scope of the claims to the embodiments disclosed in the specification or divorcing the claim language from the specification.

In Vitronics, this court grappled with the same problem and set forth guidelines for reaching the correct claim construction and not imposing improper limitations on claims. 90 F.3d at 1582. The underlying goal of our decision in Vitronics was to increase the likelihood that a court will comprehend how a person of ordinary skill in the art would understand the claim terms. See id. at 1584. In that process, we recognized that there is no magic formula or catechism for conducting claim construction. Nor is the court barred from considering any particular sources or required to analyze sources in any specific sequence, as long as those sources are not used to contradict claim, and in . We now turn to the application of those principles to the case at bar. meaning that is unambiguous in light of the intrinsic evidence. See id. at 1583-84; Intel Corp. v. VIA Techs., Inc., 319 F.3d 1357, 1367 (Fed. Cir. 2003). For example, a judge who encounters a claim term while reading a patent might consult a general purpose or specialized dictionary to begin to understand the meaning of the term, before reviewing the remainder of the patent to determine how the patentee has used the term. The sequence of steps used by the judge in consulting various sources is not important; what matters is for the court to attach the appropriate weight to be assigned to those sources in light of the statutes and policies that inform patent law. Vitronics, 90 F.3d at 1582. In Vitronics, we did not attempt to provide a rigid algorithm for claim construction, but simply attempted to explain why, in general, certain types of evidence are more valuable than others. Today, we adhere to that approach and reaffirm the approach to claim construction outlined in that case, in MarkmanInnova

IV

A

The critical language of claim 1 of the '798 patent—"further means disposed inside the shell for increasing its load bearing capacity comprising internal steel baffles extending inwardly from the steel shell walls"—imposes three clear requirements with respect to the baffles. First, the baffles must be made of steel. Second, they must be part of the load-bearing means for the wall section. Third, they must be pointed inward from the walls. Both parties, stipulating to a dictionary definition, also conceded that the term "baffles" refers to objects that check, impede, or obstruct the flow of something. The intrinsic evidence confirms that a person of skill in the art would understand that the term "baffles," as used in the '798 patent, would have that generic meaning.

The other claims of the '798 patent specify particular functions to be served by the baffles. For example, dependent claim 2 states that the baffles may be "oriented with the panel sections disposed at angles for deflecting projectiles such as bullets able to penetrate the steel plates." The inclusion of such a specific limitation on the term "baffles" in claim 2 makes it likely that the patentee did not contemplate that the term "baffles" already contained that limitation. See Dow Chem. Co. v. United States, 226 F.3d 1334, 1341-42 (Fed. Cir. 2000) (concluding that an independent claim should be given broader scope than a dependent claim to avoid rendering the dependent claim redundant). Independent claim 17 further supports that proposition. It states that baffles are placed "projecting inwardly from the outer shell at angles tending to deflect projectiles that penetrate the outer shell." That limitation would be unnecessary if persons of skill in the art understood that the baffles inherently served such a function. See TurboCare, 264 F.3d at 1123 (claim terms should not be read to contain a limitation "where another claim restricts the invention in exactly the [same] manner"). Dependent claim 6 provides an additional requirement for the baffles, stating that "the internal baffles of both outer panel sections overlap and interlock at angles providing deflector panels extending from one end of the module to the other." If the baffles recited in claim 1 were inherently placed at specific angles, or interlocked to form an intermediate barrier, claim 6 would be redundant.

The specification further supports the conclusion that persons of ordinary skill in the art would understand the baffles recited in the '798 patent to be load-bearing objects, 999 F.2d 1557, 1561 (Fed. Cir. 1993). that serve to check, impede, or obstruct flow. At several points, the specification discusses positioning the baffles so as to deflect projectiles. See '798 patent, col. 2, ll. 13-15; id., col. 5, ll. 17-19. The patent states that one advantage of the invention over the prior art is that "[t]here have not been effective ways of dealing with these powerful impact weapons with inexpensive housing." Id., col. 3, ll. 28-30. While that statement makes clear the invention envisions baffles that serve that function, it does not imply that in order to qualify as baffles within the meaning of the claims, the internal support structures must serve the projectile-deflecting function in all the embodiments of all the claims. The specification must teach and enable all the claims, and the section of the written description discussing the use of baffles to deflect projectiles serves that purpose for claims 2, 6, 17, and 23, which specifically claim baffles that deflect projectiles. See In re Wright

The specification discusses several other purposes served by the baffles. For example, the baffles are described as providing structural support. The patent states that one way to increase load-bearing capacity is to use "at least in part inwardly directed steel baffles 15, 16." '798 patent, col. 4, ll. 14-15. The baffle 16 is described as a "strengthening triangular baffle." Id., col. 4, line 37. Importantly, Figures 4 and 6 do not show the baffles as part of an "intermediate interlocking, but not solid, internal barrier." In those figures, the baffle 16 simply provides structural support for one of the walls, as depicted below:

Other uses for the baffles are listed in the specification as well. In Figure 7, the overlapping flanges "provide for overlapping and interlocking the baffles to produce substantially an intermediate barrier wall between the opposite [wall] faces":

'798 patent, col. 5, ll. 26-29. Those baffles thus create small compartments that can be filled with either sound and thermal insulation or rock and gravel to stop projectiles. Id., col. 5, ll. 29-34. By separating the interwall area into compartments (see, e.g., compartment 55 in Figure 7), the user of the modules can choose different types of material for each compartment, so that the module can be "easily custom tailored for the specific needs of each installation." Id., col. 5, ll. 36-37. When material is placed into the wall during installation, the baffles obstruct the flow of material from one compartment to another so that this "custom tailoring" is possible.

The fact that the written description of the '798 patent sets forth multiple objectives to be served by the baffles recited in the claims confirms that the term "baffles" should not be read restrictively to require that the baffles in each case serve all of the recited functions. We have held that "[t]he fact that a patent asserts that an invention achieves several objectives does not require that each of the claims be construed as limited to structures that are capable of achieving all of the objectives." Liebel-Flarsheim, 358 F.3d at 908; see also Resonate Inc. v. Alteon Websystems, Inc., 338 F.3d 1360, 1367 (Fed. Cir. 2003). Although deflecting projectiles is one of the advantages of the baffles of the '798 patent, the patent does not require that the inward extending structures always be capable of performing that function. Accordingly, we conclude that a person of skill in the art would not interpret the disclosure and claims of the '798 patent to mean that a structure extending inward from one of the wall faces is a "baffle" if it is at an acute or obtuse angle, but is not a "baffle" if it is disposed at a right angle.

B

Invoking the principle that "claims should be so construed, if possible, as to sustain their validity," Rhine v. Casio, Inc., 183 F.3d 1342, 1345 (Fed Cir. 1999), AWH argues that the term "baffles" should be given a restrictive meaning because if the term is not construed restrictively, the asserted claims would be invalid.

While we have acknowledged the maxim that claims should be construed to preserve their validity, we have not applied that principle broadly, and we have certainly not endorsed a regime in which validity analysis is a regular component of claim construction. See Nazomi Communications, 403 F.3d at 1368-69. Instead, we have limited the maxim to cases in which "the court concludes, after applying all the available tools of claim construction, that the claim is still ambiguous." Liebel-Flarsheim, 358 F.3d at 911; see also Generation II Orthonics Inc. v. Med. Tech. Inc., 263 F.3d 1356, 1365 (Fed. Cir. 2001) ("[C]laims can only be construed to preserve their validity where the proposed claim construction is 'practicable,' is based on sound claim construction principles, and does not revise or ignore the explicit language of the claims."); Elekta Instrument S.A. v. O.U.R. Scientific Int'l, Inc., 214 F.3d 1302, 1309 (Fed. Cir. 2000) ("having concluded that the amended claim is susceptible of only one reasonable construction, we cannot construe the claim differently from its plain meaning in order to preserve its validity"); E.I. du Pont de Nemours & Co. v. Phillips Petroleum Co., 849 F.2d 1430, 1434 (Fed. Cir. 1988) (rejecting argument that limitations should be added to claims to preserve the validity of the claims). In such cases, we have looked to whether it is reasonable to infer that the PTO would not have issued an invalid patent, and that the ambiguity in the claim language should therefore be resolved in a manner that would preserve the patent's validity.

That is the rationale that gave rise to the maxim in the first place. In Klein v. Russell, 86 U.S. (19 Wall.) 433, 466 (1873), the owner of a reissued patent argued for a narrow construction of the patent, while the accused infringer argued for a broader construction. The Court noted that the law "required that the reissue should be for the same invention as the original patent." Id. Because the reissue, which was granted under the predecessor to 35 U.S.C. § 251, would have been improper under the broader construction, the Court "presumed the Commissioner did his duty" and did not issue an invalid patent. For that reason, among others, the Court construed the disputed claim language in a manner that "sustain[ed] the patent and the construction claimed by the patentee," since that "can be done consistently with the language which he has employed." Id. The applicability of the doctrine in a particular case therefore depends on the strength of the inference that the PTO would have recognized that one claim interpretation would render the claim invalid, and that the PTO would not have issued the patent assuming that to be the proper construction of the term.

In this case, unlike in Klein and other cases in which the doctrine of construing claims to preserve their validity has been invoked, the claim term at issue is not ambiguous. Thus, it can be construed without the need to consider whether one possible construction would render the claim invalid while the other would not. The doctrine of construing claims to preserve their validity, a doctrine of limited utility in any event, therefore has no applicability here.

In sum, we reject AWH's arguments in favor of a restrictive definition of the term "baffles." Because we disagree with the district court's claim construction, we reverse the summary judgment of noninfringement. In light of our decision on claim construction, it is necessary to remand the infringement claims to the district court for further proceedings.

V

With respect to Mr. Phillips's allegation of misappropriation of trade secrets, we agree with the panel's decision upholding the district court's ruling on that issue, in which the district court dismissed the trade secret claim on statute of limitations grounds. See Phillips, 363 F.3d at 1214-1216. Accordingly, based on the panel's disposition of that issue, we affirm the district court's dismissal of the trade secret claim. With respect to AWH's cross-appeal, we also agree with the panel's reasoning and its conclusion that the cross-appeal is improper. See id. at 1216. We therefore dismiss the cross-appeal.

VI

In our order granting rehearing en banc, we asked the parties to brief various questions, including the following: "Consistent with the Supreme Court's decision in Markman v. Westview Instruments, 517 U.S. 370 (1996), and our en banc decision in Cybor Corp. v. FAS Technologies, Inc., 138 F.3d 1448 (Fed. Cir. 1998), is it appropriate for this court to accord any deference to any aspect of trial court claim construction rulings? If so, on what aspects, in what circumstances, and to what extent?" After consideration of the matter, we have decided not to address that issue at this time. We therefore leave undisturbed our prior en banc decision in Cybor.

Each party shall bear its own costs for this appeal.

AFFIRMED IN PART, REVERSED IN PART, DISMISSED IN PART, and REMANDED.

Courtesy of David A. Allgeyer, Lindquist & Vennum PLLP

APPENDIX J

IN RE SEAGATE TECHNOLOGY, LLC

United States Court of Appeals for the Federal Circuit

Miscellaneous Docket No. 830

IN RE SEAGATE TECHNOLOGY, LLC,
Petitioner.

DECIDED: August 20, 2007

Before NEWMAN, MAYER, LOURIE, RADER, SCHALL, BRYSON, GAJARSA, LINN, DYK, and PROST, Circuit Judges.

* Chief Judge Michel and Circuit Judge Moore took no part in the consideration of the merits of this case.

Opinion for the court filed by Circuit Judge MAYER, in which Circuit Judges NEWMAN, LOURIE, RADER, SCHALL, BRYSON, GAJARSA, LINN, DYK, and PROST join.

Concurring opinion filed by Circuit Judge GAJARSA, in which Circuit Judge NEWMAN joins. Concurring opinion filed by Circuit Judge NEWMAN.

MAYER, Circuit Judge.

Seagate Technology, LLC ("Seagate") petitions for a writ of mandamus directing the United States District Court for the Southern District of New York to vacate its orders compelling disclosure of materials and testimony that Seagate claims is covered by the attorney-client privilege and work product protection. We ordered en banc review, and now grant the petition. We overrule Underwater Devices Inc. v. Morrison-Knudsen Co., 717 F.2d 1380 (1983), and we clarify the scope of the waiver of attorney-client privilege and work product protection that results when an accused patent infringer asserts an advice of counsel defense to a charge of willful infringement.

Background

Convolve, Inc. and the Massachusetts Institute of Technology (collectively "Convolve") sued Seagate on July 13, 2000, alleging infringement of U.S. Patent Nos. 4,916,635 ("the '635 patent") and 5,638,267 ("the '267 patent"). Subsequently, U.S. Patent No. 6,314,473 ("the '473 patent") issued on November 6, 2001, and Convolve amended its complaint on January 25, 2002, to assert infringement of the '473 patent. Convolve also alleged that Seagate willfully infringed the patents.

Prior to the lawsuit, Seagate retained Gerald Sekimura to provide an opinion concerning Convolve's patents, and he ultimately prepared three written opinions.

Seagate received the first opinion on July 24, 2000, shortly after the complaint was filed.

This opinion analyzed the '635 and '267 patents and concluded that many claims were invalid and that Seagate's products did not infringe. The opinion also considered Convolve's pending International Application WO 99/45535 ("the '535 application"), which recited technology similar to that disclosed in the yet-to-be-issued '473 patent.

On December 29, 2000, Sekimura provided an updated opinion to Seagate. In addition to his previous conclusions, this opinion concluded that the '267 patent was possibly unenforceable. Both opinions noted that not all of the patent claims had been reviewed, and that the '535 application required further analysis, which Sekimura recommended postponing until a U.S. patent issued. On February 21, 2003, Seagate received a third opinion concerning the validity and infringement of the by-then-issued '473 patent.

There is no dispute that Seagate's opinion counsel operated separately and independently of trial counsel at all times.

In early 2003, pursuant to the trial court's scheduling order, Seagate notified Convolve of its intent to rely on Sekimura's three opinion letters in defending against willful infringement, and it disclosed all of his work product and made him available for deposition. Convolve then moved to compel discovery of any communications and work product of Seagate's other counsel, including its trial counsel.[8]

On May 28, 2004, the trial court concluded that Seagate waived the attorney-client privilege for all communications between it and any counsel, including its trial attorneys and in-house counsel,[9] concerning the subject matter of Sekimura's opinions, i.e., infringement, invalidity, and enforceability. It further determined that the waiver began when Seagate first gained knowledge of the patents and would last until the alleged infringement ceased. Accordingly, the court ordered production of any requested documents and testimony concerning the subject matter of Sekimura's opinions. It provided for in camera review of documents relating to trial strategy, but said that any advice from trial counsel that undermined the reasonableness of relying on Sekimura's opinions would warrant disclosure. The court also determined that protection of work product communicated to Seagate was waived.

Based on these rulings, Convolve sought production of trial counsel opinions relating to infringement, invalidity, and enforceability of the patents, and also noticed depositions of Seagate's trial counsel. After the

---

[8] Specifically, Convolve sought to obtain the following: internal communications on the same subjects as the formal [Sekimura] opinions, communications between Seagate and any attorneys on the same subjects as the formal opinions, documents reflecting outside counsel's opinion as to the same subjects of the formal opinions, documents reviewed or considered, or forming the basis for outside counsel's opinion as to the subject matter of the formal opinions, and documents reflecting when oral communications concerning the subjects of the opinions occurred between Compaq and outside counsel. Convolve, Inc. v. Compaq Comp. Corp., 224 F.R.D. 98, 101(S.D.N.Y. 2004).

[9] We do not address the trial court's discovery orders pertaining to Seagate's in-house counsel. The questions presented for en banc review do not encompass this issue. See Kirkendall v. Dep't of the Army, 479 F.3d 830, 835 n.2 (Fed. Cir. 2007) (en banc) ("As a general rule, the scope of our en banc review is limited to the issues set out in the en banc order."). That is not remarkable because Seagate's petition sought relief only as to trial counsel. Moreover, the nature and role of in-house counsel in this litigation is entirely unclear on the record before us. For the same reason, we do not address the separate opinion of Judge Gajarsa, post.

trial court denied Seagate's motion for a stay and certification of an interlocutory appeal, Seagate petitioned for a writ of mandamus.

We stayed the discovery orders and, recognizing the functional relationship between our willfulness jurisprudence and the practical dilemmas faced in the areas of attorney-client privilege and work product protection, sua sponte ordered en banc review of the petition. The en banc order set out the following questions:

1. Should a party's assertion of the advice of counsel defense to willful infringement extend waiver of the attorney-client privilege to communications with that party's trial counsel? See In re EchoStar Commc'n Corp., 448 F.3d 1294 (Fed. Cir. 2006).

2. What is the effect of any such waiver on work-product immunity?

3. Given the impact of the statutory duty of care standard announced in Underwater Devices, Inc. v. Morrison-Knudsen Co., 717 F.2d 1380 (Fed. Cir. 1983), on the issue of waiver of attorney-client privilege, should this court reconsider the decision in Underwater Devices and the duty of care standard itself? In re Seagate Tech., LLC, Misc. Docket No. 830 (Fed. Cir. Jan. 26, 2007).

Mandamus

A party seeking a writ of mandamus bears the burden of proving that it has no other means of attaining the relief desired, Mallard v. U.S. Dist. Court for the S. Dist. Of Iowa, 490 U.S. 296, 309 (1989), and that the right to issuance of the writ is "clear and indisputable," Allied Chem. Corp. v. Daiflon, Inc., 449 U.S. 33, 35 (1980). In appropriate cases, a writ of mandamus may issue "to prevent the wrongful exposure of privileged communications." In re Regents of the Univ. of Cal., 101 F.3d 1386, 1387 (Fed. Cir. 1996). Specifically, "mandamus review may be granted of discovery orders that turn on claims of privilege when (1) there is raised an important issue of first impression, (2) the privilege would be lost if review were denied until final judgment, and (3) immediate resolution would avoid the development of doctrine that would undermine the privilege." Id. at 1388. This case meets these criteria.

We review the trial court's determination of the scope of waiver for an abuse of discretion. In re Echostar Commc'ns. Corp., 448 F.3d 1294, 1300 (Fed. Cir. 2006); In re Pioneer Hi-Bred Int'l, Inc., 238 F.3d 1370, 1373 n.2 (Fed. Cir. 2001). Because willful infringement and the scope of waiver accompanying the advice of counsel defense invoke substantive patent law, we apply the law of this circuit. Echostar, 448 F.3d at 1298.

Discussion

Because patent infringement is a strict liability offense, the nature of the offense is only relevant in determining whether enhanced damages are warranted. Although a trial court's discretion in awarding enhanced damages has a long lineage in patent law,[10] the current statute, similar to its predecessors, is devoid of any standard for awarding them.[11]

Absent a statutory guide, we have held that an award of enhanced damages requires a showing of willful infringement. Beatrice Foods Co. v. New England Printing & Lithographing Co., 923 F.2d 1576, 1578 (Fed. Cir. 1991); see also Jurgens v. CBK, Ltd., 80 F.3d 1566, 1570 (Fed. Cir. 1996) (holding that bad faith infringement, which is a type of willful infringement, is required for enhanced damages). This well-established standard accords with Supreme Court precedent. See Aro Mfg. Co. v. Convertible Top

---

[10] Trial courts have had statutory discretion to enhance damages for patent infringement since 1836. 35 U.S.C. § 284 (2000); Act of Aug. 1, 1946, 60 Stat. 778; Patent Act of 1870, ch. 230, § 59, 16 Stat. 198, 207 (1870) (providing that "the court may enter judgment thereon for any sum above the amount found by the verdict as the actual damages sustained, according to the circumstances of the case, not exceeding three times the amount of such verdict, together with the costs"); Patent Act of 1836, ch. 357, 5 Stat. 117 (1836) (stating that "it shall be in the power of the court to render judgment for any sum above the amount found by such verdict . . . not exceeding three times the amount thereof, according to the circumstances of the case").

[11] The current statute, enacted in 1952 and codified at 35 U.S.C. § 284, provides: Upon finding for the claimant the court shall award the claimant damages adequate to compensate for the infringement, but in no event less than a reasonable royalty for the use made of the invention by the infringer, together with interest and costs as fixed by the court. When the damages are not found by a jury, the court shall assess them. In either event the court may increase the damages up to three times the amount found or assessed. Increased damages under this paragraph shall not apply to provisional rights under section 154(d) of this title. The court may receive expert testimony as an aid to the determination of damages or of what royalty would be reasonable under the circumstances.

Replacement Co., 377 U.S. 479, 508 (1961) (enhanced damages were available for willful or bad faith infringement); see also Dowling v. United States, 473 U.S. 207, 227 n.19 (1985) (enhanced damages are available for "willful infringement"); Seymour v. McCormick, 57 U.S. 480, 489 (1853) ("wanton or malicious" injury could result in exemplary damages). But, a finding of willfulness does not require an award of enhanced damages; it merely permits it. See 35 U.S.C. § 284; Odetics, Inc. v. Storage Tech. Corp., 185 F.3d 1259, 1274 (Fed. Cir. 1999); Jurgens, 80 F.3d at 1570.

This court fashioned a standard for evaluating willful infringement in Underwater Devices Inc. v. Morrison-Knudsen Co., 717 F.2d 1380, 1389-90 (Fed. Cir. 1983):

"Where . . . a potential infringer has actual notice of another's patent rights, he has an affirmative duty to exercise due care to determine whether or not he is infringing. Such an affirmative duty includes, inter alia, the duty to seek and obtain competent legal advice from counsel before the initiation of any possible infringing activity." (citations omitted). This standard was announced shortly after the creation of the court, and at a time "when widespread disregard of patent rights was undermining the national innovation incentive." Knorr-Bremse Systeme Fuer Nutzfahreuge GmbH v. Dana Corp., 383 F.3d 1337, 1343 (Fed. Cir. 2004) (en banc) (citing Advisory Committee on Industrial Innovation Final Report, Dep't of Commerce (Sep. 1979)). Indeed, in UnderwaterDevices, an attorney had advised the infringer that "[c]ourts, in recent years, have—in patent infringement cases—found [asserted patents] invalid in approximately 80% of the cases," and on that basis the attorney concluded that the patentee would not likely sue for infringement. 717 F.2d at 1385. Over time, our cases evolved to evaluate willfulness and its duty of due care under the totality of the circumstances, and we enumerated factors informing the inquiry. E.g., Read Corp. v. Portec, Inc., 970 F.2d 816, 826-27 (Fed. Cir. 1992); Rolls-Royce Ltd. v. GTE Valeron Corp., 800 F.2d 1101, 1110 (Fed. Cir. 1986).

In light of the duty of due care, accused willful infringers commonly assert an advice of counsel defense. Under this defense, an accused willful infringer aims to establish that due to reasonable reliance on advice from counsel, its continued accused activities were done in good faith. Typically, counsel's opinion concludes that the patent is invalid, unenforceable, and/or not infringed. Although an infringer's reliance on favorable advice of counsel, or conversely his failure to proffer any favorable advice, is not dispositive of the willfulness inquiry, it is crucial to the analysis. E.g., Electro Med. Sys., S.A. v. Cooper Life Scis., Inc., 34 F.3d 1048, 1056 (Fed. Cir. 1994) ("Possession of a favorable opinion of counsel is not essential to avoid a willfulness determination; it is only one factor to be considered, albeit an important one.").

Since Underwater Devices, we have recognized the practical concerns stemming from our willfulness doctrine, particularly as related to the attorney-client privilege and work product doctrine. For instance, Quantum Corp. v. Plus Development Corp., 940 F.2d 642, 643 (Fed. Cir. 1991), observed that "[p]roper resolution of the dilemma of an accused infringer who must choose between the lawful assertion of the attorney-client privilege and avoidance of a willfulness finding if infringement is found, is of great importance not only to the parties but to the fundamental values sought to be preserved by the attorney-client privilege." We cautioned there that an accused infringer "should not, without the trial court's careful consideration, be forced to choose between waiving the privilege in order to protect itself from a willfulness finding, in which case it may risk prejudicing itself on the question of liability, and maintaining the privilege, in which case it may risk being found to be a willful infringer if liability is found." Id. at 643-44. We advised that in camera review and bifurcating trials in appropriate cases would alleviate these concerns. Id. However, such procedures are often considered too onerous to be regularly employed.

Recently, in Knorr-Bremse, we addressed another outgrowth of our willfulness doctrine. Over the years, we had held that an accused infringer's failure to produce advice from counsel "would warrant the conclusion that it either obtained no advice of counsel or did so and was advised that its [activities] would be an infringement of valid U.S. Patents." Knorr-Bremse, 383 F.3d at 1343 (quoting Kloster Speedsteel AB v. Crucible Inc., 793 F.2d 1565, 1580 (Fed. Cir. 1986)). Recognizing that this inference imposed "inappropriate burdens on the attorney-client relationship," id., we held that invoking the attorney-client privilege or work product protection does not give rise to an adverse inference, id. at 1344-45. We further held that an accused infringer's failure to obtain legal advice does not give rise to an adverse inference with respect to willfulness. Id. at 1345-46.

More recently, in Echostar we addressed the scope of waiver resulting from the advice of counsel defense. First, we concluded that relying on in-house counsel's advice to refute a charge of willfulness triggers waiver of the attorney-client privilege. Echostar, 448 F.3d at 1299. Second, we held that asserting the advice of counsel defense waives work product protection and the attorney-client privilege for all communications on the same subject matter, as well as any documents memorializing attorney-client communications. Id. at 1299, 1302-03. However, we held that waiver did not extend to work product that was not communicated to an accused infringer. Id. at 1303-04. Echostar did not consider waiver of the advice of counsel defense as it relates to trial counsel.

In this case, we confront the willfulness scheme and its functional relationship to the attorney-client privilege and work product protection. In light of Supreme Court opinions since Underwater Devices and the practical concerns facing litigants under the current regime, we take this opportunity to revisit our willfulness doctrine and to address whether waiver resulting from advice of counsel and work product defenses extend to trial counsel. See Knorr-Bremse, 383 F.3d at 1343-44.

I. Willful Infringement

The term willful is not unique to patent law, and it has a well-established meaning in the civil context. For instance, our sister circuits have employed a recklessness standard for enhancing statutory damages for copyright infringement. Under the Copyright Act, a copyright owner can elect to receive statutory damages, and trial courts have discretion to enhance the damages, up to a statutory maximum, for willful infringement. 17 U.S.C. § 504(c). Although the statute does not define willful, it has consistently been defined as including reckless behavior. See, e.g., Yurman Design, Inc. v. PAJ, Inc., 262 F.3d 101, 112 (2d Cir. 2001) ("Willfulness in [the context of statutory damages for copyright infringement] means that the defendant 'recklessly disregarded' the possibility that 'its conduct represented infringement.'") (quoting Hamil Am., Inc. v. GFI, Inc., 193 F.3d 92, 97 (2d Cir. 1999) (additional citations omitted)); Wildlife Express Corp. v. Carol

Wright Sales, 18 F.3d 502, 511-12 (7th Cir. 1994) (same); RCA/Ariola Int'l, Inc. v. Thomas & Grayston Co., 845 F.2d 773, 779 (8th Cir. 1988) (same); see also eBay Inc. v. MercExchange, L.L.C., 126 S. Ct. 1837, 1840 (2006) (noting with approval that its resolution of the permanent injunction standard in the patent context created harmony with copyright law).

Just recently, the Supreme Court addressed the meaning of willfulness as a statutory condition of civil liability for punitive damages. Safeco Ins. Co. of Am. v. Burr, 551 U.S. ___, Nos. 06-84, -100, slip op. (June 4, 2007). Safeco involved the Fair Credit Reporting Act ("FCRA"), which imposes civil liability for failure to comply with its requirements. Whereas an affected consumer can recover actual damages for negligent violations of the FCRA, 15 U.S.C. § 1681o(a), he can also recover punitive damages for willful ones, 15 U.S.C. § 1681n(a). Addressing the willfulness requirement in this context, the Court concluded that the "standard civil usage" of "willful" includes reckless behavior. Id., slip op. at 7; accord McLaughlin v. Richland Shoe Co., 486 U.S. 128, 132-33 (1988) (concluding that willful violations of the Fair Labor Standards Act include reckless violations); Trans World Airlines, Inc. v. Thurston, 469 U.S. 111, 128 (1985). Significantly, the Court said that this definition comports with the common law usage, "which treated actions in 'reckless disregard' of the law as 'willful' violations." Id., slip op. at 7 (citing W. Keeton, D. Dobbs, R. Keeton, & D. Owen, Prosser and Keeton on Law of Torts § 34, p. 212 (5th ed. 1984)).

In contrast, the duty of care announced in Underwater Devices sets a lower threshold for willful infringement that is more akin to negligence. This standard fails to comport with the general understanding of willfulness in the civil context, Richland Shoe Co., 486 U.S. at 133 ("The word 'willful' . . . is generally understood to refer to conduct that is not merely negligent."), and it allows for punitive damages in a manner inconsistent with Supreme Court precedent, see, e.g., Safeco, slip op. at 6-7,18-19, 21 n.20; Smith v Wade, 461 U.S. 30, 39-49 (1983). Accordingly, we overrule the standard set out in Underwater Devices and hold that proof of willful infringement permitting enhanced damages requires at least a showing of objective recklessness. Because we abandon the affirmative duty of due care, we also reemphasize that there is no affirmative obligation to obtain opinion of counsel.

We fully recognize that "the term [reckless] is not self-defining." Farmer v. Brennan, 511 U.S. 825, 836 (1994). However, "[t]he civil law generally calls a person reckless who acts . . . in the face of an unjustifiably high risk of harm that is either known or so obvious that it should be known." Id. (citing Prosser and Keeton § 34, pp. 213-14; Restatement (Second) of Torts § 500 (1965)). Accordingly, to establish willful infringement, a patentee must show by clear and convincing evidence that the infringer acted despite an objectively high likelihood that its actions constituted infringement of a valid patent. See Safeco, slip op. at 19 ("It is [a] high risk of harm, objectively assessed, that is the essence of recklessness at common law."). The state of mind of the accused infringer is not relevant to this objective inquiry. If this threshold objective standard is satisfied, the patentee must also demonstrate that this objectively-defined risk (determined by the record developed in the infringement proceeding) was either known or so obvious that it should have been known to the accused infringer. We leave it to future cases to further develop the application of this standard.[12]

Finally, we reject the argument that revisiting our willfulness doctrine is either improper or imprudent, as Convolve contends. The ultimate dispute in this case is the proper scope of discovery. While it is true that the issue of willful infringement, or even infringement for that matter, has not been decided by the trial court, it is indisputable that the proper legal standard for willful infringement informs the relevance of evidence relating to that issue and, more importantly here, the proper scope of discovery. See United States Nat'l Bank of Or. v. Indep. Ins. Agents of Am., Inc., 508 U.S. 439, 447 (1993) ("[A] court may consider an issue 'antecedent to . . . and ultimately dispositive of' the dispute before it, even an issue the parties fail to identify and brief." (quoting Arcadia v. Ohio Power Co., 498 U.S. 73, 77 (1990))); see also Fed. R. Civ. Pro. R. 26(b) (limiting discovery to relevant, not necessarily admissible, information); accord Singleton v. Wulff, 428 U.S. 106, 121 (1976) ("The matter of what questions may be taken up and resolved for the first time on appeal is one left primarily to the discretion of the courts of appeals, to be exercised on the facts of individual cases."); Forshey v. Principi, 284 F.3d 1335, 1355-59 (Fed. Cir. 2002) (en banc). Accordingly, addressing willfulness is neither hypothetical nor advisory.

---

[12] We would expect, as suggested by Judge Newman, post at 2, that the standards of commerce would be among the factors a court might consider.

II. Attorney-Client Privilege

We turn now to the appropriate scope of waiver of the attorney-client privilege resulting from an advice of counsel defense asserted in response to a charge of willful infringement. Recognizing that it is "the oldest of the privileges for confidential communications known to the common law," we are guided by its purpose "to encourage full and frank communication between attorneys and their clients and thereby promote broader public interests in the observance of law and administration of justice." Upjohn Co. v. United States, 449 U.S. 383, 389 (1981). The privilege also "recognizes that sound legal advice or advocacy serves public ends and that such advice or advocacy depends upon the lawyer's being fully informed by the client." Id.

The attorney-client privilege belongs to the client, who alone may waive it. E.g., Knorr-Bremse, 383 F.3d at 1345; Am. Standard, Inc. v. Pfizer, Inc., 828 F.2d 734, 745 (Fed. Cir. 1987). "The widely applied standard for determining the scope of a waiver . . . is that the waiver applies to all other communications relating to the same subject matter." Fort James Corp. v Solo Cup Corp., 412 F.3d 1340, 1349 (Fed. Cir. 2005).

This broad scope is grounded in principles of fairness and serves to prevent a party from simultaneously using the privilege as both a sword and a shield; that is, it prevents the inequitable result of a party disclosing favorable communications while asserting the privilege as to less favorable ones. Echostar, 448 F.3d at 1301; Fort James, 412 F.3d at 1349. Ultimately, however, "[t]here is no bright line test for determining what constitutes the subject matter of a waiver, rather courts weigh the circumstances of the disclosure, the nature of the legal advice sought and the prejudice to the parties of permitting or prohibiting further disclosures." Fort James, 412 F.3d at 1349-50.

In considering the scope of waiver resulting from the advice of counsel defense, district courts have reached varying results with respect to trial counsel. Some decisions have extended waiver to trial counsel, e.g., Informatica Corp. v. Bus. Objects Data Integration, Inc., 454 F. Supp. 2d 957 (N.D. Cal. 2006), whereas others have declined to do so, e.g., Collaboration Props., Inc. v. Polycom, Inc., 224 F.R.D. 473, 476 (N.D. Cal

2004); Ampex Corp. v. Eastman Kodak Co., 2006 U.S. Dist. LEXIS 48702 (D. Del. July 17, 2006). Still others have taken a middle ground and extended waiver to trial counsel only for communications contradicting or casting doubt on the opinions asserted. E.g., Intex Recreation Corp. v. Team Worldwide Corp., 439 F. Supp. 2d 46 (D.D.C. 2006); Beneficial Franchise Co., Inc. v. Bank One, N.A., 205 F.R.D. 212 (N.D. Ill. 2001); Micron Separations, Inc. v. Pall Corp., 159 F.R.D. 361 (D. Mass. 1995).

Recognizing the value of a common approach and in light of the new willfulness analysis set out above, we conclude that the significantly different functions of trial counsel and opinion counsel advise against extending waiver to trial counsel. Whereas opinion counsel serves to provide an objective assessment for making informed business decisions, trial counsel focuses on litigation strategy and evaluates the most successful manner of presenting a case to a judicial decision maker. And trial counsel is engaged in an adversarial process. We previously recognized this distinction with respect to our prior willfulness standard in Crystal Semiconductor Corp. v. TriTech Microelectronics International, Inc., 246 F.3d 1336, 1352 (Fed. Cir. 2001), which concluded that "defenses prepared [by litigation counsel] for a trial are not equivalent to the competent legal opinion of non-infringement or invalidity which qualify as 'due care' before undertaking any potentially infringing activity." Because of the fundamental difference between these types of legal advice, this situation does not present the classic "sword and shield" concerns typically mandating broad subject matter waiver.

Therefore, fairness counsels against disclosing trial counsel's communications on an entire subject matter in response to an accused infringer's reliance on opinion counsel's opinion to refute a willfulness allegation.

Moreover, the interests weighing against extending waiver to trial counsel are compelling. The Supreme Court recognized the need to protect trial counsel's thoughts in Hickman v. Taylor, 329 U.S. 495, 510-11 (1947):

[I]t is essential that a lawyer work with a certain degree of privacy, free from unnecessary intrusion by opposing parties and their counsel. Proper preparation of a client's case demands that he assemble information, sift

269

what he considers to be the relevant from the irrelevant facts, prepare his legal theories and plan his strategy without undue and needless interference. That is the historical and the necessary way in which lawyers act within the framework of our system of jurisprudence to promote justice and to protect their clients' interests.

The Court saw that allowing discovery of an attorney's thoughts would result in "[i]nefficiency, unfairness and sharp practices," that "[t]he effect on the legal profession would be demoralizing" and thus "the interests of the clients and the cause of justice would be poorly served." Id. at 511. Although Hickman concerned work product protection, the attorney-client privilege maintained with trial counsel raises the same concerns in patent litigation. In most cases, the demands of our adversarial system of justice will far outweigh any benefits of extending waiver to trial counsel. See Jaffee v. Redmond, 518 U.S. 1, 9 (1996) ("Exceptions from the general rule disfavoring testimonial privileges may be justified, however, by a 'public good transcending the normally predominant principle of utilizing all rational means for ascertaining the truth.'" (quoting Trammel, 445 U.S. 40, 50 (1980) (quoting Elkins v. United States, 364 U.S. 206 (1960) (Frankfurter, J., dissenting))) (additional internal quotation marks omitted).

Further outweighing any benefit of extending waiver to trial counsel is the realization that in ordinary circumstances, willfulness will depend on an infringer's prelitigation conduct. It is certainly true that patent infringement is an ongoing offense that can continue after litigation has commenced. However, when a complaint is filed, a patentee must have a good faith basis for alleging willful infringement. Fed. R. Civ. Pro. 8, 11(b). So a willfulness claim asserted in the original complaint must necessarily be grounded exclusively in the accused infringer's pre-filing conduct. By contrast, when an accused infringer's post-filing conduct is reckless, a patentee can move for a preliminary injunction, which generally provides an adequate remedy for combating post-filing willful infringement. See 35 U.S.C. § 283; Amazon.com, Inc. v. Barnesandnoble.com, Inc., 239 F.3d 1343, 1350 (Fed. Cir. 2001). A patentee who does not attempt to stop an accused infringer's activities in this manner should not be allowed to accrue enhanced damages based solely on the infringer's post-filing conduct. Similarly, if a patentee attempts to secure injunctive relief but fails, it is likely the infringement did not rise to the level of recklessness.

We fully recognize that an accused infringer may avoid a preliminary injunction by showing only a substantial question as to invalidity, as opposed to the higher clear and convincing standard required to prevail on the merits. Amazon.com, 239 F.3d at 1359 ("Vulnerability is the issue at the preliminary injunction stage, while validity is the issue at trial. The showing of a substantial question as to invalidity thus requires less proof than the clear and convincing showing necessary to establish invalidity itself.").

However, this lessened showing simply accords with the requirement that recklessness must be shown to recover enhanced damages. A substantial question about invalidity or infringement is likely sufficient not only to avoid a preliminary injunction, but also a charge of willfulness based on post-filing conduct.

We also recognize that in some cases a patentee may be denied a preliminary injunction despite establishing a likelihood of success on the merits, such as when the remaining factors are considered and balanced. In that event, whether a willfulness claim based on conduct occurring solely after litigation began is sustainable will depend on the facts of each case.

Because willful infringement in the main must find its basis in prelitigation conduct, communications of trial counsel have little, if any, relevance warranting their disclosure, and this further supports generally shielding trial counsel from the waiver stemming from an advice of counsel defense to willfulness. Here, the opinions of Seagate's opinion counsel, received after suit was commenced, appear to be of similarly marginal value. Although the reasoning contained in those opinions ultimately may preclude Seagate's conduct from being considered reckless if infringement is found, reliance on the opinions after litigation was commenced will likely be of little significance.

In sum, we hold, as a general proposition, that asserting the advice of counsel defense and disclosing opinions of opinion counsel do not constitute waiver of the attorney-client privilege for communications with trial counsel. We do not purport to set out an absolute rule. Instead, trial courts remain free to exercise their discretion in unique circumstances to extend waiver to trial counsel, such as if a party or counsel engages in chicanery. We believe this view comports with Supreme Court precedent, which has made clear that rules concerning privileges are subject to review and revision, when necessary. See Jaffee, 518 U.S. at 9 (noting that federal courts are "to 'continue the evolutionary development of testimonial privileges.'" (quoting Trammel, 445 U.S. at 47)).

III. Work Product Protection

An advice of counsel defense asserted to refute a charge of willful infringement may also implicate waiver of work product protection. Again, we are here confronted with whether this waiver extends to trial counsel's work product. We hold that it does not, absent exceptional circumstances.

The work product doctrine is "designed to balance the needs of the adversary system: promotion of an attorney's preparation in representing a client versus society's general interest in revealing all true and material facts to the resolution of a dispute." In re Martin Marietta Corp., 856 F.2d 619, 624 (4th Cir. 1988). Unlike the attorney-client privilege, which provides absolute protection from disclosure, work product protection is qualified and may be overcome by need and undue hardship. Fed. R. Civ. Pro. 26(b)(3). However, the level of need and hardship required for discovery depends on whether the work product is factual, or the result of mental processes such as plans, strategies, tactics, and impressions, whether memorialized in writing or not. Whereas factual work product can be discovered solely upon a showing of substantial need and undue hardship, mental process work product is afforded even greater, nearly absolute, protection. See id.; Upjohn Co. v. United States, 449 U.S. 383, 400 (1981); Holmgren v. State Farm Mut. Auto. Ins., 976 F.2d 573, 577 (9th Cir. 1992) (holding that work product "may be discovered and admitted when mental impressions are at issue in a case and the need for the material is compelling"); see also Office of Thrift Supervision v. Vinson & Elkins, LLP, 124 F.3d 1304, 1307 (D.C. Cir. 1997) ("virtually undiscoverable"). But see Nat'l Union Fire Ins. Co. v. Murray Sheet Metal Co., 967 F.2d 980, 984 (4th Cir. 1992) ("'absolutely' immune from discovery").

Like the attorney-client privilege, however, work product protection may be waived. United States v. Nobles, 422 U.S. 225, 239 (1975). Here, the same rationale generally limiting waiver of the attorney-client privilege with trial counsel applies with even greater force to so limiting work product waiver because of the nature of the work product doctrine. Protecting lawyers from broad subject matter of work product disclosure "strengthens the adversary process, and . . . may ultimately and ideally further the search for the truth." Martin Marietta, 856 F.2d at 626; accord Echostar, 448 F.3d at 1301 ("[W]ork-product immunity . . . promotes a fair and efficient adversarial system . . . ."); Coastal States Gas Corp. v. Dep't of Energy, 617 F.2d 854, 864 (D.C. Cir. 1980) ("The purpose of the privilege, however, is not to protect any interest of the attorney . . . but to protect the adversary trial process itself. It is believed that the integrity of our system would suffer if adversaries were entitled to probe each other's thoughts and plans concerning the case."). In addition, trial counsel's mental processes, which fall within Convolve's discovery requests, enjoy the utmost protection from disclosure; a scope of waiver commensurate with the nature of such heightened protection is appropriate. See Martin Marietta, 856 F.2d at 625-26.

The Supreme Court has approved of narrowly restricting the scope of work product waiver. In United States v. Nobles, a criminal case, an accused armed robber presented the testimony of an investigator in an attempt to discredit the two eyewitnesses. When they testified for the prosecution, the defense attorney relied on the investigator's report in cross-examining the eyewitnesses. 422 U.S. at 227. After the prosecution rested, the defense attempted to call the investigator to testify. The trial court, however, ruled that if the investigator testified, his affirmative testimony would mandate disclosure of the portions of his report relating to his testimony. Id. at 229.

The Supreme Court agreed that the investigator's affirmative testimony waived work product protection, but it approvingly noted the "quite limited" scope of waiver imposed by the trial court and its refusal to allow a general "fishing expedition" into the defense files or even the investigator's report. Id. at 239-40. Similarly, Convolve has been granted access to the materials relating to Seagate's opinion counsel's opinion, and he was made available for deposition. The extent of this waiver accords with the principles and spirit of Nobles.

Accordingly, we hold that, as a general proposition, relying on opinion counsel's work product does not waive work product immunity with respect to trial counsel. Again, we leave open the possibility that situations may arise in which waiver may be extended to trial counsel, such as if a patentee or his counsel engages in chicanery. And, of course, the general principles of work product protection remain in force, so that a party may obtain discovery of work product absent waiver upon a sufficient showing of need and hardship, bearing in mind that a higher burden must be met to obtain that pertaining to mental processes. See Fed. R. Civ. Pro. 26(b)(3).

Finally, the work product doctrine was partially codified in Rule 26(b)(3) of the Federal Rules of Civil Procedure, which applies work product protection to "documents and tangible things." Courts continue to apply Hickman v. Taylor, 329 U.S. 495, to "nontangible" work product. See, e.g., In re Cendant Corp. Sec. Litig., 343 F.3d 658, 662-63 (3d Cir. 2003); United States v. One Tract of Real Property, 95 F.3d 422, 428 n.10 (6th Cir. 1996). This is relevant here because Convolve sought to depose Seagate's trial counsel. We agree that work product protection remains available to "nontangible" work product under Hickman. Otherwise, attorneys' files would be protected from discovery, but attorneys themselves would have no work product objection to depositions.

Conclusion

Accordingly, Seagate's petition for a writ of mandamus is granted, and the district court will reconsider its discovery orders in light of this opinion.

United States Court of Appeals for the Federal Circuit

Miscellaneous Docket No. 830

IN RE SEAGATE TECHNOLOGY, LLC,
Petitioner.

GAJARSA, Circuit Judge, concurring, with whom Circuit Judge
NEWMAN joins.

I agree with the court's decision to grant the writ of mandamus; however, I write separately to express my belief that the court should take the opportunity to eliminate the grafting of willfulness onto section 284. As the court's opinion points out, although the enhanced damages clause of that section "is devoid of any standard for awarding [such damages]," ante at 6, this court has nevertheless read a willfulness standard into the statute, see, e.g., Beatrice Foods Co. v. New England Printing & Lithographing Co., 923 F.2d 1576, 1578 (Fed. Cir. 1991); Leesona Corp. v. United States, 599 F.2d 958, 969 (Ct. Cl. 1979). Because the language of the statute unambiguously omits any such requirement, see 35 U.S.C. § 284 ("[T]he court may increase the damages up to three times the amount found or assessed."), and because there is no principled reason for continuing to engraft a willfulness requirement onto section 284, I believe we should adhere to the plain meaning of the statute and leave the discretion to enhance damages in the capable hands of the district courts. Accordingly, I agree that Underwater Devices, Inc. v. Morrison-Knudsen Co., 717 F.2d 1380 (Fed. Cir. 1983), should be overruled and the affirmative duty of care eliminated. I would also take the opportunity to overrule the Beatrice Foods line of cases to the extent those cases engraft willfulness onto the statute. I would vacate the district court's order and remand for the court to reconsider its ruling in light of the clear and unambiguous language of section 284.

In order to reach this conclusion that enhanced damages should not be limited by willfulness, it is appropriate to place the issue of enhanced damages in the proper historical perspective. Treble damages were first introduced into American patent law by the Act of February 21, 1793, which allowed the patentee to recover, in an action at law, "a sum, that shall be at least equal to three times the price, for which the patentee has usually sold or licensed to other persons, the use of [the invention]." Act of Feb. 21, 1793, ch. 11, § 5, 1 Stat. 318, 322. The Act of April 17, 1800, allowed the patentee to recover, also in an action at law, "a sum equal to three times the actual damage sustained by [the] patentee." Act of Apr. 17, 1800, ch. 25, § 3, 2 Stat. 37, 38. Notably, however, neither of these acts permitted the courts discretion in assessing treble damages.

Such discretion was not conferred upon the courts until the Act of July 4, 1836, which provided that "it shall be in the power of the court to render judgment for any sum above the amount found by [the] verdict as the actual damages sustained by the plaintiff, not exceeding three times the amount thereof, according to the circumstances of the case." Act of July 4, 1836, ch. 357, § 14, 5 Stat. 117, 123 (emphasis added). Nothing in the phrase "according to the circumstances of the case" implies that the district court's discretion to award enhanced damages is contingent upon a finding of willfulness.

Indeed, one deficiency identified in pre-1836 patent law was the insufficiency of damages in compensating deserving patentees. Sen. John Ruggles, S. Report Accompanying Senate Bill No. 239, at 6 (Apr. 28, 1836) (explaining that pre-1836 patent law "offer[ed] an inadequate remedy for the [infringement] injury, by giving an action of damages"). At the same time, pre-1836 patent law was criticized for its limited standards regarding the granting of patents, which led to abusive wielding of the treble-damages club by undeserving patentees. See id. at 3-4 (describing the "reprehensible" practice of patentees in possession of "patents for what has been long in public use, and what every one has therefore a right to use," who, "being armed with the apparent authority of the Government, having the sanction of its highest officers the seal of state, scour[] the country, and by threats of prosecution, compel[] those who are found using the thing patented, to pay the patent price or commutation tribute"). It would appear, then, that the 1836 Act was intended to control not only the grant of unwarranted patents, but also to restore the flexibility of remedy that is the traditional judicial province.

Moreover, due to the division of law and equity, a patentee having no basis for invoking the equitable jurisdiction of a federal court was limited to legal remedies in an action on the case. Though the court's equitable powers—

such as the power to grant discovery into a defendant's affairs in order to determine damages—might still be accessible to the patentee, access to such powers was not guaranteed. See Sinclair Refining Co. v. Jenkins Petroleum Process Co., 289 U.S. 689, 696 (1933) ("To hold that the plaintiff in an action at law may have discovery of damages is not to say that the remedy will be granted as a matter of course, or that protection will not be given to his adversary against impertinent intrusion."). Even if discovery was granted in an action on the case, the patentee had no basis for collecting the infringer's profits through an equitable action for an injunction and accounting. See Root v. Ry., 105 U.S. 189, 215-216 (1882). As such, actual damages provable at law—though not "inadequate" in the equitable sense—could nevertheless be less than sufficient to compensate the patentee. In such a case, a discretionary enhancement of damages would be appropriate for entirely remedial reasons, irrespective of the defendant's state of mind.

Apart from the difficulties created by the old law and equity division, a district court might decide to enhance a patentee's damages to overcome other obstacles. For example, assume that a substantial portion of a defendant's sales data is inadvertently but irretrievably lost prior to discovery. In such a case, a successful plaintiff, through no fault of its own, might be unable to prove the real extent of damage caused by the infringement. It would be entirely reasonable, in my judgment, for the district court to exercise its statutory discretion and enhance the damage award by some measure.

Another foreseeable situation is one in which a plaintiff, having successfully secured a damage award for past infringement, moves for a permanent injunction. However, in order to avoid manifest injustice, a multiplicity of suits, etc., the district court might reasonably determine that monetary relief in the form of enhanced damages is more appropriate than an injunction. See, e.g., City of Harrisonville v. W. S. Dickey Clay Mfg. Co., 289 U.S. 334 (1933); New York City v. Pine, 185 U.S. 93 (1902); Restatement (Second) of Torts § 951 (1979); see also eBay Inc. v. MercExchange L.L.C., 547 U.S. ___, 126 S. Ct. 1837, 1839 (2006) ("The decision to grant or deny permanent injunctive relief is an act of equitable discretion by the district court, reviewable on appeal for abuse of discretion."). Yet, by reading a willfulness requirement into the statute, we are unnecessarily confining enhanced damages to a subset of cases where punitive awards are appropriate, and thereby restricting district courts from exercising legitimate, remedial options of the type discussed above.

In spite of our seemingly unequivocal holding in cases like Beatrice Foods, our case law has not been entirely consistent with respect to enhanced damages. We have recognized a remedial aspect of such damages in at least three precedential opinions. See King Instrs. Corp. v. Perego, 65 F.3d 941, 951 n.6 (Fed. Cir. 1995) ("The problem of inadequate compensation when damages are based on a reasonable royalty has been expressly recognized in several cases. . . . The solutions suggested include awards of treble damages, attorney fees and prejudgment interest, . . . , and discretionary awards of greater than a reasonable royalty[.] . . . Such discretionary increases may be appropriate where plaintiffs cannot prove direct and foreseeable damages in the form of lost profits." (emphasis added)); Rite-Hite Corp. v. Kelley Co., 819 F.2d 1120, 1126 (Fed. Cir. 1987) ("Whether or not 'willfulness' is found, the court has authority to consider the degree of culpability of the tortfeasor. The measure of damages, as indeed the assessment of attorney fees, provides an opportunity for the trial court to balance equitable concerns as it determines whether and how to recompense the successful litigant." (quoting S.C. Johnson & Son, Inc. v. Carter-Wallace, Inc., 781 F.2d 198, 201 (Fed. Cir. 1986)) (emphasis added)); Stickle v. Heublein, Inc., 716 F.2d 1550, 1563 (Fed. Cir. 1983) ("As a final matter we would add that the trial court may award an amount of damages greater than a reasonable royalty so that the award is 'adequate to compensate for the infringement.' . . . Such an increase, which may be stated by the trial court either as a reasonable royalty for an infringer (as in Panduit) or as an increase in the reasonable royalty determined by the court, is left to its sound discretion." (emphasis altered)).[13]

---

[13] And in one nonprecedential opinion, see Fed. Cir. R. 37.1(d), this court actually remanded a case for the district court to consider increasing damages for remedial reasons: As to the claim for increased damages under 35 U.S.C. § 284, contrary to the district court's holding, the authority to increase damages is not restricted to exceptional circumstances. Damages should be increased where necessary to afford full compensation for infringement. See General Motors Corp. v. Devex Corp., [461 U.S. 648 (1983)]. Under the circumstances of this case and considering that there will be a trial on damages, we remand on the question of increased damages so that the district court can take the evidence at trial on damages into account in determining that question. Sherman Indus., Inc. v. Proto-Vest, Inc., 732 F.2d 168 (Fed. Cir. 1984) (table) (emphasis added);

Our occasional recognition of this remedial aspect of section 284 is not surprising because it is practically dictated by the Supreme Court's reasoning in General Motors Corp. v. Devex Corp., 461 U.S. 648 (1983) ("GM" or "Devex"), which deals with the standard for awarding interest under the very same statute. Prior to 1946, the patent laws of the United States did not contain a provision relating to any interest due to a prevailing patentee in a suit for infringement; however, interest was nevertheless awarded under the common law rule—referred to as the Duplate standard—that, in the absence of bad faith on the part of the defendant, interest did not accrue on unliquidated damages. See, e.g., Duplate Corp. v. Triplex Safety Glass Co. of N. Am. 298 U.S. 448, 459 (1936). In 1946, however, Congress statutorily made available to prevailing patentees "interest, as may be fixed by the court." Act of Aug. 1, 1946, Pub. L. No. 79-587, 60 Stat. 778. In 1952, this provision underwent minor, non-substantive modification, to become today's statute, i.e., 35 U.S.C. § 284 (providing to prevailing patentees "interest . . . as fixed by the court"). Act of July 19, 1952, Pub. L. No. 82-593, 66 Stat. 792, 813. As is evident from the plain language of both the 1946 and the 1952 Acts, Congress did not answer with these enactments the question of whether the Duplate standard should apply to interest awards under these statutory provisions.

That question was squarely presented in GM, and the Supreme Court held that no bad-faith standard should be read into section 284. Id. at 653 ("On the face of § 284, a court's authority to award interest is not restricted to exceptional circumstances, and there is no warrant for imposing such a limitation. When Congress wished to limit an element of recovery in a patent infringement action, it said so explicitly. With respect to attorney's fees, Congress expressly provided that a court could award such fees to a prevailing party only 'in exceptional cases.' 35 U. S. C. § 285. The power to award interest was not similarly restricted."). The Court also observed that "[t]he standard governing the award of prejudgment interest under § 284 should be consistent with Congress' overriding purpose of affording patent

---

see also Code-Alarm, Inc. v. Electromotive Techs. Corp., Nos. 96- 1368, 96-1369, and 96-1385, 1997 U.S. App. LEXIS 13031, at *4 (Fed. Cir. 1997) (nonprecedential) ("In cases where awarding damages based on a reasonable royalty does not adequately compensate the patentee, it is also within the district court's discretion to award damages that exceed a reasonable royalty."); Aptargroup, Inc. v. Summit Packaging Sys., Nos. 97-1475 and 97-1484, 1998 U.S. App. LEXIS 28047, at *24-*25 (Fed. Cir. 1998) (nonprecedential) (same).

owners complete compensation." Id. at 655. Thus, because "an award of prejudgment interest is necessary to ensure that the patent owner is placed in as good a position as he would have been in had the infringer entered into a reasonable royalty agreement," id. at 655, the Court held that "prejudgment interest should be awarded under § 284 absent some justification for withholding such an award," id. at 657.

While the issue in GM was "[t]he standard governing the award of prejudgment interest under § 284," id. at 655, the rationale underlying the GM holding applies with equal force to enhanced damages, and it is in direct dialectic tension with some of this court's case law concerning the standard governing the award of such damages. The statutory-language argument applies with equal force to both interest and enhanced damages; just as prejudgment interest may be awarded in other than "exceptional cases" under the plain language of the statute, so too may enhanced damages.

Moreover, discretionary use of enhanced damages to achieve remedial goals is likewise "consistent with Congress' overriding purpose of affording patent owners complete compensation." Id.

The fact that the interest provision of section 284 was previously only a creature of common law does not diminish the applicability of GM to the provision for enhanced damages. In GM, the Court explained:

There is no basis for inferring that Congress' adoption of the provision concerning interest merely incorporated the Duplate standard. This is not a case in which Congress has reenacted statutory language that the courts had interpreted in a particular way. In such a situation, it may well be appropriate to infer that Congress intended to adopt the established judicial interpretation. See, e. g., Herman & MacLean v. Huddleston, 459 U.S. 375, 384-386 (1983); Lorillard v. Pons, 434 U.S. 575, 580-581 (1978). In this case, however, the predecessor statute did not contain any reference to interest, and the 1946 amendments specifically added a provision concerning interest in patent infringement actions. We cannot agree with petitioner that the only significance of Congress' express provision for the award of interest was the incorporation of a common-law standard that developed in the absence of any specific provision concerning interest. GM,

461 U.S. at 653-54. But unlike prejudgment interest, a provision for enhanced damages has been a part of nearly every patent act since 1790. Therefore, we can reasonably and logically conclude that the enhanced damages permitted by section 284 are not inherently exempt from the inference that Congress was merely reenacting consistently-interpreted statutory language with the 1952 Act.

Nevertheless, the inference is not warranted in this case because pre-1952 interpretations of the enhanced damages statutes have at times explicitly recognized a remedial aspect. See, e.g., Clark v. Wooster, 119 U.S. 322, 326 (1886) ("It is a general rule in patent causes, that established license fees are the best measure of damages that can be used. There may be damages beyond this, such as the expense and trouble the plaintiff has been put to by the defendant; and any special inconvenience he has suffered from the wrongful acts of the defendant; but these are more properly the subjects of allowance by the court, under the authority given to it to increase the damages."); Birdsall v. Coolidge, 93 U.S. 64, 69-70 (1876) (explaining that the provision making treble damages available in equity helps ameliorate the "manifest injustice . . . done to the complainant in equity suits [under prior law], by withholding from him a just compensation for the injury he sustained by the unlawful invasion of his exclusive rights").

It is also noted that the Supreme Court cases cited in this court's opinion—only one of which pre-dates the 1952 Act—do not hold that a finding of willfulness is necessary to support an award of enhanced damages. See ante at 6-7. At most, those cases merely stand for the uncontroversial proposition that a finding of willfulness is sufficient to support an award of enhanced damages. See Dowling v. United States, 473 U.S. 207, 227 (1985) ("Despite its undoubted power to do so, however, Congress has not provided criminal penalties for distribution of goods infringing valid patents. . . . [n.19] Congress instead has relied on provisions affording patent owners a civil cause of action. 35 U. S. C. §§ 281-294. Among the available remedies are treble damages for willful infringement."); Aro Mfg. Co. v. Convertible Top Replacement Co., 377 U.S. 476, 508 (1964) (explaining that the patentee "could in a case of willful or bad-faith infringement recover punitive or 'increased' damages under the statute's trebling provision"); Seymour v. McCormick, 57 U.S. 480, 489 (1854) ("The power to inflict vindictive or punitive damages is committed to the discretion and judgment of the court within the limit of trebling the actual damages found by the jury."). Those cases cannot be interpreted to mean that enhanced damages are limited to a finding of willfulness.

To the extent this court relies on interpretations of other statutes to support its reading of 35 U.S.C. § 284, those statutes fail to ground the postulate. For example, the court analogizes section 284 to 17 U.S.C. § 504(c) of the Copyright Act in order to demonstrate that a showing of recklessness is required to support an award of enhanced damages. Ante at 10-11. That comparison is unconvincing, however, because section 504(c) actually uses the word "willfully" to describe the threshold state of mind necessary to justify an award of enhanced damages, whereas section 284 does not. The court draws a similar analogy between section 284 and 15 U.S.C. § 1681n(a) of the Fair Credit Reporting Act ("FCRA"), the latter having recently been interpreted by the Supreme Court to require a showing of objective recklessness to support enhanced damages. Safeco Ins. Co. of Am., Inc. v. Burr, 551 U.S. ___, 127 S. Ct. 2201 (2007).

By contrasting the language of 15 U.S.C. § 1681n(a)—which uses the word "willfully" to describe the threshold state of mind necessary to justify an award of enhanced damages under the FCRA—with the language of 15 U.S.C. § 1681o(a)—which uses the word "negligent" to describe the threshold state of mind necessary to justify an award of actual damages under the FCRA—this court concludes that the negligence-like state of mind established by Underwater Devices as necessary and generally sufficient to justify an award of enhanced damages under section 284 of the Patent Act is inconsistent with the objective recklessness standard of Safeco. Ante at 11-12. As with the copyright statute, the problem with this court's logic is that it depends on the assumption that section 284 also uses the word "willfully," which of course it does not. This assumption, unwarranted for several reasons already discussed, is additionally discordant with the Supreme Court's emphasis in Safeco on adherence to statutory language. See 127 S. Ct. at 2209 (relying on the "interpretive assumption that Congress knows how we construe statutes and expects us to run true to form"); cf. eBay, Inc. v. Mercexchange, L.L.C., 547 U.S. ___, 126 S. Ct. 1837, 1839 (2006) ("Nothing in the Patent Act indicates that Congress intended . . . a departure [from the traditions of equity in granting injunctions]. To the contrary, the Patent Act expressly provides that injunctions 'may' issue 'in accordance with the principles of equity.'"). We should take this opportunity to bring patent law regarding damages into the mainstream of the general law and avoid the necessity of carving a special niche for the realm of patent law.

It is also important to note several other contexts in which enhanced damages allowed by statute have a remedial purpose. See, e.g., 15 U.S.C. § 1117(a) (discretionary award of up to three times actual damages "shall constitute compensation and not a penalty"); Cook County v. United States, 538 U.S. 119, 130 (2003) ("To begin with it is important to realize that treble damages have a compensatory side, serving remedial purposes in addition to punitive objectives. . . . While the tipping pointbetween pay-back and punishment defies general formulation, being dependent on the workings of a particular statute and the course of particular litigation, the facts about the FCA show that the damages multiplier has compensatory traits along with the punitive."); Agency Holding Corp. v. Malley-Duff & Associates, Inc., 483 U.S. 143, 151 (1987) ("Both RICO and the Clayton Act are designed to remedy economic injury by providing for the recovery of treble damages, costs, and attorney's fees."); Am. Soc'y of Mech. Eng'rs v. Hydrolevel Corp., 456 U.S. 556, 575 (1982) ("It is true that antitrust treble damages were designed in part to punish past violations of the antitrust laws. . . .But treble damages were also designed to deter future antitrust violations. . .

Moreover, the antitrust private action was created primarily as a remedy for the victims of antitrust violations."); Brunswick Corp. v. Pueblo Bowl-O-Mat, Inc., 429 U.S. 477, 485-86 (1977) ("Section 4 [of the Clayton Act], in contrast, is in essence a remedial provision. It provides treble damages to '[a]ny person who shall be injured in his business or property by reason of anything forbidden in the antitrust laws . . . .' Of course, treble damages also play an important role in penalizing wrongdoers and deterring wrongdoing, as we also have frequently observed. . . . It nevertheless is true that the treble-damages provision, which makes awards available only to injured parties, and measures the awards by a multiple of the injury actually proved, is designed primarily as a remedy.").

Simply put, interpretations of the precursors to section 284, of section 284 itself, and of any other enhanced damages statutes give rise to no inference that Congress was merely reenacting consistently-interpreted statutory language with the 1952 Act.

That inconsistency seems to abound in the case law is nothing new. According to Professor Chisum, "[w]hether the purpose of an increased damage award should be exemplary (i.e. to punish and deter flagrant acts of patent infringement) or compensatory (i.e. to compensate the patent owner for immeasurable expenses and losses) is a longstanding controversy in the law. Perhaps the best view is that increased awards combine both purposes." 7 Donald S. Chisum, Chisum on Patents § 20.03[4][b][iii] (2002).[14]

Thus, while some courts have held that a finding of willfulness is necessary to support an award of enhanced damages, other courts have taken a remedial view of the statute. See, e.g., Saturn Mfg., Inc. v. Williams Patent Crusher & Pulverizer Co., 713 F.2d 1347, 1358 (8th Cir. 1983) ("It appears that the district court imposed a higher standard, the exceptional circumstances standard, in denying increased damages. Although an award of increased damages is discretionary under the statute and the decided cases, nonetheless in view of the analysis in Devex that section 284 does not incorporate the exceptional circumstances standard of section 285, . . . we feel it appropriate to remand this issue to the district court for further consideration in light of Devex.");[15] Trio Process Corp. v. L. Goldstein's Sons, Inc., 638 F.2d 661, 663 (3d Cir. 1981) ("Because it is often difficult in patent litigation to measure with mathematical precision a patentee's damages, the enhancement provision of the statute is designed to permit,

---

[14] Without citation, Chisum summarily asserts that "[t]he power to increase is triggered only when the infringer's conduct warrants an exemplary award." 7 Chisum § 20.03[4][b][iii]. No Supreme Court case supports this proposition. I also discern no principled basis for inferring such a proposition. If Congress was concerned with ensuring that patentees are fully compensated for infringement, there would seem to be no reason to condition full compensation upon a showing of culpable conduct.

[15] In Saturn, the district court appears to have drawn a distinction between willfulness and "exceptional circumstances," holding the latter to require proof of more egregious behavior. The Eighth Circuit reversed, instructing the district court that its finding of willfulness could support an award of enhanced damages. Importantly, however, the Eighth Circuit did not hold that willfulness is required to make such an award.

inter alia, adequate compensation for an infringement where strict legal rules would not afford it.").[16]

To be sure, the majority rule has been that an award of enhanced damages pursuant to section 284 requires a finding of willfulness. 7 Chisum § 20.03[4][b][iii].

However, the existence of this "longstanding controversy" adequately demonstrates that Congress was not merely reenacting consistently-interpreted statutory language with the 1952 Act so as to justify the inference suggested in GM. Therefore, I am of the judgment that this court should not continue to read a willfulness requirement into section 284, to support the enhancement of damages. That said, willfulness remains a relevant consideration under section 284. Thus, to the extent Convolve seeks to demonstrate that Seagate is willfully infringing its patents, I agree with the court that it is appropriate to follow the Supreme Court's statutory interpretation in Safeco. See 127 S. Ct at 2209 (explaining that its interpretation of "willfully" adheres to "the general rule that a common law term in a statute comes with a common law meaning"). Under my reading of Safeco, which I believe is consistent with that of this court, Convolve must show, by clear and convincing evidence, (1) that Seagate's theory of noninfringement/invalidity, was not only incorrect, but was objectively unreasonable, and (2) that Seagate ran a risk of infringing Convolve's patents substantially greater than the risk associated with a theory of noninfringement/invalidity that was merely careless. See id. at 2215 (holding that a defendant "does not act in reckless disregard of [a statute] unless the action is not only a violation under a reasonable reading of the statute's terms, but shows that the [defendant] ran a risk of violating the law substantially greater than the risk associated with a reading that was merely careless").

If Convolve is unable to show the former, Seagate cannot be found to have willfully infringed, regardless of any evidence of its subjective beliefs. See id. at 2216 n.20 ("To the extent that [the plaintiffs] argue that evidence of subjective bad faith can support a willfulness finding even when the [defendant's] reading of the statute is objectively reasonable, their argument

---

[16] These cases, while not binding on this court, are persuasive authority nonetheless.

is unsound."); see also id. at 2215 (explaining that "there is no need to pinpoint the negligence/recklessness line [where the defendant's] reading of the statute, albeit erroneous, was not objectively unreasonable"). Thus, Seagate's subjective beliefs may become relevant only if Convolve successfully makes this showing of objective unreasonableness. See id. at 2216 n.20 (leaving open the possibility that "good-faith reliance on legal advice should render [defendants] immune to claims [of willfulness]"). Because no finding of objective unreasonableness has yet been made in this case, the issues of attorney-client privilege and work product may not even need to be confronted. As such, it is premature to comment on the scope of the waiver of the attorney-client privilege and work-product protection.

United States Court of Appeals for the Federal Circuit

Miscellaneous Docket No. 830

IN RE SEAGATE TECHNOLOGY, LLC,
Petitioner.

NEWMAN, Circuit Judge, concurring.

I join the court's holding that a voluntary waiver of the attorney-client privilege and work product protection as to patent opinion counsel is not a waiver of any privilege or protection as to litigation counsel. I also agree with the separate decision to overrule Underwater Devices, but only because that case has been misapplied, in the extremis of high-stakes litigation, to mean that "due care" requires more than the reasonable care that a responsible enterprise gives to the property of others. The obligation to obey the law is not diminished when the property is "intellectual." However, experience, and the exhortations of the amici curiae, have persuaded me that we should reduce the opportunities for abusive gamesmanship that the "due care" standard apparently has facilitated.

The thrust of Underwater Devices was that patent property should receive the same respect that the law imposes on all property. Industrial innovation would falter without the order that patent property contributes to the complexities of investment in technologic R&D and commercialization in a competitive marketplace. The loser would be not only the public, but also the nation's economic vigor. So I am sympathetic when told of the disproportionate burdens that a rigorous reading of Underwater Devices has placed on otherwise law-abiding commercial enterprise. Thus, to the extent that Underwater Devices has been applied as a per se rule that every possibly related patent must be exhaustively studied by expensive legal talent, lest infringement presumptively incur treble damages, I agree that the standard should be modified.

Although new uncertainties are introduced by the court's evocation of "objective standards" for such inherently subjective criteria as "recklessness" and "reasonableness," I trust that judicial wisdom will come to show the way, in the common-law tradition. The standards of behavior by which a possible infringer evaluates adverse patents should be the standards of fair commerce, including reasonableness of the actions taken in the particular circumstances. It cannot be the court's intention to tolerate the intentional disregard or destruction of the value of the property of another, simply because that property is a patent; yet the standard of "recklessness" appears to ratify intentional disregard, and to reject objective standards requiring a reasonable respect for property rights.

The remedial and deterrent purposes of multiplied damages, and their measure for a particular case, are best established by the district court in light of the original purposes of 35 U.S.C. '284, as set forth in Judge Gajarsa's concurring opinion. The fundamental issue remains the reasonableness, or in turn the culpability, of commercial behavior that violates legally protected property rights.

Courtesy of David A. Allgeyer, Lindquist & Vennum PLLP

APPENDIX K

KSR INTERNATIONAL CO., PETITIONER
v. TELEFLEX INC. ET AL.

Opinion of the Court

NOTICE: This opinion is subject to formal revision before publication in the preliminary print of the United States Reports. Readers are requested to notify the Reporter of Decisions, Supreme Court of the United States, Washington, D. C. 20543, of any typographical or other formal errors, in order that corrections may be made before the preliminary print goes to press.

SUPREME COURT OF THE UNITED STATES

No. 04–1350

KSR INTERNATIONAL CO., PETITIONER
v. TELEFLEX INC. ET AL.

ON WRIT OF CERTIORARI TO THE UNITED STATES
COURT OF APPEALS FOR THE FEDERAL CIRCUIT

[April 30, 2007]

JUSTICE KENNEDY delivered the opinion of the Court.

Teleflex Incorporated and its subsidiary Technology Holding Company—both referred to here as Teleflex—sued KSR International Company for patent infringement. The patent at issue, United States Patent No. 6,237,565B1, is entitled "Adjustable Pedal Assembly With Electronic Throttle Control." Supplemental App. 1. The patentee is Steven J. Engelgau, and the patent is referred to as "the Engelgau patent." Teleflex holds the exclusive license to the patent.

Claim 4 of the Engelgau patent describes a mechanism for combining an electronic sensor with an adjustable automobile pedal so the pedal's position can be transmitted to a computer that controls the throttle in the vehicle's engine. When Teleflex accused KSR of infringing the Engelgau patent by adding an electronic sensor to one of KSR's previously designed pedals, KSR countered that claim 4 was invalid under the Patent Act, 35 U. S. C. §103, because its subject matter was obvious.

Section 103 forbids issuance of a patent when "the differences between the subject matter sought to be patented and the prior art are such that the subject matter as a whole would have been obvious at the time the invention was made to a person having ordinary skill in the art to which said subject matter pertains."

In Graham v. John Deere Co. of Kansas City, 383 U. S. 1 (1966), the Court set out a framework for applying the statutory language of §103, language itself based on the logic of the earlier decision in Hotchkiss v. Greenwood, 11 How. 248 (1851), and its progeny. See 383 U. S., at 15–17. The analysis is objective:

"Under §103, the scope and content of the prior art are to be determined; differences between the prior art and the claims at issue are to be ascertained; and the level of ordinary skill in the pertinent art resolved. Against this background the obviousness or nonobviousness of the subject matter is determined. Such secondary considerations as commercial success, long felt but unsolved needs, failure of others, etc., might be utilized to give light to the circumstances surrounding the origin of the subject matter sought to be patented." Id., at 17–18.

While the sequence of these questions might be reordered in any particular case, the factors continue to define the inquiry that controls. If a court, or patent examiner, conducts this analysis and concludes the claimed subject matter was obvious, the claim is invalid under §103.

Seeking to resolve the question of obviousness with more uniformity and consistency, the Court of Appeals for the Federal Circuit has employed an approach referred to by the parties as the "teaching, suggestion, or motivation" test (TSM test), under which a patent claim is only proved obvious if "some motivation or suggestion to combine the prior art teachings" can be found in the prior art, the nature of the problem, or the knowledge of a person having ordinary skill in the art. See, e.g., Al-Site Corp. v. VSI 3 Int'l, Inc., 174 F. 3d 1308, 1323–1324 (CA Fed. 1999). KSR challenges that test, or at least its application in this case. See 119 Fed. Appx. 282, 286–290 (CA Fed. 2005). Because the Court of Appeals addressed the question of obviousness in a manner contrary to §103 and our precedents, we granted certiorari, 547 U. S ___ (2006). We now reverse.

I

A

In car engines without computer-controlled throttles, the accelerator pedal interacts with the throttle via cable or other mechanical link. The pedal arm acts as a lever rotating around a pivot point. In a cable-actuated throttle control the rotation caused by pushing down the pedal pulls a cable, which in turn pulls open valves in the carburetor or fuel injection unit. The wider the valves open, the more fuel and air are released, causing combustion to increase and the car to accelerate. When the driver takes his foot off the pedal, the opposite occurs as the cable is released and the valves slide closed.

In the 1990's it became more common to install computers in cars to control engine operation. Computer-controlled throttles open and close valves in response to electronic signals, not through force transferred from the pedal by a mechanical link. Constant, delicate adjustments of air and fuel mixture are possible. The computer's rapid processing of factors beyond the pedal's position improves fuel efficiency and engine performance.

For a computer-controlled throttle to respond to a driver's operation of the car, the computer must know what is happening with the pedal. A cable or mechanical link does not suffice for this purpose; at some point, an electronic sensor is necessary to translate the mechanical operation into digital data the computer can understand.

Before discussing sensors further we turn to the mechanical design of the pedal itself. In the traditional design a pedal can be pushed down or released but cannot have its position in the footwell adjusted by sliding the pedal forward or back. As a result, a driver who wishes to be closer or farther from the pedal must either reposition himself in the driver's seat or move the seat in some way. In cars with deep footwells these are imperfect solutions for drivers of smaller stature. To solve the problem, inventors, beginning in the 1970's, designed pedals that could be adjusted to change their location in the footwell. Important for this case are two adjustable pedals disclosed in U. S. Patent Nos. 5,010,782 (filed July 28, 1989) (Asano) and 5,460,061 (filed Sept. 17, 1993) (Redding). The Asano patent reveals a support structure that houses the pedal so that even when the pedal location is adjusted relative to the driver, one of the pedal's pivot points stays fixed. The pedal is also designed so that the force necessary to push the pedal down is the same regardless of adjustments to its location. The Redding patent reveals a different, sliding mechanism where both the pedal and the pivot point are adjusted.

We return to sensors. Well before Engelgau applied for his challenged patent, some inventors had obtained patents involving electronic pedal sensors for computer-controlled throttles. These inventions, such as the device disclosed in U. S. Patent No. 5,241,936 (filed Sept. 9, 1991) ('936), taught that it was preferable to detect the pedal's position in the pedal assembly, not in the engine. The '936 patent disclosed a pedal with an electronic sensor on a pivot point in the pedal assembly. U. S. Patent No. 5,063,811 (filed July 9, 1990) (Smith) taught that to prevent the wires connecting the sensor to the computer from chafing and wearing out, and to avoid grime and damage from the driver's foot, the sensor should be put on a fixed part of the pedal assembly rather than in or on the pedal's footpad.

In addition to patents for pedals with integrated sensors inventors obtained patents for self-contained modular sensors. A modular sensor is designed independently of a given pedal so that it can be taken off the shelf and attached to mechanical pedals of various sorts, enabling the pedals to be used in automobiles with computer-controlled throttles. One such sensor was disclosed in U. S. Patent No. 5,385,068 (filed Dec. 18, 1992) ('068). In 1994, Chevrolet manufactured a line of trucks using modular sensors "attached to the pedal support bracket, adjacent to the pedal and engaged with the pivot shaft about which the pedal rotates in operation." 298 F. Supp. 2d 581, 589 (ED Mich. 2003).

The prior art contained patents involving the placement of sensors on adjustable pedals as well. For example, U. S. Patent No. 5,819,593 (filed Aug. 17, 1995) (Rixon) discloses an adjustable pedal assembly with an electronic sensor for detecting the pedal's position. In the Rixon pedal the sensor is located in the pedal footpad. The Rixon pedal was known to suffer from wire chafing when the pedal was depressed and released.

This short account of pedal and sensor technology leads to the instant case.

B

KSR, a Canadian company, manufactures and supplies auto parts, including pedal systems. Ford Motor Company hired KSR in 1998 to supply an adjustable pedal system for various lines of automobiles with cable-actuated throttle controls. KSR developed an adjustable mechanical pedal for Ford and obtained U. S. Patent No. 6,151,976(filed July 16, 1999) ('976) for the design. In 2000, KSR was chosen by General Motors Corporation (GMC or GM)to supply adjustable pedal systems for Chevrolet and GMC light trucks that used engines with computer-controlled throttles. To make the '976 pedal compatible with the trucks, KSR merely took that design and added a modular sensor.

Teleflex is a rival to KSR in the design and manufacture of adjustable pedals. As noted, it is the exclusive licensee of the Engelgau patent. Engelgau filed the patent application on August 22, 2000 as a continuation of a previous application for U. S. Patent No. 6,109,241, which was filed on January 26, 1999. He has sworn he invented the patent's subject matter on February 14, 1998. The Engelgau patent discloses an adjustable electronic pedal described in the specification as a "simplified vehicle control pedal assembly that is less expensive, and which uses fewer parts and is easier to package within the vehicle." Engelgau, col. 2, lines 2–5, Supplemental App. 6. Claim 4 of the patent, at issue here, describes:

"A vehicle control pedal apparatus comprising: a support adapted to be mounted to a vehicle structure;

an adjustable pedal assembly having a pedal arm moveable in for[e] and aft directions with respect to said support;

a pivot for pivotally supporting said adjustable pedal assembly with respect to said support and defining a pivot axis; and an electronic control attached to said support for controlling a vehicle system;

said apparatus characterized by said electronic control being responsive to said pivot for providing a signal that corresponds to pedal arm position as said pedal arm pivots about said pivot axis between rest and applied positions wherein the position of said pivot remains constant while said pedal arm moves in fore and aft directions with respect to said pivot." Id., col. 7 Cite as: 550 U. S. _____ (2007) 6, lines 17–36, Supplemental App. 8 (diagram numbers omitted).

We agree with the District Court that the claim discloses "a position-adjustable pedal assembly with an electronic pedal position sensor attached to the support member of the pedal assembly. Attaching the sensor to the support member allows the sensor to remain in a fixed position while the driver adjusts the pedal." 298 F. Supp. 2d, at 586–587.

Before issuing the Engelgau patent the U. S. Patent and Trademark Office (PTO) rejected one of the patent claims that was similar to, but broader than, the present claim 4. The claim did not include the requirement that the sensor be placed on a fixed pivot point. The PTO concluded the claim was an obvious combination of the prior art disclosed in Redding and Smith, explaining:

"'Since the prior ar[t] references are from the field of endeavor, the purpose disclosed . . . would have been recognized in the pertinent art of Redding. Therefore it would have been obvious . . . to provide the device of Redding with the . . . means attached to a support member as taught by Smith.'" Id., at 595.

In other words Redding provided an example of an adjustable pedal and Smith explained how to mount a sensor on a pedal's support structure, and the rejected patent claim merely put these two teachings together.

Although the broader claim was rejected, claim 4 was later allowed because it included the limitation of a fixed pivot point, which distinguished the design from Redding's. Ibid. Engelgau had not included Asano among the prior art references, and Asano was not mentioned in the patent's prosecution. Thus, the PTO did not have before it an adjustable pedal with a fixed pivot point. The patent issued on May 29, 2001 and was assigned to Teleflex.

Upon learning of KSR's design for GM, Teleflex sent a warning letter informing KSR that its proposal would violate the Engelgau patent. "'Teleflex believes that any supplier of a product that combines an adjustable pedal with an electronic throttle control necessarily employs technology covered by one or more'" of Teleflex's patents. Id., at 585. KSR refused to enter a royalty arrangement with Teleflex; so Teleflex sued for infringement, asserting KSR's pedal infringed the Engelgau patent and two other patents. Ibid. Teleflex later abandoned its claims regarding the other patents and dedicated the patents to the public. The remaining contention was that KSR's pedal system for GM infringed claim 4 of the Engelgau patent. Teleflex has not argued that the other three claims of the patent are infringed by KSR's pedal, nor has Teleflex argued that the mechanical adjustable pedal designed by KSR for Ford infringed any of its patents.

C

The District Court granted summary judgment in KSR's favor. After reviewing the pertinent history of pedal design, the scope of the Engelgau patent, and the relevant prior art, the court considered the validity of the contested claim. By direction of 35 U. S. C. §282, an issued patent is presumed valid. The District Court applied Graham's framework to determine whether under summary-judgment standards KSR had overcome the presumption and demonstrated that claim 4 was obvious in light of the prior art in existence when the claimed subject matter was invented. See §102(a). The District Court determined, in light of the expert testimony and the parties' stipulations, that the level of ordinary skill in pedal design was "'an undergraduate degree in mechanical engineering (or an equivalent amount of industry experience) [and] familiarity with pedal control systems for vehicles.'" 298 F. Supp. 2d, at 590. The court then set forth the relevant prior art, including the patents and pedal designs described above.

Following Graham's direction, the court compared the teachings of the prior art to the claims of Engelgau. It found "little difference." 298 F. Supp. 2d, at 590. Asano taught everything contained in claim 4 except the use of a sensor to detect the pedal's position and transmit it to the computer controlling the throttle. That additional aspect was revealed in sources such as the '068 patent and the sensors used by Chevrolet.

Under the controlling cases from the Court of Appeals for the Federal Circuit, however, the District Court was not permitted to stop there. The court was required also to apply the TSM test. The District Court held KSR had satisfied the test. It reasoned (1) the state of the industry would lead inevitably to combinations of electronic sensors and adjustable pedals, (2) Rixon provided the basis for these developments, and (3) Smith taught a solution to the wire chafing problems in Rixon, namely locating the sensor on the fixed structure of the pedal. This could lead to the combination of Asano, or a pedal like it, with a pedal position sensor.

The conclusion that the Engelgau design was obvious was supported, in the District Court's view, by the PTO's rejection of the broader version of claim 4. Had Engelgau included Asano in his patent application, it reasoned, the PTO would have found claim 4 to be an obvious combination of Asano and Smith, as it had found the broader version an obvious combination of Redding and Smith. Asa final matter, the District Court held that the secondary factor of Teleflex's commercial success with pedals based on Engelgau's design did not alter its conclusion. The District Court granted summary judgment for KSR.

With principal reliance on the TSM test, the Court of Appeals reversed. It ruled the District Court had not been strict enough in applying the test, having failed to make "'finding[s] as to the specific understanding or principle within the knowledge of a skilled artisan that would have motivated one with no knowledge of [the] invention' . . . toattach an electronic control to the support bracket of the Asano assembly." 119 Fed. Appx., at 288 (brackets in original) (quoting In re Kotzab, 217 F. 3d 1365, 1371 (CA Fed. 2000)). The Court of Appeals held that the District Court was incorrect that the nature of the problem to be solved satisfied this requirement because unless the "prior art references address[ed] the precise problem that the patentee was trying to solve," the problem would not motivate an inventor to look at those references. 119 Fed. Appx., at 288.

Here, the Court of Appeals found, the Asano pedal was designed to solve the "'constant ratio problem'"—that is, to ensure that the force required to depress the pedal is the same no matter how the pedal is adjusted—whereas

Engelgau sought to provide a simpler, smaller, cheaper adjustable electronic pedal. Ibid. As for Rixon, the court explained, that pedal suffered from the problem of wire chafing but was not designed to solve it. In the court's view Rixon did not teach anything helpful to Engelgau's purpose. Smith, in turn, did not relate to adjustable pedals and did not "necessarily go to the issue of motivation to attach the electronic control on the support bracket of the pedal assembly." Ibid. When the patents were interpreted in this way, the Court of Appeals held, they would not have led a person of ordinary skill to put a sensor on the sort of pedal described in Asano.

That it might have been obvious to try the combination of Asano and a sensor was likewise irrelevant, in the court's view, because "''[o]bvious to try" has long been held not to constitute obviousness.'" Id., at 289 (quoting In re Deuel, 51 F. 3d 1552, 1559 (CA Fed. 1995)).

The Court of Appeals also faulted the District Court's consideration of the PTO's rejection of the broader version of claim 4. The District Court's role, the Court of Appeals explained, was not to speculate regarding what the PTO might have done had the Engelgau patent mentioned Asano. Rather, the court held, the District Court was obliged first to presume that the issued patent was valid and then to render its own independent judgment of obviousness based on a review of the prior art. The fact that the PTO had rejected the broader version of claim 4, the Court of Appeals said, had no place in that analysis.

The Court of Appeals further held that genuine issues of material fact precluded summary judgment. Teleflex had proffered statements from one expert that claim 4 "'was a simple, elegant, and novel combination of features,'" 119 Fed. Appx., at 290, compared to Rixon, and from another expert that claim 4 was nonobvious because, unlike in Rixon, the sensor was mounted on the support bracket rather than the pedal itself. This evidence, the court concluded, sufficed to require a trial.

II

A

We begin by rejecting the rigid approach of the Court of Appeals. Throughout this Court's engagement with the question of obviousness, our cases have set forth an expansive and flexible approach inconsistent with the way the Court of Appeals applied its TSM test here. To be sure, Graham recognized the need for "uniformity and definiteness." 383 U. S., at 18. Yet the principles laid down in Graham reaffirmed the "functional approach" of Hotchkiss, 11 How. 248. See 383 U. S., at 12. To this end, Graham set forth a broad inquiry and invited courts, where appropriate, to look at any secondary considerations that would prove instructive. Id., at 17.

Neither the enactment of §103 nor the analysis in Graham disturbed this Court's earlier instructions concerning the need for caution in granting a patent based on the combination of elements found in the prior art. For over a half century, the Court has held that a "patent for a combination which only unites old elements with no change in their respective functions . . . obviously withdraws what is already known into the field of its monopoly and diminishes the resources available to skillful men." Great Atlantic & Pacific Tea Co. v. Supermarket Equipment Corp., 340 U. S. 147, 152 (1950). This is a principal reason for declining to allow patents for what is obvious. The combination of familiar elements according to known methods is likely to be obvious when it does no more than yield predictable results. Three cases decided after Graham illustrate the application of this doctrine.

In United States v. Adams, 383 U. S. 39, 40 (1966), a companion case to Graham, the Court considered the obviousness of a "wet battery" that varied from prior designs in two ways: It contained water, rather than the acids conventionally employed in storage batteries; and its electrodes were magnesium and cuprous chloride, rather than zinc and silver chloride. The Court recognized that when a patent claims a structure already known in the prior art that is altered by the mere substitution of one element for another known in the field, the combination must do more than yield a predictable result. 383 U. S., at 50–51. It nevertheless rejected the Government's claim that Adams's battery was obvious. The Court relied upon the corollary principle that when the prior art teaches away from combining certain known elements, discovery of a successful means of combining them is more likely to be nonobvious. Id., at 51–52. When Adams designed his battery, the prior art warned that risks were involved in using the types of electrodes he employed. The fact that the elements worked together in an unexpected and fruitful manner supported the conclusion that Adams's design was not obvious to those skilled in the art.

In Anderson's-Black Rock, Inc. v. Pavement Salvage Co., 396 U. S. 57 (1969), the Court elaborated on this approach.

The subject matter of the patent before the Court was a device combining two pre-existing elements: a radiant-heat burner and a paving machine. The device, the Court concluded, did not create some new synergy: The radiant-heat burner functioned just as a burner was expected to function; and the paving machine did the same. The two in combination did no more than they would in separate, sequential operation. Id., at 60–62. In those circumstances, "while the combination of old elements performed a useful function, it added nothing to the nature and quality of the radiant-heat burner already patented," and the patent failed under §103. Id., at 62 (footnote omitted).

Finally, in Sakraida v. AG Pro, Inc., 425 U. S. 273 (1976), the Court derived from the precedents the conclusion that when a patent "simply arranges old elements with each performing the same function it had been known to perform" and yields no more than one would expect from such an arrangement, the combination is obvious. Id., at 282.

The principles underlying these cases are instructive when the question is whether a patent claiming the combination of elements of prior art is obvious. When a work is available in one field of endeavor, design incentives and other market forces can prompt variations of it, either in the same field or a different one. If a person of ordinary skill can implement a predictable variation, §103 likely bars its patentability. For the same reason, if a technique has been used to improve one device, and a person of ordinary skill in the art would recognize that it would improve similar devices in the same way, using the technique is obvious unless its actual application is beyond his or her skill. Sakraida and Anderson's-Black Rock are illustrative—a court must ask whether the improvement is more than the predictable use of prior art elements according to their established functions.

Following these principles may be more difficult in other cases than it is here because the claimed subject matter may involve more than the simple substitution of one known element for another or the mere application of a known technique to a piece of prior art ready for the improvement. Often, it will be necessary for a court to look to interrelated teachings of multiple patents; the effects of demands known to the design community or present in the marketplace; and the background knowledge possessed by a person having ordinary skill in the art, all in order to determine whether there was an apparent reason to combine the known elements in the fashion claimed by the patent at issue. To facilitate review, this analysis should be made explicit. See In re Kahn, 441 F. 3d 977, 988 (CA Fed. 2006) ("[R]ejections on obviousness grounds cannot be sustained by mere conclusory statements; instead, there must be some articulated reasoning with some rational underpinning to support the legal conclusion of obviousness"). As our precedents make clear, however, the analysis need not seek out precise teachings directed to the specific subject matter of the challenged claim, for a court can take account of the inferences and creative steps that a person of ordinary skill in the art would employ.

B

When it first established the requirement of demonstrating a teaching, suggestion, or motivation to combine known elements in order to show that the combination is obvious, the Court of Customs and Patent Appeals captured a helpful insight. See Application of Bergel, 292 F. 2d 955, 956–957 (1961). As is clear from cases such as Adams, a patent composed of several elements is not proved obvious merely by demonstrating that each of its elements was, independently, known in the prior art. Although common sense directs one to look with care at a patent application that claims as innovation the combination of two known devices according to their established functions, it can be important to identify a reason that would have prompted a person of ordinary skill in the relevant field to combine the elements in the way the claimed new invention does. This is so because inventions in most, if not all, instances rely upon building blocks longsince uncovered, and claimed discoveries almost of necessity will be combinations of what, in some sense, is already known.

Helpful insights, however, need not become rigid and mandatory formulas; and when it is so applied, the TSM test is incompatible with our precedents. The obviousness analysis cannot be confined by a formalistic conception of the words teaching, suggestion, and motivation, or by overemphasis on the importance of published articles and the explicit content of issued patents. The diversity of inventive pursuits and of modern technology counsels against limiting the analysis in this way. In many fields it may be that there is little discussion of obvious techniques or combinations, and it often may be the case that market demand, rather than scientific literature, will drive design trends. Granting patent protection to advances that would occur in the ordinary course without real innovation retards progress and may, in the case of patents combining previously known elements, deprive prior inventions of their value or utility.

In the years since the Court of Customs and Patent Appeals set forth the essence of the TSM test, the Court of Appeals no doubt has applied the test in accord with these principles in many cases. There is no necessary inconsistency between the idea underlying the TSM test and the Graham analysis. But when a court transforms the general principle into a rigid rule that limits the obviousness inquiry, as the Court of Appeals did here, it errs.

C

The flaws in the analysis of the Court of Appeals relate for the most part to the court's narrow conception of the obviousness inquiry reflected in its application of the TSM test. In determining whether the subject matter of a patent claim is obvious, neither the particular motivation nor the avowed purpose of the patentee controls. What matters is the objective reach of the claim. If the claim extends to what is obvious, it is invalid under §103. One of the ways in which a patent's subject matter can be proved obvious is by noting that there existed at the time of invention a known problem for which there was an obvious solution encompassed by the patent's claims.

The first error of the Court of Appeals in this case was to foreclose this reasoning by holding that courts and patent examiners should look only to the problem the patentee was trying to solve. 119 Fed. Appx., at 288. The Court of Appeals failed to recognize that the problem motivating the patentee may be only one of many addressed by the patent's subject matter. The question is not whether the combination was obvious to the patentee but whether the combination was obvious to a person with ordinary skill in the art. Under the correct analysis, any need or problem known in the field of endeavor at the time of invention and addressed by the patent can provide a reason for combining the elements in the manner claimed.

The second error of the Court of Appeals lay in its assumption that a person of ordinary skill attempting to solve a problem will be led only to those elements of prior art designed to solve the same problem. Ibid. The primary purpose of Asano was solving the constant ratio problem; so, the court concluded, an inventor considering how to put a sensor on an adjustable pedal would have no reason to consider putting it on the Asano pedal. Ibid. Common sense teaches, however, that familiar items may have obvious uses beyond their primary purposes, and in many cases a person of ordinary skill will be able to fit the teachings of multiple patents together like pieces of a puzzle. Regardless of Asano's primary purpose, the design provided an obvious example of an adjustable pedal with a fixed pivot point; and the prior art was replete with patents indicating that a fixed pivot point was an ideal mount for a sensor. The idea that a designer hoping to make an adjustable electronic pedal would ignore Asano because Asano was designed to solve the constant ratio problem makes little sense. A person of ordinary skill is also a person of ordinary creativity, not an automaton.

The same constricted analysis led the Court of Appeals to conclude, in error, that a patent claim cannot be proved obvious merely by showing that the combination of elements was "obvious to try." Id., at 289 (internal quotation marks omitted). When there is a design need or market pressure to solve a problem and there are a finite number of identified, predictable solutions, a person of ordinary skill has good reason to pursue the known options within his or her technical grasp. If this leads to the anticipated success, it is likely the product not of innovation but of ordinary skill and common sense. In that instance the fact that a combination was obvious to try might show that it was obvious under §103.

The Court of Appeals, finally, drew the wrong conclusion from the risk of courts and patent examiners falling prey to hindsight bias. A fact finder should be aware, of course, of the distortion caused by hindsight bias and must be cautious of arguments reliant upon ex post reasoning. See Graham, 383 U. S., at 36 (warning against a "temptation to read into the prior art the teachings of the invention in issue" and instructing courts to "'guard against slipping into the use of hindsight'" (quoting Monroe Auto Equipment Co. v. Heckethorn Mfg. & Supply Co., 332 F. 2d 406, 412 (CA6 1964))). Rigid preventative rules that deny fact finders recourse to common sense, however, are neither necessary under our case law nor consistent with it.

We note the Court of Appeals has since elaborated a broader conception of the TSM test than was applied in the instant matter. See, e.g., DyStar Textilfarben GmbH & Co. Deutschland KG v. C. H. Patrick Co., 464 F. 3d 1356, 1367 (2006) ("Our suggestion test is in actuality quite flexible and not only permits, but requires, consideration of common knowledge and common sense"); Alza Corp. v. Mylan Labs., Inc., 464 F. 3d 1286, 1291 (2006) ("There is flexibility in our obviousness jurisprudence because a motivation may be found implicitly in the prior art. We do not have a rigid test that requires an actual teaching to combine . . ."). Those decisions, of course, are not now before us and do not correct the errors of law made by the Court of Appeals in this case. The extent to which they may describe an analysis more consistent with our earlier precedents and our decision here is a matter for the Court of Appeals to consider in its future cases. What we hold is that the fundamental misunderstandings identified above led the Court of Appeals in this case to apply a test inconsistent with our patent law decisions.

III

When we apply the standards we have explained to the instant facts, claim 4 must be found obvious. We agree with and adopt the District Court's recitation of the relevant prior art and its determination of the level of ordinary skill in the field. As did the District Court, we see little difference between the teachings of Asano and Smith and the adjustable electronic pedal disclosed in claim 4 of the Engelgau patent. A person having ordinary skill in the art could have combined Asano with a pedal position sensor in a fashion encompassed by claim 4, and would have seen the benefits of doing so.

A

Teleflex argues in passing that the Asano pedal cannot be combined with a sensor in the manner described by claim 4 because of the design of Asano's pivot mechanisms. See Brief for Respondents 48–49, and n. 17. Therefore, Teleflex reasons, even if adding a sensor to Asano was obvious, that does not establish that claim 4 encompasses obvious subject matter. This argument was not, however, raised before the District Court. There Teleflex was content to assert only that the problem motivating the invention claimed by the Engelgau patent would not lead to the solution of combining of Asano with a sensor. See Teleflex's Response to KSR's Motion for Summary Judgment of Invalidity in No. 02–74586 (ED Mich.), pp. 18–20, App. 144a–146a. It is also unclear whether the current argument was raised before the Court of Appeals, where Teleflex advanced the nonspecific, conclusory contention that combining Asano with a sensor would not satisfy the limitations of claim 4. See Brief for Plaintiffs-Appellants in No. 04–1152 (CA Fed.), pp. 42–44. Teleflex's own expert declarations, moreover, do not support the point Teleflex now raises. See Declaration of Clark J. Radcliffe, Ph.D., Supplemental App. 204–207; Declaration of Timothy L. Andresen, id., at 208–210. The only statement in either declaration that might bear on the argument is found in the Radcliffe declaration:

"Asano . . . and Rixon . . . are complex mechanical linkage-based devices that are expensive to produce and assemble and difficult to package. It is exactly these difficulties with prior art designs that [Engelgau] resolves. The use of an adjustable pedal with a single pivot reflecting pedal position combined with an electronic control mounted between the support and the adjustment assembly at that pivot was a simple, elegant, and novel combination of features in the Engelgau '565 patent." Id., at 206, ¶16.

Read in the context of the declaration as a whole this is best interpreted to mean that Asano could not be used to solve "[t]he problem addressed by Engelgau '565[:] to provide a less expensive, more quickly assembled, and smaller package adjustable pedal assembly with electronic control." Id., at 205, ¶10.

The District Court found that combining Asano with a pivot-mounted pedal position sensor fell within the scope of claim 4. 298 F. Supp. 2d, at 592–593. Given the sigificance of that finding to the District Court's judgment, it is apparent that Teleflex would have made clearer challenges to it if it intended to preserve this claim. In light of Teleflex's failure to raise the argument in a clear fashion, and the silence of the Court of Appeals on the issue, we take the District Court's conclusion on the point to be correct.

B

The District Court was correct to conclude that, as of the time Engelgau designed the subject matter in claim 4, it was obvious to a person of ordinary skill to combine Asano with a pivot-mounted pedal position sensor. There then existed a marketplace that created a strong incentive to convert mechanical pedals to electronic pedals, and the prior art taught a number of methods for achieving this advance. The Court of Appeals considered the issue too narrowly by, in effect, asking whether a pedal designer writing on a blank slate would have chosen both Asano and a modular sensor similar to the ones used in the Chevrolet truck line and disclosed in the '068 patent. The District Court employed this narrow inquiry as well, though it reached the correct result nevertheless. The proper question to have asked was whether a pedal designer of ordinary skill, facing the wide range of needs created by developments in the field of endeavor, would have seen a benefit to upgrading Asano with a sensor. In automotive design, as in many other fields, the interaction of multiple components means that changing one component often requires the others to be modified as well. Technological developments made it clear that engines using computer-controlled throttles would become standard. As a result, designers might have decided to design new pedals from scratch; but they also would have had reason to make pre-existing pedals work with the new engines. Indeed, upgrading its own pre-existing model led KSR to design the pedal now accused of infringing the Engelgau patent.

For a designer starting with Asano, the question was where to attach the sensor. The consequent legal question, then, is whether a pedal designer of ordinary skill starting with Asano would have found it obvious to put the sensor on a fixed pivot point. The prior art discussed above leads us to the conclusion that attaching the sensor where both KSR and Engelgau put it would have been obvious to a person of ordinary skill.

The '936 patent taught the utility of putting the sensor on the pedal device, not in the engine. Smith, in turn, explained to put the sensor not on the pedal's footpad but instead on its support structure. And from the known wire-chafing problems of Rixon, and Smith's teaching that "the pedal assemblies must not precipitate any motion in the connecting wires," Smith, col. 1, lines 35–37, Supplemental App. 274, the designer would know to place the sensor on a nonmoving part of the pedal structure. The most obvious nonmoving point on the structure from which a sensor can easily detect the pedal's position is a pivot point. The designer, accordingly, would follow Smith in mounting the sensor on a pivot, thereby designing an adjustable electronic pedal covered by claim 4.

Just as it was possible to begin with the objective to upgrade Asano to work with a computer-controlled throttle, so too was it possible to take an adjustable electronic pedal like Rixon and seek an improvement that would avoid the wire-chafing problem. Following similar steps to those just explained, a designer would learn from Smith to avoid sensor movement and would come, thereby, to Asano because Asano disclosed an adjustable pedal with a fixed pivot.

Teleflex indirectly argues that the prior art taught away from attaching a sensor to Asano because Asano in its view is bulky, complex, and expensive. The only evidence Teleflex marshals in support of this argument, however, is the Radcliffe declaration, which merely indicates that Asano would not have solved Engelgau's goal of making a small, simple, and inexpensive pedal. What the declaration does not indicate is that Asano was somehow so flawed that there was no reason to upgrade it, or pedals like it, to be compatible with modern engines. Indeed, Teleflex's own declarations refute this conclusion. Dr. Radcliffe states that Rixon suffered from the same bulk and complexity as did Asano. See id., at 206. Teleflex's other expert, however, explained that Rixon was itself designed by adding a sensor to a pre-existing mechanical pedal. See id., at 209. If Rixon's base pedal was not tooflawed to upgrade, then Dr. Radcliffe's declaration does not show Asano was either. Teleflex may have made a plausible argument that Asano is inefficient as compared to Engelgau's preferred embodiment, but to judge Asano against Engelgau would be to engage in the very hindsight bias Teleflex rightly urges must be avoided. Accordingly, Teleflex has not shown anything in the prior art that taught away from the use of Asano.

Like the District Court, finally, we conclude Teleflex has shown no secondary factors to dislodge the determination that claim 4 is obvious. Proper application of Graham and our other precedents to these facts therefore leads to the conclusion that claim 4 encompassed obvious subject matter. As a result, the claim fails to meet the requirement of §103.

We need not reach the question whether the failure to disclose Asano during the prosecution of Engelgau voids the presumption of validity given to issued patents, for claim 4 is obvious despite the presumption. We nevertheless think it appropriate to note that the rationale underlying the presumption—that the PTO, in its expertise, has approved the claim—seems much diminished here.

IV

A separate ground the Court of Appeals gave for reversing the order for summary judgment was the existence of a dispute over an issue of material fact. We disagree with the Court of Appeals on this point as well. To the extent the court understood the Graham approach to exclude the possibility of summary judgment when an expert provides a conclusory affidavit addressing the question of obviousness, it misunderstood the role expert testimony plays in the analysis. In considering summary judgment on that question the district court can and should take into account expert testimony, which may resolve or keep open certain questions of fact. That is not the end of the issue, however. The ultimate judgment of obviousness is a legal determination. Graham, 383 U. S., at 17. Where, as here, the content of the prior art, the scope of the patent claim, and the level of ordinary skill in the art are not in material dispute, and the obviousness of the claim is apparent in light of these factors, summary judgment is appropriate. Nothing in the declarations proffered by Teleflex prevented the District Court from reaching the careful conclusions underlying its order for summary judgment in this case.

* * * We build and create by bringing to the tangible and palpable reality around us new works based on instinct, simple logic, ordinary inferences, extraordinary ideas, and sometimes even genius. These advances, once part of our shared knowledge, define a new threshold from which innovation starts once more. And as progress beginning from higher levels of achievement is expected in the normal course, the results of ordinary innovation are not the subject of exclusive rights under the patent laws. Were it otherwise patents might stifle, rather than promote, the progress of useful arts. See U. S. Const., Art. I, §8, cl. 8. These premises led to the bar on patents claiming obvious subject matter established in Hotchkiss and codified in §103. Application of the bar must not be confined within atest or formulation too constrained to serve its purpose.

KSR provided convincing evidence that mounting a modular sensor on a fixed pivot point of the Asano pedal was a design step well within the grasp of a person of ordinary skill in the relevant art. Its arguments, and the record, demonstrate that claim 4 of the Engelgau patent is obvious. In rejecting the District Court's rulings, the Court of Appeals analyzed the issue in a narrow, rigid manner inconsistent with §103 and our precedents. The judgment of the Court of Appeals is reversed, and the case remanded for further proceedings consistent with this opinion.

It is so ordered.

(Slip Opinion) October Term, 2006

Syllabus

NOTE: *Where it is feasible, a syllabus (headnote) will be released, as is being done in connection with this case, at the time the opinion is issued. The syllabus constitutes no part of the opinion of the Court but has been prepared by the Reporter of Decisions for the convenience of the reader. See United States v. Detroit Timber & Lumber Co., 200 U. S. 321, 337.*

SUPREME COURT OF THE UNITED STATES

Syllabus

KSR INTERNATIONAL CO. v. TELEFLEX INC. ET AL.

CERTIORARI TO THE UNITED STATES COURT OF APPEALS FOR THE FEDERAL CIRCUIT

No. 04–1350. Argued November 28, 2006—Decided April 30, 2007

To control a conventional automobile's speed, the driver depresses or releases the gas pedal, which interacts with the throttle via a cable or other mechanical link. Because the pedal's position in the footwell normally cannot be adjusted, a driver wishing to be closer or farther from it must either reposition himself in the seat or move the seat, both of which can be imperfect solutions for smaller drivers in cars with deep footwells. This prompted inventors to design and patent pedals that could be adjusted to change their locations. The Asano patent reveals a support structure whereby, when the pedal location is adjusted, one of the pedal's pivot points stays fixed. Asano is also designed so that the force necessary to depress the pedal is the same regardless of location adjustments. The Redding patent reveals a different, sliding mechanism where both the pedal and the pivot point are adjusted. In newer cars, computer-controlled throttles do not operate through force transferred from the pedal by a mechanical link, but open and close valves in response to electronic signals. For the computer to know what is happening with the pedal, an electronic sensor must translate the mechanical operation into digital data. Inventors had obtained a number of patents for such sensors. The so-called '936 patent taught that it was preferable to detect the pedal's position in the pedal mechanism, not in the engine, so the patent disclosed a pedal with an electronic sensor on a pivot point in the pedal assembly. The Smith patent taught that to prevent the wires connecting the sensor to the computer from chafing and wearing out, the sensor should be put on a fixed part of the pedal assembly rather than in or on the pedal's footpad. Inventors had also patented self-contained modular sensors, which can be taken off the shelf and attached to any mechanical pedal to allow it to function with a computer-controlled throttle. The '068 patent disclosed one such sensor. Chevrolet also manufactured trucks using modular sensors attached to the pedal support bracket, adjacent to the pedal and engaged with the pivot shaft about which the pedal rotates. Other patents disclose electronic sensors attached to adjustable pedal assemblies. For example, the Rixon patent locates the sensor in the pedal footpad, but is known for wire chafing.

After petitioner KSR developed an adjustable pedal system for cars with cable-actuated throttles and obtained its '976 patent for the design, General Motors Corporation (GMC) chose KSR to supply adjustable pedal systems for trucks using computer-controlled throttles. To make the '976 pedal compatible with the trucks, KSR added a modular sensor to its design. Respondents (Teleflex) hold the exclusive license for the Engelgau patent, claim 4 of which discloses a position-adjustable pedal assembly with an electronic pedal position sensor attached a fixed pivot point. Despite having denied a similar, broader claim, the U. S. Patent and Trademark Office (PTO) had allowed claim 4 because it included the limitation of a fixed pivot position, which distinguished the design from Redding's. Asano was neither included among the Engelgau patent's prior art references nor mentioned in the patent's prosecution, and the PTO did not have before it an adjustable pedal with a fixed pivot point. After learning of KSR's design for GMC, Teleflex sued for infringement, asserting that KSR's pedal system infringed the Engelgau patent's claim 4. KSR countered that claim 4 was invalid under §103 of the Patent Act, which forbids issuance of a patent when "the differences between the subject matter sought to be patented and the prior art are such that the subject matter as a whole would have been obvious at the time the invention was made to a person having ordinary skill in the art."

Graham v. John Deere Co. of Kansas City, 383 U. S. 1, 17–18, set out an objective analysis for applying §103: "[T]he scope and content of the prior art are . . . determined; differences between the prior art and the claims at issue are . . . ascertained; and the level of ordinary skill in the pertinent art resolved. Against this background the obviousness or nonobviousness of the subject matter is determined. Such secondary considerations as commercial success, long felt but unsolved needs, failure of others, etc., might be utilized to give light to the circumstances surrounding the origin of the subject matter sought to be patented." While the sequence of these questions might be reordered in any particular case, the factors define the controlling inquiry. However, seeking to resolve the obviousness question with more uniformity and consistency, the Federal Circuit has employed a "teaching, suggestion, or motivation" (TSM) test, under which a patent claim is only proved obvious if the prior art, the problem's nature, or the knowledge of a person having ordinary skill in the art reveals some motivation or suggestion to combine the prior art teachings.

The District Court granted KSR summary judgment. After reviewing pedal design history, the Engelgau patent's scope, and the relevant prior art, the court considered claim 4's validity, applying Graham's framework to determine whether under summary-judgment standards KSR had demonstrated that claim 4 was obvious. The court found "little difference" between the prior art's teachings and claim 4: Asano taught everything contained in the claim except using a sensor to detect the pedal's position and transmit it to a computer controlling the throttle. That additional aspect was revealed in, e.g., the '068 patent and Chevrolet's sensors. The court then held that KSR satisfied the TSM test, reasoning (1) the state of the industry would lead inevitably to combinations of electronic sensors and adjustable pedals, (2) Rixon provided the basis for these developments, and (3) Smith taught a solution to Rixon's chafing problems by positioning the sensor on the pedal's fixed structure, which could lead to the combination of a pedal like Asano with a pedal position sensor.

Reversing, the Federal Circuit ruled the District Court had not applied the TSM test strictly enough, having failed to make findings as to the specific understanding or principle within a skilled artisan's knowledge that would have motivated one with no knowledge of the invention to attach an electronic control to the Asano assembly's support bracket. The Court of

Appeals held that the District Court's recourse to the nature of the problem to be solved was insufficient because, unless the prior art references addressed the precise problem that the patentee was trying to solve, the problem would not motivate an inventor to look at those references. The appeals court found that the Asano pedal was designed to ensure that the force required to depress the pedal is the same no matter how the pedal is adjusted, whereas Engelgau sought to provide a simpler, smaller, cheaper adjustable electronic pedal. The Rixon pedal, said the court, suffered from chafing but was not designed to solve that problem and taught nothing helpful to Engelgau's purpose. Smith, in turn, did not relate to adjustable pedals and did not necessarily go to the issue of motivation to attach the electronic control on the pedal assembly's support bracket. So interpreted, the court held, the patents would not have led a person of ordinary skill to put a sensor on an Asano-like pedal. That it might have been obvious to try that combination was likewise irrelevant. Finally, the court held that genuine issues of material fact precluded summary judgment.

Held: The Federal Circuit addressed the obviousness question in a narrow, rigid manner that is inconsistent with §103 and this Court's precedents. KSR provided convincing evidence that mounting an available sensor on a fixed pivot point of the Asano pedal was a design step well within the grasp of a person of ordinary skill in the relevant art and that the benefit of doing so would be obvious. Its arguments, and the record, demonstrate that the Engelgau patent's claim 4 is obvious. Pp. 11–24.

1. Graham provided an expansive and flexible approach to the obviousness question that is inconsistent with the way the Federal Circuit applied its TSM test here. Neither §103's enactment nor Graham's analysis disturbed the Court's earlier instructions concerning the need for caution in granting a patent based on the combination of elements found in the prior art. See Great Atlantic & Pacific Tea Co. v. Supermarket Equipment Corp., 340 U. S. 147, 152. Such a combination of familiar elements according to known methods is likely to be obvious when it does no more than yield predictable results. See, e.g., United States v. Adams, 383 U. S. 39, 50–52. When a work is available in one field, design incentives and other market forces can prompt variations of it, either in the same field or in another. If a person of ordinary skill in the art can implement a predictable variation, and would see the benefit of doing so, §103 likely bars its patentability. Moreover, if a

technique has been used to improve one device, and a person of ordinary skill in the art would recognize that it would improve similar devices in the same way, using the technique is obvious unless its actual application is beyond that person's skill. A court must ask whether the improvement is more than the predictable use of prior-art elements according to their established functions. Following these principles may be difficult if the claimed subject matter involves more than the simple substitution of one known element for another or the mere application of a known technique to a piece of prior art ready for the improvement. To determine whether there was an apparent reason to combine the known elements in the way a patent claims, it will often be necessary to look to interrelated teachings of multiple patents; to the effects of demands known to the design community or present in the marketplace; and to the background knowledge possessed by a person having ordinary skill in the art. To facilitate review, this analysis should be made explicit. But it need not seek out precise teachings directed to the challenged claim's specific subject matter, for a court can consider the inferences and creative steps a person of ordinary skill in the art would employ. Pp. 11–14.

(b) The TSM test captures a helpful insight: A patent composed of several elements is not proved obvious merely by demonstrating that each element was, independently, known in the prior art. Although common sense directs caution as to a patent application claiming as innovation the combination of two known devices according to their established functions, it can be important to identify a reason that would have prompted a person of ordinary skill in the art to combine the elements as the new invention does. Inventions usually rely upon building blocks long since uncovered, and claimed discoveries almost necessarily will be combinations of what, in some sense, is already known. Helpful insights, however, need not become rigid and mandatory formulas. If it is so applied, the TSM test is incompatible with this Court's precedents. The diversity of inventive pursuits and of modern technology counsels against confining the obviousness analysis by a formalistic conception of the words teaching, suggestion, and motivation, or by overemphasizing the importance of published articles and the explicit content of issued patents. In many fields there may be little discussion of obvious techniques or combinations, and market demand, rather than scientific literature, may often drive design trends. Granting patent protection to advances that would occur in the ordinary course without real innovation retards progress and may, for patents combining previously known elements, deprive prior inventions of their value or utility. Since the TSM test was devised, the Federal Circuit doubtless has applied it in accord with these principles in many cases. There is no necessary inconsistency between the test and the Graham analysis. But a court errs where, as here, it transforms general principle into a rigid rule limiting the obviousness inquiry. Pp. 14–15.

(c) The flaws in the Federal Circuit's analysis relate mostly to its narrow conception of the obviousness inquiry consequent in its application of the TSM test. The Circuit first erred in holding that courts and patent examiners should look only to the problem the patentee was trying to solve. Under the correct analysis, any need or problem known in the field and addressed by the patent can provide a reason for combining the elements in the manner claimed. Second, the appeals court erred in assuming that a person of ordinary skill in the art attempting to solve a problem will be led only to those prior art elements designed to solve the same problem. The court wrongly concluded that because Asano's primary purpose was solving the constant ratio problem, an inventor considering how to put a sensor on an adjustable pedal would have no reason to consider putting it on the Asano pedal. It is common sense that familiar items may have obvious uses beyond their primary purposes, and a person of ordinary skill often will be able to fit the teachings of multiple patents together like pieces of a puzzle. Regardless of Asano's primary purpose, it provided an obvious example of an adjustable pedal with a fixed pivot point, and the prior art was replete with patents indicating that such a point was an ideal mount for a sensor. Third, the court erred in concluding that a patent claim cannot be proved obvious merely by showing that the combination of elements was obvious to try. When there is a design need or market pressure to solve a problem and there are a finite number of identified, predictable solutions, a person of ordinary skill in the art has good reason to pursue the known options within his or her technical grasp. If this leads to the anticipated success, it is likely the product not of innovation but of ordinary skill and common sense. Finally, the court drew the wrong conclusion from the risk of courts and patent examiners falling prey to hindsight bias. Rigid preventative rules that deny recourse to common sense are neither necessary under, nor consistent with, this Court's case law. Pp. 15–18.

2. Application of the foregoing standards demonstrates that claim 4 is obvious. Pp. 18–23.

(a) The Court rejects Teleflex's argument that the Asano pivot mechanism's design prevents its combination with a sensor in the manner claim 4 describes. This argument was not raised before the District Court, and it is unclear whether it was raised before the Federal Circuit. Given the significance of the District Court's finding that combining Asano with a pivot-mounted pedal position sensor fell within claim 4's scope, it is apparent that Teleflex would have made clearer challenges if it intended to preserve this claim. Its failure to clearly raise the argument, and the appeals court's silence on the issue, lead this Court to accept the District Court's conclusion. Pp. 18– 20.

(b) The District Court correctly concluded that when Engelgau designed the claim 4 subject matter, it was obvious to a person of ordinary skill in the art to combine Asano with a pivot-mounted pedal position sensor. There then was a marketplace creating a strong incentive to convert mechanical pedals to electronic pedals, and the prior art taught a number of methods for doing so. The Federal Circuit considered the issue too narrowly by, in effect, asking whether a pedal designer writing on a blank slate would have chosen both Asano and a modular sensor similar to the ones used in the Chevrolet trucks and disclosed in the '068 patent. The proper question was whether a pedal designer of ordinary skill in the art, facing the wide range of needs created by developments in the field, would have seen an obvious benefit to upgrading Asano with a sensor. For such a designer starting with Asano, the question was where to attach the sensor. The '936 patent taught the utility of putting the sensor on the pedal device. Smith, in turn, explained not to put the sensor on the pedal footpad, but instead on the structure. And from Rixon's known wire-chafing problems, and Smith's teaching that the pedal assemblies must not precipitate any motion in the connecting wires, the designer would know to place the sensor on a nonmoving part of the pedal structure. The most obvious such point is a pivot point. The designer, accordingly, would follow Smith in mounting the sensor there. Just as it was possible to begin with the objective to upgrade Asano to work with a computer-controlled throttle, so too was it possible to take an adjustable electronic pedal like Rixon and seek an improvement that would avoid the wire-chafing problem. Teleflex has not shown anything in the prior art that taught away from the use of Asano, nor any secondary factors to dislodge the determination that claim 4 is obvious. Pp. 20–23.

3. The Court disagrees with the Federal Circuit's holding that genuine issues of material fact precluded summary judgment. The ultimate judgment of obviousness is a legal determination. Graham, 383 U. S., at 17. Where, as here, the prior art's content, the patent claim's scope, and the level of ordinary skill in the art are not in material dispute and the claim's obviousness is apparent, summary judgment is appropriate. P. 23. 119 Fed. Appx. 282, reversed and remanded.

KENNEDY, J., delivered the opinion for a unanimous Court.

Courtesy of David A. Allgeyer, Lindquist & Vennum PLLP